WAS ISRAEL EVER IN EGYPT?

OR, A LOST TRADITION

BY

G. H. BATESON WRIGHT, D.D.

QUEEN'S COLLEGE, OXFORD; HEAD MASTER, QUEEN'S COLLEGE, HONG KONG
AUTHOR OF "A CRITICAL REVISED TRANSLATION OF THE BOOK OF JOB"

ISBN: 978-1-63923-958-0

All Rights reserved. No part of this book maybe reproduced without written permission from the publishers, except by a reviewer who may quote brief passages in a review to be printed in a newspaper or magazine.

Printed: March 2023

Published and Distributed By:
Lushena Books
607 Country Club Drive, Unit E
Bensenville, IL 60106
www.lushenabks.com

ISBN:978-1-63923-958-0

CONTENTS

CHAPTER I

CRITICISM

PAR.
1. Criticism, the highest mental exercise
2. Mental processes observable in the individual identical with those of the human race
3. Hebrew authors, by critical studies, make eclectic use of ideas common to other nations
4. Evolution of Hebrew religion; search into origins: ritual and canon; Greek philosophy engrafted
5. Christ's religion, God and man. He quotes, but declines to discuss Hebrew narratives
6. Paul, the apostle of dogma
7. Dogma produces heresy, which is doomed to be misunderstood and misrepresented
8. Church of Rome and progressive dogma
9. Dark Ages and Renaissance
10. Reformation attacks tradition, repudiates later dogmas of Rome
11. Reuchlin, the prophet of enlightened, untrammelled criticism
12. English Reformation, exotic in its origin
13. Scientific activity of the 17th and 18th centuries, paves the way for labours of the 19th
14. Search into origins, the first (par. 4) and last phases of critical enterprise
15-18. The objection "*what is new is not true*" considered; Criticism seeks to recover old standpoint

§1. Gilead, two stories
§2. Bethel
§3. Penuel
§4. Reflections

CHAPTER IV

GENEALOGIES

§5. Importance attached to these, a characteristic of the Jews
§6. Need of them first felt on the return from Captivity
§7. Lists in Chronicles, worthy of careful study
§8. But a Domesday book, not genealogy
§9. 1 Chron. 1–8. Embryo state of the first seven books of the Bible
90. In Hexateuch, history of Joseph set forth as history of Israel
91. Ordinary explanations of historical difficulties applicable to Hebrew genealogies
92. Historico-geographical value and purpose of Hebrew genealogies
93. Names ending in –n, Arabic plural
94. Names of tribes and of men, not interchangeable
95. Subject of enquiry
96. Missing generations
97. Forty years to a generation, reckoned only in doubtful history
98. Adam to capture of Jerusalem by Nebuchadrezzar—a Jubilee of generations
99. Pedigrees testifying to missing generations
100. Scribes conscious of these lacunæ
101. Were Heman, Asaph and Ethan, the names of individuals at all?
102. Suspicious elements in the pedigrees (99)
103–105. Genealogy and chronology differ about the duration of Egyptian sojourn

PAR.
106. Impossible rate of propagation, especially
107. In view of other nations derived from Abram
108. Reference to contradictions; detailed treatment deferred
109. Curious coincidences, even in later lists
110. High-priest's genealogy
111, 112. 1 Chron. ix. and Nehemiah xi. compared
113. High priests mentioned in royal history do not correspond, in names or numbers, with the genealogies
114. Genealogies not kept prior to Captivity

CHAPTER V

HEBREW FEASTS AND CUSTOMS

115. General remarks
116. Editions of Hebrew history, B.C. 850–700 Prophetical edition
           625 Deuteronomy
           480 Ritual and Numbers
117. Sabbath, ancient Babylonian observance
 118. A holiday, restrictions of later date
 119. Associated with Exodus, then thrown back to Creation
 120. Two novelettes on its strict observance in Moses' days
 121. Antiquity of its observance
122. Circumcision. First instance at Gilgal
 123. Absence of circumcision during the wanderings
 124. Ritual uncleanness for Passover, physical weakness for Battle
 125. Gilgal—three derivations
 126. Circumcision thrown back to Moses and
 127. Then to Abraham, being not confined to Israel
128. Passover. Two feasts combined and developed
 129. History of its spasmodic observance
 130. Unleavened bread, ancient feast at New Year, before eating new corn

152. Passover, and crossing the line — several Paschal incidents
    Notables crossing the Expanses
    Jacob   .   .   Jabbok
    Moses   .   .   Red Sea
    Joshua   .   .   Jordan
    Elijah   .   .   .
    Elisha   .   .   .
    all associated with introduction to a new life
152. Sacrifice of first-born originally observed at this feast
153. Double feast at Autumnal Equinox
154. Sacrifice
155. Methods of igniting sacrifices
156. Ark. Its size, mode of conveyance, absence of cherubim
157. Holy Place. 4 Sacred trees
    138. Matzzebeth permitted
    139. Asherah (Groves)
    140. Both connected with ancestral worship
    141. Hills
    142. Altars
    143. One only Holy Place
144. High-priest. The Power represented in the Hexateuch, unknown till the Captivity
    145. King could make and unmake high-priests
    146. Wellhausen quoted on occasion for the rise of high-priestly office
    147. Summary

CHAPTER VI

ELEMENTS OF IMPROBABILITY IN THE HEXATEUCH NARRATIVE

148. Revelation
149. Inspiration
    150. Degrees of inspiration
    151. Wider range for inspiration

PAR.
152. God. Heathen practices of patriarchs
 153. Saturn worship in the wilderness
 154. Sun and moon worship
 155. Nature worship maintained till the Captivity
 156. Baal worship concurrent with Yahveh worship
 157. Other deities ; 'Am, Zur, Yechudh, &c.
 158. Shaddai, of doubtful antiquity
 159. Yahveh not unknown to other nations
 160. Yahveh's jealousy
 161. Yahveh's eternal wrath against his own people, written from a later standpoint
 162. No evidence of a self-revelation of God
 163. Description of God inconsistent with his self-revelation
 164. Hebrews groped after God, as well as other nations. Acts xvii. 27
165. Creation. Two discordant accounts. Insupportable premises, Universe made for the world ; the world made for man, *i.e.*, the Israelites
 166. The sun a portable lamp; Joshua and Isaiah
167. Fall of Man
 168. Perfection, from a Hebrew point of view, absence of change
 169. Life is negative, being a struggle against mortal tendency
 170. The three curses
 171. Serpent myths in the Scriptures
172. The Flood. Two conflicting narratives
 173. Enormous mass of water required
174. Call of Abram
175. Survey of patriarchal tales
176. Joseph; details of his life drawn from Samuel
177. Moses ; massacre of the infants
 178. The Ten Plagues
 179. Forty years' wandering
180. Joshua

CHAPTER VII

ENQUIRY INTO ORIGIN OF THE NAMES OF THE PATRIARCHS

PAR.
181. The present chapter an Onomasticon
182. Abram. Nothing is known of him, save that the ancestor of Hebrew and other races migrated from the East
   183. No derivation of this name suggested in Genesis. Is Abbir, Abhir, the root?
184. Abraham. Pater Orchamus
   185. Abu-rachman
186. Hagar. Ancestress of the Hagarenes
187. Sarah   ,,   ,, I(sra)elites
188. Iscah   ,,   ,, Iskites (Isaacites)
189. Isaac = Iskites, identified with Hyksos
190. Rebecca, Ribqah connected with Qirjath-'Arba'
191. Ishmael = Semali
192. Se'ir = Wild-goat
193. 'Esau = Se'ir
194. Edom = Red-sandstone
195. Jacob = Nomad
196. Israel. Various Derivations
   (1) Prince or Warrior of God; *c.f.*, Sarah and Seraiah
   (2) Man sees God
   (3) Upright
      (a) Jeshurun
      (b) Book of Jasher
      (c) Jashar for Israel, Numbers xxiii. 10, Psalms xxx. 36
      (d) Used by Christ, John i. 47
   (4) God directs his way
   (5) Perhaps connected with Asherah (?)
197. Reuben, very ancient name
   198. Evidence of presence of letter 'Ain

Contents

PAR
- 199–1. In Syriac &c., supports presence of 'Ain
- 200. Ruchubi (Rechobon), old form
- 201. Traces of Rechoboth, in and out of Palestine
- 202. Judah's marriage with Rachab represents absorption of territory of Reuben. Rechobon
- 203. Sime'on connected with Ishmaelites
- 204. Levi = Bond
    - (1) Between husband and wife
    - (2) „ two brothers
    - (3) Consecrated by massacre of idolaters
    - (4) Taken as a substitute for first-born
    - (5) Bound as servants to high-priest
- 205. Lewan = Priests, associated with Moses
- 206. Levites, not properly scattered over Israel, but found in various localities
- 207. Early history of high-priest, unknown
- 208. Samuel, a Qenite
- 209. Levites used as soldiers by David
- 210. Levites are Qenites
- 211. Rechabites are Qenites, Levites
- 212. Qenites known as Lewan, or priests
- 213. Chebronites
- 214. Organisation of Levites in Hexateuch, a Prolepsis
- 215. Sketch of history of Levites
- 216. Qohath, Gershom Merari
- 217. Gershom = Expulsion
- 218. Merari = Miriam, sons of Machol = Dance-music
- 219. Mushi = Mosites
- 220. Confusion of names in David's officers
- 221. Qorachites
- 222. A branch of Chebronite Qenites
- 223. Neglect of ark proves non-existence of Levites
- 224. David first to organise Levites
- 225. David pays no special reverence to *the* tabernacle

Contents

230. History shows accounts of Levites in Hexateuch unfounded
231. Judah
    232. Named after Yechudh, Phœnician God
    233. Which appears in composition in Israelite names
    234. Story of the man, Judah, unhistoric, written by Josephites
    231. Ezrachites = Indigenous
    232. Perizzites, adopted tribes
    233. Chezron, ,, ,,
    234. Royal descent from Chezron, doubtful
    235. Play on Caleb, in Jacob's blessing
    236. Five genealogies of one Caleb
    237. Identity of Caleb the Chezronite with Caleb the Qenizzite
    238. Qenizzite root of Yephunneh
    239. Royal house of Judah, of Qenizzite origin
    240. Influence of Qenites and Qenizzites on history of Israel
    241. Shelah = Shilonites
242. Joseph. Puns on his name suggest details of story
    243. Joseph a later accretion of Israel
    244. Ephraim = Fruitful, name of district, before Joseph came out of Egypt. History of Judah in early times connected with this locality
    245. Jacob's blessing refers to Joseph's coming to Shiloh, and consequent partition of kingdom
    246. Genesis xlix. 10, play on the name Qohathites confirms this
    247. Achiyah's the Shilonite's part in the secession, further corroboration
    248. Manasseh = Fugitives
    249. Early history of this district also associated with Judah
    250. Caleb's connexion with Gilead
    251. Sselophehad's daughters
252. Benjamin = Southerners
    253. Se'irite Aborigines, 'Anaq
    254. Traces of Edomites
    255. 'Anaq called after 'Anah, goddess of strength

PAR.
- 256. Ben-'oni refers to sons of 'Anah, previous occupants
- 257. Another list of Benjamites
- 258. Dan, perhaps curtailed from Adon
- 259. 1 Chronicles vii. 12 explained
- 260. Danites on Benjamite territory
- 261. Origin of Samson's father's name
- 262. Naphthali = Wooded heights, instance of gross misderivation
- 263. Gad = Luck
- 264. Moabite stone shows Hebrew story incorrect
- 265. Issachar, really a literary tribe
- 266. Zebulun = Dwelling of Baal

CHAPTER VIII

SYNTHESIS

- 267. Mathematical precision impossible
- 268. Postulates
- 269. Axioms
- 270. Definitions
- 271. A lost tradition
- 272. Canaan prior to Abram's advent
- 273. Abrahamides
- 274. Gradual appearance of Jacobean tribes
- 275. Hyksos and Exodus
- 276. Joshua and Union
- 277. Abram B.C. 2350
- 278. Exodus B.C. 1325
- 279. Zoan founded B.C. 1806
- 280. Stories of Exodus unreliable
- 281. Forty years' wandering unreliable
- 282. Joseph alone reported as coming out of Egypt
- 283. " Jacob and Joseph;" "Judah and Israel" indicate separate histories of Jacob and Israel, of Judah and Joseph

PAR.
284. Israel assumed as national name, at Shechem after union
285. History of Jacobeans in Canaan, while Joseph was in Egypt
286. Other pre-Mosaic stories
287. Sihon and Og doubtful cotemporaries of Moses
288. Difficulties of accepted story of Exodus, and conquest of Canaan recognised by Ewald ;
    289. ,,   Wellhausen ;
    290. ,,   Kuenen ;
    291. ,,   Renan
292. History of Israel, written in the north accounts for suppression of pre-Mosaic history of other tribes
293. Stories to discredit of Judah
294.   ,,   ,,   Reuben
295. Judah's acquiescence in his own misrepresented history
296. Religious character of history prevented subsequent rejection

CHAPTER IX

HEBREW AND CHINESE HISTORY AND RELIGION :
A PARALLEL

297. Both nations without great architectural monuments
298. Each a mystery
299. Each now subject to persecution
300. Self-conceit a characteristic of each ; its cause shown
301. Tenacity of historic life
302. Chinese a living monument might repay for research into primitive relics of antiquity
303. Comparison of history
        Fabulous periods, ten sections ;
        Three patriarchs almost cotemporary ;
        Golden Epoch   ,,   ,,
        National degradation ,,   ,,

PAR.
304. Accadian influence on both
305. Chinese originally a pastoral tribe
306. Isolation of Chinese, natural; of Hebrews, artificial
307. Simplest form of primitive religion to be sought in China
308, 309. Identical conditions in criticism
310. Inspiration
311. Legendary matter.
312. Exaggeration, and aim at symmetry
313. Bamboo annals
314. Historiographers' notes expanded; clerical errors supported and explained away; specimen of curt ancient form of history
315. Vividness of colouring and detail in Tso Chuen
316. Predictions
317. Intentional perversion of truth, with religious motive
318. Ascription of works to Confucius, which he could not have penned
319. Parallelism, a prominent feature in both Hebrew and Chinese poetry and prose
320. Dr. Legge quoted on religious ideas of the Chinese; no priestly class; burnt offerings; God's personality, supremacy, unity
321. Personality of God recognised by later Chinese writers
322. Ignorance of immortality common to Chinese and Hebrew races
323. Divination
324. Creation; Chaos; *Rest* on the *Seventh* day
325. Filial piety; concubinage; adoption; early marriage; genealogies
326. Ancestral worship; worship of trees and stones: new moon; full moon; new year; Equinox
327. Body, soul and spirit; self-respect; guilt and affliction; purity of motive
328. Interference of prophets

CHAPTER X

CONCLUSION

PAR.
329. Confessions
330. Original purpose, a study of genealogies
331. Enquiry into the historicity of the Exodus necessitated research into history of passover and of Hebrew feasts and customs
332. Stories, based on derivation of names, convey reference to later events
333. Critical motive of Hebrew authors
334. Chapter I. Critical faculty and religious motive
335. *Subjective* criticism suggested as a substitute for "*Higher*" criticism
336. Chapter II. Hebrew history discredited by stories based on derivations
337. Specimens of such stories
338. Chapter IV. Hebrew genealogies
339. Chapter V. Hebrew method of assigning to institutions, dates more and more remote
340. Same backward method applied to history generally
341. Chapter VI. Revelation, inspiration, &c.
342. Chapter VII. Application of above principles to history of the patriarchs
343. Important lesson from parallel of Hebrew and Chinese history. Chapter IX
344. Existence of writing, not incompatible with unreliable history
345. This book not designed as a reply to Professor Sayce's "Higher Criticism"
346. Recollections of Queen's College, Oxford, twenty years ago
347. Subjective critics misrepresented, as exaggerating trivial mistakes ;
348. As ransacking the scriptures for testimony against itself ;
349. As not according full weight to the presence of the word *Shel* on a coin of the 8th century B.C.

PAR.
350. As basing their arguments on the inability of Moses to write
351. The " Verdict of the Monuments " tells both ways
352. The discovery of mere names cannot establish the form and clothing of history
353. Composite character of Pentateuch accepted by Professor Sayce in one place, but discredited in another
354. The criticism of Hebrew literature cannot be modelled after the criticism of isolated monuments
355. Strange prolepsis of history in Tel el-Amarna correspondence
356. Ramses III.'s list of Palestine races differs from Khu-n-Aten's
357. Verdict of monuments discredits Hebrew chronology
358. Tel el-Amarna only shows *sources* of Hebrew authors, not the correctness of their association with certain heroes
359. Position of " Higher Critics " not affected by discoveries at Tel el-Amarna
360. Miracles
361. Prophecies
362. Fulfilment exaggerated ; unfulfilled prophecy ignored
363. Miracles and prophecy evidence of late composition
364. Quousque tandem ?
365. Ministers of different denominations admit some element of legend
366. Only two courses open : to forbid the study of the scriptures ; or to give to our children a more rational account
367. Author, not a judge nor a critic, but one of a large class of the thinking public

APPENDIX (*see* Par. 322)

THE DOCTRINE OF IMMORTALITY IN THE OLD TESTAMENT

368. Confucius' Refusal to discuss the doctrine
369. Evidence of Chinese popular belief in it
370. Hebrew experience identical

Contents

PAR.
371. "Transitory promises"
372. Method of investigation
373. Death a sleep and an eternal one
    374. The grave a bed
    375. Blackness of night
    376. Unconscious condition
    377-379. The grave outside Yahveh's jurisdiction
380. We proceed to investigate Hebrew expressions
381. And observe that there is no mention of immortality, by the aged
382. Nor by the sick
    383. Job's case deferred
    384. Caution against taking "raising up" as equivalent to resurrection
    385. Especially in Hosea vi. 2
386. Nor by the bereaved
387. Immortality eliminated from the moral government of the world
388. The Book of Job silent upon this topic
    389. Despairing utterances
    390. Job wishes Resurrection were feasible
    391. Chapter xix. 25-27 has nothing to do with resurrection
    392 But with restitution in this life
393. The vivifying principle returns to God
394. Immortality of fame
395.   "   " name
396.   "   " the race, not of the individual
397. Gradual introduction of the doctrine after the Exile
398. "Mountain of the North"
399. Allegorical use of resurrection as applied to the nation
400. Evidence of popular belief
401. Necromancy
402. Miracles of resurrection and translation
403. Motive for long periods of mourning

PAR.
404. Rephaim
405. Prophets intentionally suppress this doctrine
406. Danger of the doctrine in early times
407. Rabbis unable to prove existence of doctrine in Pentateuch
408. Immortality, a doctrine more suited to the aged
409. And therefore to the maturer life of the Hebrew nation

LIST OF BOOKS CHIEFLY REFERRED TO.

Ewald : " History of Israel "
       "Antiquities of Israel "
       " Lehrbuch der Hebräischen Sprache."
Kuenen : " Religion of Israel "
       " The Hexateuch."
Wellhausen : " History of Israel. Prolegomena.'
Renan : " Histoire du Peuple d'Israël."
Sayce : " Hibbert Lectures "
       " Ancient Empires of the East
       " Verdict of the Monuments."
Schrader : " Cuneiform Inscriptions."
" Corpus Inscriptionum Semiticarum." Part I.
Driver : " Introduction to the Literature of the Old Testament."
Weber : " Die Lehren des Talmud."

                And

Legge's : " Chinese Classics." Vols. I-V. Part 2
       " Sacred Books of the East," XVI. XXVI. XXVII.
Mayer : " Chinese Reader's Manual."
Williams : " Middle Kingdom."
Dyer Ball: " Things Chinese."

WAS ISRAEL EVER IN EGYPT?

CHAPTER I

CRITICISM

1. IDEA, thought, opinion, judgment, criticism: such appears to be the order of operation, from the simplest to the most complex exercise of the mental faculties. Thought bears the same relation to idea as observation does to sight; the former is a more conscious act than the latter. As the observant man sees more in the same view than ninety-nine men out of a hundred equally endued with sight; so the thoughtful man nurtures and multiplies the ideas which flash into all brains alike. Opinion is the crystallisation of thought into definite regulated formation, and is the first-fruit of personal choice and effort. From entertaining an opinion, a phrase suggestive of remaining vagueness and uncertainty, we proceed by comparison of the varying and conflicting opinions of ourselves and others to a more definite and final conclusion, which is dignified by the name of judgment. When judgment is habitually exercised in one field of thought, till one has obtained a more complete mastery of the subject under consideration, the critical faculty is developed;

the judgments themselves would have a higher value, and the mature fruit is criticism.

2. Stopford Brooke has shown that the life of the poet and the history of poetry reveal the same phases of progressive thought, as exemplified by the treatment successively of the subjects—religion, love, history, nature, man. This thought may be more fully generalised: the experience of the individual and of the race is identical, the former being the microcosm. As, then, we know that the criticism of the youth is of a not higher level than the ideas of the full-grown man, so we may expect to find that the judgments and criticisms of two thousand or three thousand years ago assume now the less proportions of mere thoughts and ideas. When we speak of uncritical ages, we must not in our fancied superiority overlook the immense but gradual development that has been meanwhile effected by the universal law of evolution. We, the "heirs of ages," are apt to pride ourselves on our personal acquisitions, rather than gratefully acknowledge the legacies of past generations. In our arrogance, too, we are prone to speak slightingly of stories or legends, which not only embody the ideas and thoughts of long ago, but actually reveal processes of selection and rejection which claim for them the credit of critical labours.

3. I propose to apply this line of thought to the Hebrew religious ideas and the Christian development of them, endeavouring to show that a steady principle of applied criticism is discernible throughout. The stories of Creation and the Flood are clearly derived from very ancient, probably Hindu, sources, through an Assyrian medium; but they have been subjected to critical revision, and that, too, by more than one inde-

pendent Hebrew author. To critical labours also is due the theory of the Fall of man and origin of Death, which are engrafted as absolute dogmas on to the old legend known to us elsewhere as the apples of the Hesperides. At a first glance, all these might too readily be classified as mere speculative ideas. But the systematic principle of unity that pervades them all, insists on their ascription to a definite critical school of thought; they are not mere bald reproductions of existing fables, but are rewritten with a specific purpose. The development of the idea of the Deity may be traced to the same cause. First, we have the indefinite personification of a divine man, with all its gross anthropomorphisms, whereby El Shaddai is represented as walking, talking, and eating with man; next we have the national God, Yahveh, now no longer with body and parts (except in the apparition to Moses at Horeb), but certainly not yet without passions—individual passions of hate and jealousy, gross partiality towards his partisans are undeniable characteristics; and lastly, the latter prophets originate or adopt the idea of a god of the universe, who is lord of life and death, light and darkness, good and evil, Israelites and the world at large. It is probably a fact that the first conceptions of a Deity would be largely pervaded with ideas compounded from human experience; but it may be doubted whether the Hebrew and Greek anthropomorphic tales were not rather the imaginings of later generations as to what the religious notions of their ancestors were, than a preservation by tradition of those actual notions themselves. If anthropomorphic theology were common to the infancy of mankind, it would appear remarkable that no trace of it survives amongst so ancient a race as the Chinese, with its hoary literature.

4. Availing itself freely of Egyptian, Phœnician, and Assyrian traditions, Hebrew criticism appears early to have found scope for its enterprise in the search into origins—the origin of the world, of man, of woman, of sin and death, of the Israelite and other nations. Purer ethical problems, justice and righteousness, involving the enunciation of socialistic ideas, distinguished the later prophetic age. The return from Babylon was signalised by a critical edition of the ritual, and attempts to assign limits to the canon of the classical works; and for centuries the stamp thus heavily impressed upon the sphere of Hebrew activity remained uneffaced. Morality manifestly suffered by protracted discussion, often of the most puerile character, over unedifying details. The Alexandrian Jews found a refuge from the unhealthy atmosphere of their native dogmatism in the purer air of Greek philosophy. Cold as their writings appear in comparison with prophetic fires, they produced a bracing effect in those enervated times, and the marriage of logical philosophy and Hebrew religious thought, then solemnised, was destined to bear fruit in the birth of the Alexandrine Christian School, which developed Paulinism.

5. The Advent of Christ inaugurated the true school of Higher Criticism, the distinguishing characteristic of which should be the search for lost and hidden truth and the wholesale rejection of more modern accretions. He discarded the labours of the scribes, and returned to the more congenial spirit of the great prophetical epoch, 800 to 500 B.C. It was only what might be expected, that the God he revealed, or rather unveiled,

was the God of Deutero-Isaiah, rather than the Yahveh of Moses; it was only reasonable that the further evolution of the divine idea should proceed from the highest development hitherto attained; God was glorified by being simplified. So true is it that by Christ and the Divine Spirit we have "access unto the Father." Christ's critical enterprise was eminently practical; God and man were the only topics that interested him. History, Ritual, and Canon concerned him not. Deeply imbued as he was with the living spirit of the Hebrew Scriptures, he never committed himself to any definite utterance requiring as a matter of faith acceptance of the historicity of Hebrew narratives. His references are all by way of illustration, which loses none of its force even if the stories quoted are merely instructive legend—*e.g.*, Noah's flood, Lot's wife, and Jonah's dolphin. Further, his simple attitude of acquiescent acceptance of the Mosaic ritual, the while he strenuously opposed its spirit, shows us with what caution we may infer his own firm belief in narratives he quotes as readily accepted by his hearers.

6. The labours of Paul were mainly directed to the systematisation of Christianity, chiefly with a view to its adaptation to the needs of the Gentiles; for which purpose he had free recourse to the ideas and expressions of Philo's Hebraised Greek Philosophy. His early devotion to the study of the Law urged him to cope with the difficult problems of Original Sin and Predestination. The expression of his opinions on such topics would read strangely in the Gospels; no man can imagine such dogmas proceeding from the mouth of Christ. Here again, then, we have a distinct advance,

in one sense, in the development of religious thought, the result of critical application.

7. Succeeding centuries followed in the direction indicated by Paul. Dogma chiefly absorbed the critical energies of the Christian Church, especially the investigation of the divinity of Christ. The particular interpretation of various passages of Scripture in support of certain views, led to the more systematic study of Old and New Testaments, and such commentaries as those of Chrysostom and Augustine arose; while Origen and Jerome have bequeathed to us monuments of learned research, that form of literary labour to which in more modern times the term criticism appears to be almost solely applied. Critical inquiry into narratives, the observation of anachronisms and other inconsistencies, were not disregarded; but, as a rule, such inquiry was condemned as inquisitive, and put to silence with the opprobrious epithet of Heresy. As these opinions only survive in fragments, preserved by quotation in the works of those who triumphantly opposed and confuted their arguments, we are unable to form a definite conception of the actual views of such men as Celsus and Marcion. It is the custom of orthodox apologists to ignore unpalatable arguments if they are strong, and unduly to emphasise side issues in which errors may be manifest, representing them as the main position assailed. The real extent of the vital vigour of belief in the dogmas of the Church in those ages may be estimated from the statement of Cardinal Newman in his History of the Arians (p. 445), that the whole Christian world would have become Arians had it not been by the grace of God that the doctrine of the eternal divine pre-existence of

Christ was too deeply imbedded in the affections of the illiterate mass of the people. "Ex uno disce omnes;" the critical labours of the learned were suppressed in favour of the religious prejudices of the ignorant; popular sentiment triumphed over calm, mature judgment.

8. With the growing conviction that tradition was a living spirit, while the letter of the Bible was dead, the power of the Church grew. A united system became an absolute necessity, and the Bishop of Rome had little difficulty in asserting and maintaining his claim to supremacy over Western Churches. This, in itself an onward step, led to several others. The doctrines of Transubstantiation and of the Immaculate Conception of the Virgin Mary were found to be necessary additions, to strengthen the logical position of the Church. Thus, from time to time new dogmas succeeded, but seldom superseded, the old; till, to secure the infallibility of the Church, so recently as a quarter of a century ago, the Pope himself was declared officially infallible. In all this we have the conscious exertion of the critical faculty, indicating weak points, advocating improvements and aiming at perfection.

9. During the Middle Ages learning became the monopoly of the Church, whose monks were more engaged in the task of carefully preserving and laboriously multiplying existing works, than in evolving new ideas. It was a time of great darkness as regards the populace at large; but the dawn was at hand, and, as might be expected, it arose in the East. The fall of Constantinople drove to Italy countless Greek professors and students, whose presence speedily awakened an interest in dead languages. A revival

of learning ensued. Manuscripts soon became too expensive and the process of production too slow to meet the demand; as a consequence, the art of printing was invented. The more generous education thus afforded, with the freer access to more general literature, enlarged men's minds, and roused a spirit of inquiry which found vent in the Reformation.

10. Partial reforms had been attempted by Wyckliffe and Huss, but Luther enjoyed the advantages of the later age. Without printing his revolution would never have become popular; hymns and pamphlets, but chiefly his translation of the Bible, found their way into the castles of dukes and the cottages of the poor. Briefly, the work of the Reformation was to deny the power of Tradition, and endeavour to revert to the simplicity of apostolic times. It was more successful in the latter than in the former attempt: so far, indeed, did they reproduce the condition of the churches in the days of Paul, that the admonition to the Corinthian Church against party dissensions might have been specially written for their behoof. In whatever light the Reformation may be regarded, as progressive or retrogressive, it cannot be denied that it owed its existence to the spirit of criticism. The discussion of such doctrines as Justification, Predestination, Original Sin, Free Will, became of vital importance, while the later dogmas of the Church were discarded.

11. The great critical genius of this epoch, however, was a man somewhat senior to Luther—*Reuchlin*. Erasmus and he were known as the two eyes of Germany. Of him Baring-Gould says he "not only became an enthusiastic student of the classic Latin and Greek authors, but also broke ground as a Hebrew

holar;" while Oehler remarks: "His immortal service nsists in this, that he was the first to claim, with the eatest emphasis, the independence of exegesis from ɛ traditions of the Church;" but he adds, with gret: "It is only too true that Reuchlin himself did t know the force of his own views; he was highly satisfied even with the Reformation." It would ɔear that Reuchlin, on the other hand, was fully ɪscious of the tendency of his theory, which was t every man should read the original Greek or brew for himself, and form his own opinion; "I e," says he, "more confidence in my own sagacity ɪ in any one's else." No wonder that he was atisfied with the Reformation of his days, which ely transferred to small knots of men the authority ɪerly held by the Church. Liberty to read the ɪe for himself was professedly claimed for every ɪ; but when the question arose of liberty of inter- ation, every section of the Protestant Church was ɪgoted in maintaining its own private view, and as ly to persecute dissentients, as the Catholic Church nst whose severity they declaimed. Good cause had ɔr dissatisfaction with the Reformation. Reuchlin's ortal fame should stand on a broader base than one assigned by Oehler: he was 400 years ahead ɪis times; he foresaw the seething turmoil that t ensue from abandoning the soothing doctrine ːcepting the infallible tradition from the hands of infallible Church; he was convinced that if the ificates of the pilots were discredited it was futile to ɔose to replace them by men who did not pretend ave any such credentials, and openly expressed ˙ contempt for, and disbelief in, their value; he bravely asserted that each man must navigate his own craft for himself, reading and interpreting the compass by the light of his own wit.

12. The Reformation in England did not centre round the name of one man; it was chiefly influenced by refugees from the Continent, who were welcomed at our universities; and it is to the liberal spirit in which all such were impartially greeted, whether from Germany, Holland, or Switzerland, that the heterogeneous character of our Articles of Religion and other Church formularies must be attributed. I do not wish to be misunderstood as denying the debt of gratitude we owe to Tyndale and others, who were martyrs to the cause of liberty; but the fact remains, that to a great extent the course of the Reformation in England was directed by a body of men who were either foreigners themselves, or persistently took foreign declarations of faith for their models and groundwork.

13. The seventeenth and the eighteenth centuries were celebrated for their great mental activity and consequent success in every field of research. Mathematics, science, history, logic, classical and Hebrew criticism are associated with such names as Newton, Priestley, Hume, Locke, Bentley, and Porson; Lowth, Hody, and Pocock. Their labours, however, were the foundation, the prelude, to the fuller music of the present century, the record of which shows Germany to hold that place formerly held by England. Never before has there been, as now, such a period of successful exploration of every branch of literature and science. Each decade heralds some fresh discovery. The impossible has become possible. It was not to be expected that

Biblical criticism should escape the influence of the prevailing genius of the nineteenth century. Apart from science, it might be stated without exaggeration, that the progress of Biblical criticism, including the history of Israel, is the distinctive feature of modern times. Whatever advance may be made in the future, the labours of such giants as Gesenius and Ewald, Kuenen and Wellhausen, will still remain the base for further operations.

14. Thus briefly have I endeavoured to represent in an imperfect sketch the course of religious critical enterprise, which is a strong characteristic of the Hebrew race, and has from them been derived by us. It began, as we have seen, with research into origins, and precisely the same is its last phase. It is claimed that the former research nearly three thousand years ago was incomplete, and not based on true scientific principles; that the study of the literature and religions of other nations has resulted in the formation of a system of critical inquiry which should legitimately be also applicable to the Hebrew literature and religion; that, though we may be in a position definitely to assert that some statements are false, others anachronisms, it does not follow that we are able, or should be required, to substitute the true version or to indicate with precision when the anachronisms were introduced. The general conclusion is, that we have no reliable information of the origin of the world, of mankind, of the people of Israel; and that such hints as we may have in this direction are not in accordance with the Hexateuch narrative.

15. When the Bedouins saw Layard attacking the ancient mounds of earth in the neighbourhood of

Nineveh, they would not have believed his assurance that he was in search of the old; it must have appeared to them that he was removing well-known landmarks and changing the face of primeval nature. It is thus that the work of the critical schools is misinterpreted to the present day; all efforts to exhume ancient truth are met, and supposed to be silenced, by the apothegm, "What is true is not new, and what is new is not true."

16. To start with: we do not know what absolute truth is. "What is truth?" asked Pilate of Christ, who had just declared that he was born to testify to truth. This petulant, half-sneering, evasive inquiry has, by the inability of generations of mankind to find its answer, been transformed into a philosophic question, ranking higher than any propounded by Socrates or Confucius. At first sight it would appear that truth must not outstep the line of demarcation traced by our conception of possibility, or even probability. Any statement is *primâ facie* true or false when it accords or not with our own experience, or the general experience of mankind, so far as we are acquainted with it by intercourse or study. Thus it is manifest that ignorance and obstinacy are the greatest enemies of truth, for it is possible to conceive of things contrary to our experience being yet true; or, indeed, for a statement of facts within this experience to be made deliberately false and even successfully to deceive. It is possible—nay, it is continually happening—that true and false, possible and impossible, change places. What can appear more impossible than that vast empires should be swayed by cities like Rome or Venice, or by small countries like Greece, Holland, and Britain? On the other hand, there is nothing intrinsically improbable in

the stories of William Tell and of Eleanor's saving Prince Edward's life; yet these have been excluded from the pages of history within our own lifetime.

17. The truths of politics, science, and medicine, are being daily extended, discovered, or rejected; history and religion cannot be exempt from this inevitable law of change, which is also the law of progress. The search for truth is thus in some sense analogous to the pursuit of pleasure; the quarry is ever just ahead; what is captured proves to be a phantom representation of the real object; the apparent success merely whets the appetite, the discovery of the illusion does not plunge the individual or the human race into despair; the chase begins afresh, and can never cease. Absolute truth postulates absolute knowledge. The sententious phrase, "What is true is not new, and what is new is not true," loses half its potency by the reflection that we do not know what is absolutely true; and is deprived of all its venom when we observe how calmly it ignores the relative value in this ancient planet of the terms new and old. What if historic truths were buried, say, two and a half millenniums ago, under heaps of disguised facts, meagre hints, legends and stories, distorted by a religious or national bias! Are we to accept the present amorphous condition of the original, or are we to dig, and, if necessary, hew, till we have excavated the old?

18. Layard, and other similar explorers in Asia Minor and Egypt, have had the satisfaction of convincing the most incredulous by that most powerful of arguments, ocular demonstration. The most stiff-necked and bigoted of opponents would scarcely have the hardihood to suggest that the Assyrian tablets and bulls in

London, the sarcophagus of Ashmanuzar at the Louvre, were manufactured at Birmingham. Very different is the case with criticism; it may demonstrate, for example, that the authors and dates assigned to certain books two thousand years ago, were at variance with the contents of those books themselves; that it is not possible for kings and priests of the most acknowledged piety to have ignored in their religious services, injunctions laid down for their guidance; that their ignorance is pure and simple; there is no hint of rebellion. This perfectly legitimate line of argument, one that would be deemed sufficiently conclusive in dealing with Greek or Latin literature, fails to influence the judgment of those who prefer tradition and cry "the old is better." The results of the herculean labours in Germany, Holland, and France, are viewed by vast numbers, in England at least, as modern and meretricious. It is in the eyes of many a new idea—not an old one brought once more to light. Having worshipped the mounds so long, the conservative believer in the verbal inspiration of Scripture grudges the removal of every spadeful of earth, though by this means the true old symmetrical outlines are gradually being exhumed.

<p style="text-align:center;">Pro magna teste vetustas
Creditur. Acceptam parce movere fidem.
Ov. <i>Fast.</i> iv. 203.</p>

19. Ovid, with the keener appreciation of religious rites and ideas enjoyed by poets, may have possibly meant, "Do not disturb my reverence for antiquity, and my consequent devout belief;" but it is more probable that, with Cicero, he was more anxious about the effect of disbelief on the ignorant common herd. Religious revolutions are liable to produce political. Anarchy

threatens when the mass of mankind suddenly lose their confidence in the faith of their childhood. Forbear, then, to open the sluices for a general inundation. It is true that there is great need of such a caution. Change is a law of Nature, but analogy teaches us that it must be effected slowly, and almost imperceptibly, to be beneficial to man. Earthquakes and other sudden transformations of Nature are always attended by horror and devastation. Still, however much the principle "let well alone" appeals to all men and nations, if it had been logically carried out, Christ would never have superseded Jupiter at Rome; Druid forms of worship would still be the State religion of Britain. And what of the progress of events since the triumph of Christianity? The motto, "Acceptam parce movere fidem," would have paralysed the first attempts at reformation. Where would have been the subsequent struggles between the various phases of conflicting religious thought; those struggles which have been the very source of life to the Church, stimulating as a tonic and rousing from a lethargic acquiescence, which is no more living faith than the hours spent in slumber are the real part of any man's life? How would religion have fared in Great Britain without Puritan and Methodist revivals, without the High Church movement of the first half, and the advance of Broad Church views in the second half of this century?

20. "Semper eadem" is the motto of the Catholic Church; still, its history shows that progress and evolution are as necessary to it as to all forms of religion which shrink from a living death. This is very evident from the most cursory review of the Great Councils, and specially so when we regard the edicts

of the Tridentine and (last) (Ecumenical Councils. The dogmas then promulgated may appear new, but they had long been held by many, being logically developed from previous tenets. Nor may we, with some, mock at the motto as vain and pretentious. The members of a family, seeing one another at frequent intervals, are unconscious of the changes effected in their character, manner, and appearance, which are sufficiently manifest to astonish a friend from a distance. A man, however, who has lived abroad for ten years or more, finds the difference in himself as freely canvassed by his relations as by his friends. And yet in both cases the man is the same; he cannot be accused of arrogance for maintaining "Ego sum," though friends and relatives cry in chorus, "Quantum mutatus ab illo." The Catholic Church, however much she has grown, and altered with her growth, is still the same. Outsiders may point to what they view as sudden changes at intervals of three hundred yards; she is quite consistent in maintaining her claim to the motto "Semper eadem."

21. Another charge brought against modern critics is, that they start with an *à priori* hostile attitude towards Revelation and Tradition; that because miracles are repugnant to their human pride or common sense, they first found theories and afterwards search for corroborative arguments. This is one of the rusty weapons from the eighteenth-century arsenal which is only slightly less effete than the assertion that theists abandoned and attacked Christianity to be able with more absolute freedom to indulge in vice. Strange to say, the same charges were brought against Paul, Luther, and many other Reformers. Let any one read

Wellhausen's Prolegomena or Kuenen's "History of Israel" carefully through two or three times, and he will be convinced that the calm spirit of almost mathematical, certainly judicial, inquiry that pervades such works entirely precludes the possibility of their having been deliberately undertaken with a hostile bias to anything but error. Read the Life of Renan, a man who not only was trained for the priesthood, but had been admitted to minor orders, a man who all his life spoke pathetically of himself as "un prêtre manqué," a phrase indicative of a spirit very far removed from antagonism to views he was logically bound to reject: surely his is not an instance of *à priori* animosity! It certainly strikes one as passing strange that it does not occur to these reasoners that their position might with more excuse be termed one of *à priori* friendly prejudice, born and bred in them.

22. The experience of Renan, referred to above, though, in its circumstances naturally peculiar, is still to a great extent typical. Silent and gradual as is the change in every man, there is at least one era in the lives of most men when the consciousness of the change is forced upon him; when suddenly it dawns upon him that his conception of himself, of the world and its problems, is quite at variance with what he hitherto held. It is not uncommon for the solitary student at first to experience a shock at the apparent incompatibility of the results of modern criticism with the religious ideas inculcated in his youth. That shock as truly marks an era, never to be forgotten, whether he resolves on attempting the task of reconciliation, or on devoting what powers in him lie to the furtherance of research.

23. Seven hundred years ago, the greatest of Chinese commentators passed through the same experience. When it is remembered that the Confucian Classic occupy in China the same revered position as the Bible does in Christian countries, the following quotation from an extract by him, appended to an edition of the Filial Piety Classic, cannot fail to excite the keenest interest: " Some time ago I read some remarks by Hu Hang-shan, Vice-President of the Board, on the Confucian Analects, where he says : ' I doubt that the Filial Piety Classic, with its quotations from the Book of Odes, is an original part of the classic.' At first I was alarmed, but by degrees, and on investigation, I began to awake to the truth of Mr. Hu's words ; and because (I discovered) that these were not the only doubtful parts of the Filial Piety Classic, I wrote a letter on the subject to Ch'ing K'o-kiu of Sha Chui, who replied : ' Without loss of time I called on Wang Twang-ming of Yu Shan, and he is of opinion that several passages have been corrected and interpolated by men subsequent to Confucius.' Thus I learned from the letter, which I had received, that my seniors read the book with every degree of cautious criticism ; and I rejoiced both at their corroboration and my own escape from a charge of beating the air and uttering vain words."

24. Here we have, long ago, in ignored—(I had almost said despised, certainly looked-down-upon)— China, a simple, unpretentious statement of the great change that takes place in thousands of human hearts and minds all over the world in the present day; when there first flashes, like an inspiration, or rather a revelation, the conviction that the old view is not correct, nor satisfactory, nor satisfying. A new standpoint is adopted, new phases of truth transport the soul. At first, we experience a revulsion, as though we were "rebels against the light"[1] but we grow calmer and more reassured as we awake to the conviction that the true work of modern criticism is restoration, not demolition; its aim is to endeavour to discover and re-establish old truth.

25. The crowning glory of the present age is the strenuous effort "to follow things that make for peace." The cordiality between Established Church and Nonconformists, the amity between Catholics and Protestants, are not the result of cold indifference, but the fruit of a definite purpose. "The scientific spirit is the great power that now sways all communities; its first disciples were mathematicians, then the students of the physical world's phenomena, and last of all the investigators of the moral world's science. A great calm has followed upon the former contentions between philosophy and religion.[2] It has been reserved for the closing half of the nineteenth century to prepare a tomb for the "Odium Theologicum," the giant ogre who has flourished for over two thousand years, whom Christ would fain have slain. The frantic outburst of fanatical opposition that nearly forty years ago greeted the publication of the "Essays and Reviews" and Colenso's "Pentateuch" is now viewed as excessive by all, and unreasonable by very many. General sympathy was accorded to a professor who was driven by a narrow-minded majority from the Scotch Church on account of his views on the so-called Higher Criticism. And quite recently a remarkable work has appeared from

[1] Job xxiv. 13.   [2] Renouf: "Science of Religion." p. 4.

the Oxford High Church School, in which it is clearly shown that the great truths and doctrines of the Church are not incompatible with an acceptance of the results of modern research. "Lux Mundi" is a splendid example of the recent growth of the true liberal spirit in religion and politics, which is thus ably extolled in P. G. Hamerton's "Intellectual Life": "As a positive increase in the morality of public sentiment, especially in the love of justice and the willingness to hear the truth, even when truth is not altogether agreeable to the listener, and in the respect paid by opponents to able and sincere men merely for their ability and sincerity. The love of justice, this patient and tolerant hearing of new truth, in which our age immeasurably surpasses all the ages that have preceded it, are the direct results of the scientific spirit, and are not only in themselves eminently moral, but conducive to moral health generally."

26. The Odium Theologicum differs, in kind, not degree, from the Odium Politicum. The significant fact, that by common consent of society, theology and politics are excluded from ordinary conversation, in mixed company at dinner tables, is evidence of this. The sneer, "See how these Christians hate one another," could as easily, and with as little truth, be employed against politicians. The fact is, that religion and politics are subjects in which every man is supposed to be interested, ignorance of which, and the absence of definite opinions concerning which, are attended with a certain amount of disgrace. Both topics are liable to be held dear in the secret recesses of each man's heart; and it is like an assault on the man himself, when what he disapproves is stoutly main-

tained, and doubts cast on what he holds precious. The heat and spirit displayed in argument are not to be attributed to inherent evils in the subjects which evoke them, but are rather tokens of the firm hold which they have on the personality of mankind. People who do not devote themselves to art and literature, can differ in opinion about the relative merits of works and fame of certain authors and artists, without condemning their opponents. It is not so easy, however, to abstain from accusations of ignorance or prejudice when Home Rule or Eternal Damnation is the topic.

27. "The essence of wisdom is double."[1] In the moral as well as the natural world, there are parts and counterparts, without either of which completeness is lacking. There are also opposing forces, which produce life and safety by their opposition. In electricity objects attracted by the negative pole are repelled by the positive; so those who find Orthodoxy and Conservatism alluring, experience a revulsion when brought in contact with Heterodoxy and Radicalism. The contention between the force of gravity and the tangential impetus is the means by which for millions of years our little planet has happily pursued its path around the sun; in regular, recurring periods each of these in turn predominates. Is there not a great analogy between these forces of nature and the moral forces under consideration; the contest is necessary and unceasing, but is in its results a promoter of harmonious working. Orthodoxy and Conservatism are not themselves central spots of calm, around which gyrate the devastating typhoons

[1] Job xi. 6.

repugnant that completes the circuit which in its perfection is so great a blessing to mankind. Opposition cannot be abolished: "A Protestant who wished to bring all men to Protestantism, a Catholic to Catholicism, an Orthodox to Orthodoxy, is under the same delusion as alchymists of former days, who tried to make gold from all metals. Gold is a metal as regards those properties which are common to all metals, but it is gold as regards the special attributes alone."[1]

29. How hopelessly we are unable to realise each other's standpoint and premises, to appreciate each other's motives and arguments, has been exemplified over and over again. Caird and Driver, Huxley and Gladstone, James Robertson[2] and Wellhausen: how vividly do these names recall to us writings which testify the utter inability of writers who start from two diametrically opposite points of vision to recognise the feelings which actuate the author who is champion on the other side. The highest attainments of scholarly learning do not seem to obviate this difficulty. Read Pusey on Daniel, or Lightfoot's reply to "Supernatural Religion;" is it possible from these works to gain anything like a real conception of, still less to reconstruct, the views opposed; the inarticulate skeleton is no more a fair representation of the living man than the Celsus of Origen or the Marcion of Tertullian, the Huxley of Gladstone or the Driver of Caird.

30. This difference of standpoint is very well illustrated by the use made, by each party, of inscriptions and other modern discoveries. To one, the chief value consists in the proportion of new words, new customs,

---
[1] Renouf: "Science of Religion."
[2] "Early History of Israel."

suggesting fresh alterations in difficult readings on other inscriptions or in the Hebrew Scriptures, or throwing fresh light on the general history of religion; by the other, welcome is only accorded to old words and old customs—*e.g.*, on the Moabite Stone, Omri, Yahveh, and David (?) attract attention, while the strange word for Altar-hearth[1] escapes their interest; if on an Assyrian inscription a name is found capable of recalling one of those names of kings in Genesis xiv. the whole historicity of that chapter is considered as thereby irrevocably established: the further question of how Abraham's life is thus thrown back three or four centuries is not considered worth mentioning. Doctors and artists alike study anatomy, but the object of the one is practical, of the other poetical, with a view to greater accuracy in pictorial effect. Very similar appears to be the difference between the critical labours of the Progressive and Conservative schools: with the latter criticism is only acceptable as affecting the poetical colouring of traditional history; the former, however, view it as a matter of business; they do not aim at a picturesque presentment of life—they desire to know the function and relation of every bone and ligature.

[1] 2 Sam. xxiii. 20; Isa. xxix. 1.

CHAPTER II

HEBREW STORY AND HISTORY

31. "The most ancient and shattered pages of tradition are dear to us, nay, dearer, perhaps, than the more copious chapters of modern times."[1] Next to the unavailing desire to penetrate the veil that shrouds the future, man suffers from an insatiable thirst to know all about the past. Hence the eager perusal of ancient tradition is not merely due to the glamour of antiquity, nor to the attractive dress of poetical words or ideas which characterise it. The personal interest awakened by tradition is one thing; the historical value afforded by it, quite another. The use recently made of all traditions, in the study of the history of religions and other comparative investigations of principles, shows us that less value is attached to each tradition as relating the particular history of any one nation, than as revealing the general ideas and providing a truer conception of the earlier human race. In every instance they must be stripped for examination; it is the bare thought, common to any certain number of them, that is after all the true tradition.

32. When we speak of tradition, we are apt to think of it as the tale of actual facts seen by some eye-

[1] Max Müller.

witness; by him recorded, and thereafter handed down through successive generations. This is very far from being the case; the truth being, that little more than the name of an ancient hero is preserved, associated with some one or more great event or personal attribute; the desire to know something of his daily life leads later generations to adapt to his surroundings stories already related elsewhere, either of his own descendants, or even as legends belonging to several races. This was the special province of the poet or maker, who, supplied with a few dry names, could, with a few dramatic touches, provide from imagination details of thought, word, and character. In proportion to the genius of the poet was the longevity of his description; others would attempt the same romance, novelties would be introduced, repetitions and contradictions would occur. "We find by experience every day that accounts which have been current but a short period have admitted very many strange elements, and in some cases have become unrecognisable. Without a perpetual miracle the oral tradition of Israel cannot have remained free from this influence."[1]

33. The tragedies at Sodom and Gomorrha, and at Gibeah of Benjamin, are only two of many such reported in the East, descriptive of the horrible abuse of the laws of hospitality, and the terrible punishment that attends their violation. The offering up of Isaac by Abraham is a Phœnician legend, of so great antiquity as to be related of the gods, and must therefore be held to have been extant long anterior to the times of Abraham, though introduced into his life as evidence that sacrifices to Moloch had been repudiated by the

[1] Kuenen, R. I.

founder of the Hebrew race. The exposure of Moses among the bulrushes is simply an indication that nothing is known of the birth and infant years of the great Deliverer; while his father's name, "Immersion," and his mother's, "Highly Honoured," or "Honoured by Yahveh," are manifest inventions. Similar tales are told of Cyrus, Romulus, and other heroes among many nations sprung from obscurity. All alike bear the stamp of improbability; why should we make an exception in favour of the Moses narrative, especially when it is remembered that the transparent reason for its introduction is, in this case, the opportunity it affords for providing a fictitious derivation of a name of foreign origin.

34. Uniform does not make a soldier, nor his robes a priest, but each is seen to best advantage, and his vocation is more manifest, when the man is in his official dress. The true tradition is the name of the hero itself wedded with some great undying fact, as the migration from Chaldæa is indissolubly connected with Abram, and the exodus from Egypt with Moses. The stories are merely the dress, but even though manufactured by different hands of materials brought from various countries, they cannot afford to be disregarded. What interest should we have in the great ancestor of the Hebrew and Arab races, if our knowledge of him were confined to the bare statement: "They went forth to go into the land of Canaan, and into the land of Canaan they came?" What could compensate mankind for the loss of the panoramic views of patriarchal life in the Pentateuch?

35. The admiration thus felt for the artistic pictures must not, however, lead us to the acceptance of the stories as history. It is to be observed, with Ewald,

that the narratives are carefully selected to preserve types of family life, as models or warnings for mankind, presenting in due series, father, son, nurse, steward, husband devoted to one wife (Rebecca), and the evils of concubinage (Sarah and Hagar), and of polygamy (Leah and Rachel). So artificial a system is plainly unhistoric; the grouping and colouring have secured universal and unqualified admiration and praise; but the effect is due rather to the imaginative skill of the gifted novelist, than to the painstaking preservation of every detail by the careful historian.

36. How many there are who, with one breath, will declare that the portrayal of these ancient times would have been impossible without the aid of revelation; and with the next, will exultingly draw attention to the fact that patriarchal life may still be seen unchanged in Palestine and Arabia! So far from corroborating the necessity here of revelation, the latter truth prejudices acceptance of the former theory. If a modern traveller, with the material now available, could with his pen draw similar pictures of patriarchal life; if the authors of the books of Job and Ruth were capable of depicting times long prior to their own so successfully that stories were long held to have been composed at the dates presupposed by their descriptive details; what compels us to the conclusion that the tales in Genesis are absolutely genuine? Why are we driven to the inference that they are either carefully preserved tradition or miraculous revelation?

37. Hebrew history and story—*i.e.*, fact and fiction —are so interwoven that it is hard to separate them, and nigh to impossible to lay the finger with precision on the point, and declare that here fiction ends and fact begins. Fiction in the early history of any people is not surprising, being the universal custom, due, as we have seen, to the important part played by poets in its manufacture. Even so late as the eighth century A.D. we find the venerable Bede solemnly recording as history fabulous events purporting to have occurred in his own times. All ancient races have striven to put on record the origin of their founder: the Hebrew is more ambitious; it aims at the presentment not only of the hero himself, but of his wife, concubine, servant, nephew, sons, &c., and in a marked manner claims that all the conversations which took place between these characters are the real original utterances, for they are pregnant with prophecies or abound with backward references. Nowhere else does early history assume the form of such lengthy consecutive detailed narrative, carefully distinguishing the characters of individuals, and steadily progressing from one point to another. This unique characteristic of early Hebrew literature is in a great measure to be attributed to the peculiar manner in which it has undergone successive courses of polishing and remodelling from a series of editors whose aim was rather to inculcate moral lessons, and publish grounds for modern belief and custom, than to describe actual events. If a later editor saw an opportunity for introducing a reference to a neglected custom, or a derivation for an unexplained name of man or place, he felt no scruple in making the necessary addition for that purpose. A novel founded on fact is the most suitable name for at least the first seven books of the Bible.

38. There is, however, a great gulf between the myths of the Hindus and Greeks and the sacred

fiction of the Hebrews. It is true that heathen mythology has been laid under contribution in several instances, as in the story of the Garden, Noah and the Flood, the sacrifice of Isaac, &c.; but the matter is so transformed and receives such new dignity as to lose its mythological meaning, while conveying some historic truth or hinting at some profound theory in explanation of some moral problem. The only unalloyed myth in the Bible would appear to be the sun-stories of Samson, for no moral lesson is attached to them.

39. The hand of God in history was the noble motto of the Hebrew historian; it is this which imparts a solemnity to his narratives, even when fictitious, and completely differentiates him from profane authors. When the Hebrews move eastwards from the land of Chaldæa this natural tendency, observable earlier in the Hittites and Egyptians, and later in Scythians, Goths, and Huns, is attributed directly to God's command. When the Jacobeans (or Josephites) were hurried out of Egypt, most probably *against* their inclination at the time, providential guidance was demonstrated by miraculous intervention and protection; and by the subsequent success of their settlement in Canaan (or the northern part of it); and consequently we find a complete narrative, stating that the *Egyptians* were *unwilling* to let them go, and solemn but highly improbable stories are told of the manner in which God, " with strong hand and uplifted arm," brought them forth from the land of bondage. The description of the occupation of Canaan is heightened into a miraculous conquest, with the same laudable purpose—the glorification of the God of Israel. We find crowded into forty years, and attributed to one God-led Josephite hero, victories and acquisitions of territory that must be distributed over at least a couple of centuries, and the honour of these must be shared by at least one Judite warrior. As a contrast to this view, the result of critical inquiry, I cannot refrain from quoting the following:[1] "The account given to us in the Book of Joshua as to the process by which the Hebrew people appropriated Palestine, is the oldest, the most authentic, and the most circumstantial account we have of the way in which any victorious race possessed itself of a conquered territory."

40. In all this we see, for the most part, not a wanton perversion of facts, but a lack of historical perspective, not remarkable in those ages, and the natural prejudices of the historian, which almost preclude the possibility of an absolutely impartial history; while, at the same time, these human defects are ennobled and beautified by the consistent reference and appeal to the guiding Deity. Ewald speaks of "the peculiar genius of the fourth narrator being practical creation."[2] When Driver says, "The Hebrew bistoriographer, as we know him, is essentially a compiler, or arranger of pre-existing documents, he is not himself an original author,"[3] we must understand him to refer to the latest editors; while Ewald's remark is one of those cautious theoretical distinctions which he disregards in practice, most frequently in footnotes, where his most advanced ideas are generally to be found.

41. In suggesting the term novel as applicable to

[1] Duke of Argyll : " Unseen Foundations of Society," p. 131.
[2] "Hist.," i. 106.   [3] Intr. 3.

these writings, I have availed myself of the only expression that appears to suit the conditions we discover. We cannot speak of myths with propriety unless some natural phenomenon is disguised in story. A legend is an ancient narrative attached to some spot, or in which some hero is almost, if not quite, deified. An allegory is a continuous expanded parable. Thus we have the Samson myth, legends of Moses and Elijah, and about Sodom and Gomorrha; and traces of allegory forming, as, it were, a pattern interwoven in the historical fabric. But what name are we to give to stories the main incidents of which, running through three or four generations, are so arranged as to present in defined order a series of pictures of patriarchal life; and that, too, when there are grave reasons for believing that the individual characters never existed in the form which is so vividly portrayed?

42. In no other language is there a book in which incidents are compiled so systematically on principles of philological derivation. Given the name of a place, which for some reason or other the author wishes to associate with some ancient saint, and immediately the form of the word suggests to him a narrative, which is accordingly introduced—*e.g.*, Bethel Jabbok. But the same word may be suggestive of more than one root; we therefore find two or three stories connected with the same place—*e.g.*, Beer-sheba, Beer-lachai-roi. Add to this, stories based on the most self-evident meanings of names of men (Edom, Jacob, &c.), several of which are clearly incorrect—Naphthali, Levi, Reuben, &c.— not forgetting the manifest attempt to prove antiquity of customs, and we have a pretty complete apparatus for tale composition.

48. As I believe that few people fully recognise the true aspect presented by the narrative of the Hexateuch, I subjoin a modernised imitation of its style and characteristics; this form of illustration having been suggested to me by Archbishop Whately's parody on the Book of Joshua, in which he pretended to throw doubts on the historic truth of the career of Napoleon Buonaparte:—

B.C. . . . Now King Celtus took unto him to wife Belga, and she bare him three daughters—Hibernia, Caledonia, and Britannia; and the sons of Hibernia were these: Ulster, Munster, Leinster, and Connaught; and Leinster was the father of Dublin.

A.D. 400. Now the sons of Teuton were these: Anglus, Saxo, Juta, Danus, and Horsa. And to Saxo were born four sons, Essex, Middlesex, Wessex, and Sussex. And the son of Juta, Kent. Now Kent sat by the sea-shore, and ordered the waves back from his chair, but lo! they surrounded him altogether; then said he unto his servants, "Call me no more a god, for God only ruleth the winds and the waves." Therefore was the name of that place called Godwin, for there strove he with God, but could not prevail. And to Danus were born sons, Northumber, Durham, and York. Now, York was a great man, and had three sons riding upon horses; to each of them gave he a province, therefore is the name of that province called Riding unto this day. And his servants conspired against him and smote off his head, and set it up on the walls of his city that he had built for himself withal; so he died; therefore they that speak in proverbs say, "Alas! poor Yorick."

A.D. 1066. And the high priest said unto him, "Thus

hath the Lord said, Get thee up and take the land, for to thee have I given it; and he said, Good is the word of the Lord: I am willing to go up:" therefore was his name called Will-i-am. Now the chief city of that land was great exceedingly, and much business was wrought there, and many a loan done; therefore called they the name of that city London.

A.D. 1314. And Bruce fled from the face of his enemies, and a woman said unto him, "Turn in, my lord;" and she was baking cakes, and the woman said unto him, "See that these cakes burn not:" and it came to pass that as his heart was heavy because the enemies of God possessed the land, lo! the cakes did burn. Therefore was that place called Bannockburn, and there did God give him great deliverance.

44. Let us suppose the above to be extracts from the only available chronicles of England, and to have been accepted unchallenged as a statement of facts, until a more critical age arose, say A.D. 3000. What an outburst of abuse and derision would at first fall on the heads of those who had the temerity to assert that the names of persons were really names of countries, races, districts, and towns; that the philology displayed in the interpretation of names was incorrect, Saxon roots being found in words of Latin or Celtic origin; how far-fetched, too, some of the substitutions would appear—*e.g.*, Riding from Trithing—that these false derivations actually gave rise to the invention or misappropriation of stories—*e.g.*, Bannockburn; that quotations from later books were thrust in out of place, in much earlier periods — *e.g.*, "Alas! poor Yorick," written by Shakespeare in 1600, called a proverb between 400 and 600.

45. The play on sounds, indulged in by the prophets of which Micah i. 10–14 is a splendid example, differs *toto cælo* from the custom in the Hexateuch of observing such a play, and authoritatively asserting that such a pun is the historical derivation of the name of a man or place. Again, observation of the manner in which incomplete puns are found among the prophets justifies us in concluding that such may reasonably be expected to be found in the earlier narratives.[1] A complete pun is Micah i. 10, *B'Gath* al tag-*gidhu*, *B'Ako* al ti*bhku*. A specimen of a latent pun, which has escaped the eye of Ewald, is noticeable at the end of the verse, where the rare word hith*pallashti* is employed as a play on *Pallesheth* = Philistia understood.

46. Thus a large proportion of so-called Hebrew tradition is based on suggestions derived from the names of men and places, many of which will not stand the light of investigation; the consideration of this trait will act as a check in according too ready an acceptance to those narratives where they most abound, for it is worthy of careful regard that such derivations gradually grow extinct as we advance into the domain of more assured history. In the Books of Samuel even, where fact more preponderates, but from which fiction is still not absent, we find but rare attempts to explain the name of men or places. As long as we are prepared to recognise as true, derivations of these words, which are purely artificial, if not absurd and impossible, room is left for our belief in their antiquity. But if—as we must, on observation of the facts—if we see in the derivations evidence of purpose, study, system, our position is changed: the tradition which

---

[1] Gen. xxv. 25, and xxxv. 18.

relies on such manufactured supports is more modern than many of us would like to admit. If the tradition is modern, what is its value? Certainly not its history. Take the two most important heroes, Abram and Moses. That we are justified in a cautious reception of the stories told of them is sufficiently apparent when it is remembered that no satisfactory derivation of either name has been given in the Hebrew books, nor definitely accepted by modern authorities, the probability being that they are not of Semitic origin at all; when further we observe that the details of their biographies are marred by conflicting statements of the traditional documents, together with the assignment to these heroes of acts long posterior to their times, we begin to be conscious that we know nothing whatever of them reliable, other than the hoary legend of their respective migrations. If then we are so ignorant of these great luminaries, we may well be supposed to know still less of the stars of smaller magnitude that are marked on the chart between them.

47. The finest Chinese and Japanese works of art are marred by a lack of perspective, and it is more than doubtful whether the owner is ever able to picture to himself the scene which was originally in the artist's mind: it is not that each figure or tree is in itself ludicrous or impossible—they may individually be monuments of high art and each possess claims to admiration and esteem; but the association and combination are improbable and unnatural. There is no story-teller to compare with the Oriental for fire, vigour, and sustained interest; but there is a lack in the Hebrew narratives of what may be termed historic perspective; there is no toning-down into the misty haziness of the distance; the remotest ages must be painted in as vivid colours and with the same minuteness of detail as quite recent times. All the figures, too, are the same life-size; the author seems to touch up the account of his heroes, that one may not be eclipsed by the other. Noah, Abram, Moses, and David would at the first glance appear to stand forth prominently; but the figures of Jacob, Joshua, and Solomon are soon seen to rival them, and that, too, with the most obvious intent. See, too, how the lesser prophet Elisha looms ever bigger and bigger, till at last he attains the proportions of his master, Elijah, the hero of Carmel and Horeb, It is not surprising that this habit should betray the authors, at least once, into a *reductio ad absurdum*, for, comparing 2 Kings xviii. 5 with xxiii. 25, we find it stated both of Hezekiah and his successor Josiah, that "there was no king like him, that was before him, neither after him arose there any like unto him;" whence it is manifest that Josiah was at the same time both greater and less than Hezekiah, which is absurd. Most of us have seen that clever illusive trick, where figures, all exactly the same height by measurement, appear to the eye to increase in size in proportion as they are further off, the effect being produced by a simple arrangement of converging lines. This to a very great extent accounts for the gigantic stature and immense age assigned to primæval man, which seems due to the attempt to draw men, at that immeasurable distance, the same size as those of modern times, while the converging lines of historic perspective complete the illusion.

48. Even the great Shakespeare, with his love of accuracy and true representation, cannot escape being

convicted of occasional anachronisms. More remarkable in the Hebrew historian is the deliberate assumption that rites and customs, prevalent in his own day, have remained unchanged since that great era, the Exodus. Such statements are as manifestly unhistoric as if, taking the conquest of England by William for the era of English history, our writers were to attribute Magna Charta, representative Parliaments, Habeas Corpus, and other gradual developments of our constitution, to William's zeal and ability for government. It is only in mythology that an Athena springs into the world from her father's head, fully equipped with arms and endowed with complete wisdom. It is not historically true, for instance, that the Levitical system, with its priestly tribe of some myriads, with its code, political, social, military, moral, and ritual, rushed into existence within twelve months of the Israelites leaving Egypt. Not only is it in itself highly improbable, as contrary to the experience of every nation, and inconsistent with the description of the ignorant mob of slaves straight from the furnaces and lime-kilns, who would have required years of special training for the judicial work immediately required of them; but the supposition of its historic truth is directly at variance with accounts of more modern times, where no motive for departing from an existing law has even been suggested. We only hear of scattered Levites till David to a certain extent organised them. Religious rites were performed everywhere by everybody, preferentially by the father of the family. There is a strange silence actually about so important an official as the high priest: the very claim of Eli and Samuel to Levitical descent is of the most shadowy, while the full Levitical ritual would appear to owe its origin to Ezekiel and post-exilic influence.

49. To take examples of more general matters. If provisions were already made (in Deuteronomy xvii. 14-16) for the election of a king, the denunciation by Samuel of the natural desire of the people for a permanent military leader is inexplicable; this, without regard to the palpable allusions to the subsequent events of Solomon's reign. If the law of dividing the spoil fairly amongst camp-followers, as well as those who had taken an active part in the battle, already existed (Numbers xxxi. 27), why does David appear as the deviser of this just rule? (1 Samuel xxx. 25.) Why, again, should David and the nation suffer for holding a census, when all details, including a tax, had been provided in the code published five hundred years previously? (Exodus xxx. 12.) How is it that Hezekiah is reported to have, with much diffidence, suggested the observance of the Passover in the second instead of the first month (2 Chronicles xxx. 2), when the difficulty of ceremonial uncleanness had been foreseen and legislated for? (Numbers ix. 11.) Very strange it is to read (Deuteronomy xxiv. 16), " The children shall not be put to death for the father," and then to observe the wholesale destruction of families for the sins of the fathers, Korah, Dathan, and Abiram, and Achan: the early doctrine was "visiting the sins of the father on the children to the third and fourth generations," and it was first combated by Jeremiah (xxxi. 29).

50. The native compilers of Israelite history are, however, on no account, as was formerly the custom, to be charged with ignorance and carelessness. Their

work of selection and preservation is stamped with evidences of system and consistency; they had an aim steadily before them, the pursuit of which has left much that puzzles and confuses minds directed by the more severe and logical canons laid down by modern ideas of the requirements of true history. It is not possible that the glaring contradictions in diverse reports of the same event could have escaped their notice; nor that in interweaving them they had the deliberate intention of deceiving future generations. Rather than reject an old traditional legend because it did not accord with another, both should be preserved; each is valuable as a relic of antiquity, sometimes also each has a moral lesson of its own. "Gather up the fragments that remain, that nothing be lost," and "Destroy not the wheat with the tares," were the guiding principles of these ancient compilers.

51. Let us take a couple of prominent instances. In Exodus xxiv. 9–11 we read that Moses, Aaron, Nadab and Abihu, and seventy of the elders of Israel, *saw the God* of Israel, and particulars of what they saw are given. According to Deuteronomy iv. 12, they heard the voice but, *saw no similitude;* and in Exodus xxxiii. 20 even Moses is allowed only a partial view of God. The contradictions preclude the acceptance of any of them as history, but the stories teem with lessons. Official privileges and intercourse with God do not prevent subsequent backsliding and its attendant punishment: the Nadab and Abihu who shared this glorious vision died later a sudden death for drunkenness when performing their priestly office. Only by solitude and fasting can man, even the holiest and greatest saint, bring his soul into communion with

God. It is also quite possible that the first story arose last of all, with a definite purpose of attributing to the direct choice and commandment of God, with a subsequent confirmation of their appointment by a special vision, the institution of the elders, first ascribed to Jethro (Exodus xviii.), or to Moses (Deuteronomy i.). If this be so, the earlier story—*i.e.*, occupying an earlier position in the books as we have them—would appear to have been later added by the schools of the prophets, when the combined wisdom of synods began to supplant the authority of the individual; and a caution would thus be administered to us, as to the degree of care with which we accept the presence of primitive ideas as evidence of antiquity.

62. As a second example, we will take Numbers xxi. 17, 18. " So Israel was wont to sing :

> Concerning the well (So LXX.)
> Sing ye to it ;
> The well, the princes sought it with a divining rod ;
> The chiefs of the people cut it with their staves."

This is clearly the original version of the twofold story of Moses striking the rock at Horeb and at Kadesh, though its identity with the second occasion is established by the reference (xxi. 16 to xx. 8). The song as it stands is of great antiquity, and its indefinite character would make it equally applicable to the wells dug by any chief, even Abram and Isaac. A reference was seen to Moses in the word *M'choqeq*, which may mean a lawgiver, but by parallelism requires here the rendering given above, which is also found in other passages. Here, then, we have a simple natural occurrence, not needlessly transformed into a miracle for the astonishment of the vulgar, but referred to the direct agency of God for the inculcation of the religious lesson, that the supply of our simplest needs, and our scientific acquaintance with the laws of nature, must not be attributed to man's unaided energy and intellect. If we accept this theory of a determination to benefit mankind by the concealed truth, rather than instruct him by unvarnished history, we shall be the gainers. Thus all the miraculous and anthropomorphic elements of the Bible are deprived of the grossness which is the cause of stumbling to many. They are written, not by, but for, the ignorant; their object was to instruct, not deceive.

53. Communing with God, prayer, confession, and repentance, would never have been so fully and easily apprehended by even the most illiterate of mankind, of all ages and countries, had they not been set forth in the guise of simple narrative. How few educated Christians derive their code of morality, their ideas of special providence, of intimacy with God, from any other source than the Old Testament! The dogmas of predestination and the like must be studied in the Epistles; but for the most part they are un-illustrated, and do not evoke the general interest of simpler hearts. It is not only children that demand books with pictures. How much larger is the number of persons who read Green's or Gardiner's Histories, than of those acquainted with May's or Hallam's Constitutional Histories! More general interest is aroused by the incidents that present to us the acts and character of living men, than by the development of ideas and systems.

54. And here in passing I cannot refrain from questioning whether the modern tendency in Education,

to condemn the old-fashioned method of teaching history, and substitute the study of customs and laws for the more sprightly narrative, is not mistaken. Boys who will dilate on the murder of Thomas à Becket have little to say about the Constitutions of Clarendon; Simon de Montfort is more associated in their minds with the battles of Lewes and Evesham, than with the formation of the first representative Parliament. Births, deaths, and marriages are within their mental grasp, and tales connected with such events assist them in some measure in realising the actual existence of men and women who otherwise are apt to pass before their mental vision as mere puppets. How little do boys know intelligently of the present government of their own country; much less can they appreciate the story of its gradual growth. The struggle excites them, but its cause acts as a soporific. Every child will listen with rapt attention to historical tales, at the same time unconsciously acquiring some of the true principles of history; but higher history as much requires special natural taste and trained intelligence as do higher mathematics and physical science.

55. The aversion from the Abstract and the preference for the Concrete were as natural to the infancy of the human race as they are observable in tastes of children of our own day. By attributing a recognition of the truth and necessity of this principle to the sacred writers, we do not expose them to the charge of wilfully deluding the ignorance of the people, nor of labouring in the interests of priestcraft. The lessons of religion and great moral truths were, in other countries, formulated into systems of philosophy

beyond the comprehension of the common people; but by presenting them in the simple but impressive form of captivating tales, the Israelite author, with equal tact and talent, solved the problem of reaching and influencing the great mass, not only of his own race, but of all mankind.

CHAPTER III

STORIES BASED ON DERIVATION

56. In the preceding chapter mention was made of the constant practice by the Hebrew authors of compiling stories based on supposed derivation of names of men and places: it may not be amiss here to give some examples, especially as in Chapter VII. this feature will be assumed as an accepted fact, by aid of which important inquiries will be prosecuted.

57. The later Priestly Code simply states that God created man, "male and female created he them, in the image of God;[1] the name of the female man is not given; their only son is Seth;[2] Seth's son and grandson are respectively, Enosh and Cainan = Cain.

58. The Yahvist document had not been content with so bare a statement; reasons and explanations must be given. Man was made out of the ground (Adhamah), *therefore* was he called Adham.[3] This fiction was suggested partly by the similarity of the above words, both connected with a root, "red," and partly from observation that corpses resolve themselves into dust;[4] but equally should all animal and vegetable creation have been described as being formed

---

[1] Gen. i. 27. [2] Gen. v. 3.
[3] Gen. ii. 7. [4] Gen. iii. 19.

by God from the dust of the earth,[1] and to all alike should the generic term Adham have been applied. A similar identity of root is, of course, noticeable in *homo* and *humus*, the latter being derived from *chthama*, an archaic form of *chama*. Have adhamah and chthama any common origin in the remote past?

59. Woman.—The curious mind of this writer was perplexed with the difficulty arising from the possibility of a male originating a race; so, to obtain a solution, he again betakes himself to the region of philology. He found in the word *Ishsha*, woman, the presence of the letter *n* assimilated with *sh*; which is an undoubted fact, and manifest in the plural *nashím*. Two roots suggested themselves: *neshi* = forgetfulness, and *nasha* = to borrow. On this he forms the narrative: Yahveh throws Adam into a sleep of *forgetfulness*, and *borrowing* a rib from him makes a woman; hence called Ishsha = borrowed, because she was taken out of man.[2] The ordinary rendering, "she was called a she-man, because she was taken out of man," is surely vapid; the female sex in animals is not so accounted for. Gesenius rests content with a very simple play on words, supported by the Samaritan Pentateuch, "called Ishsba, because she was taken from Ishah = her husband;" but this ignores the double *sh* and is therefore an unsatisfactory pun, if, indeed, worthy of the name at all.

60. Innocence.—A latent pun, but not on that account to be overlooked, is to be observed in the words for *naked* and *subtle*[3] and the following verses. The lesson inculcated is, that man's ambition for subtlety, or wisdom as he flatteringly called it,

---
[1] Gen. ii. 19. [2] Gen. ii. 23. [3] Gen. ii. 25.

resulted in the exposure of the nakedness, not of his body, but of his spiritual self.

61. Particulars pregnant with allegorical significance are consistently added of the fortunes of the first human pair. Man (Adam) marries Life (Eve), and, they bear a son, Possession (Cain), deriving the name from *qanah*, to possess : " I have *gotten* a son, namely, the life-giver," *i.e.*, the progenitor of the future human race.[1] The Hebrew strictly is, " I have gotten a man, viz., Yahveh." There is no doubt that Renan is right in asserting the original identity of the roots of Yahveh and Chavvah (Eve); the *ch* and the *h* were later subdivisions to modify meanings ; as here, *hayah* = to be, and *chavah* or *chayah* = to live. The second son of Eve was Vanity or Disappointment (Abel); a name chosen not also without regard to the Assyrian *Abil* = son, though scarcely restricting it to that meaning, which would not accord with the author's research for allegorical signification. The allegory then runs thus : Mankind, infused with Life, begat Success and Disappointment ; Success surmounted, or killed, Disappointment, and the result was Settlement, a third son.[2]

62. " Then began man to call upon the name of Yahveh,"[3] is explained at once if we recognise this author's persistent inquiry into the philological meaning of words. Enosh = sick, frail, mortal man ; it was the first appearance of sickness or epidemic, which impelled men to cry to the unseen Power. Necessity evokes prayer.

63. Whatever may have been the original form of the eight or ten names in the genealogies of Genesis iv. and v.—very probably most of them were culled from

[1] Gen. iv. 1.   [2] Seth: iv. 25.   [3] iv. 26.

a Hindu source, as Ewald thinks—still it is quite in the style of the Hebrew author to dress them in such a way as to hint at some underlying theory in his own mind; possibly somewhat as follows:

Adam	Mankind.	
Qain	Nest-men; Troglodytes (Num. xii. 24)	Races.
M-ahale-el	Tent-men.	
Irad	City-men.	
Chenok	Dedicator of city; priest.	
Methu-selah	Weapon-man.	Individuals.
Lamek	?	
Noach	Ship-man.	

In the two genealogies of Cain and Seth we are rightly told by most critics that we have a confusion of two tables which were originally identical. Thus it is suspicious that the grandson of man (Adam) should have been Man (Enosh; and that their respective sons should have been Qain and Qainan. In chapter iv. we find eight descendants from Adam through Qain; and in chapter v. the same number, with almost identical names, but disarranged order, from Enosh through Quainan:

Chap. iv.	Adam.	Chap. v.	Enosh.
	Qain.		Qainan.
	Chenok.		Mahalel.
	'Irad.		Ired.
	M'chuyael.		Chenok.
	Methusael.		Methushelach.
	Lamek.		Lamek.
	Na'amah.		Noach.

We have reciprocal evidence of this identity in both lists. The 'Ain is necessary in Chapter V. to make Ired have the signification required by the context—viz., city men; and in chapter iv. Lamek, the son of Methusael sings a sword-song more appropriate to Lamek, the son of Methuselach, the Weapon-man (chap. v.); again Na'amah in the one has the letter *m*, which is only hinted at in the derivation of the other Noach from Nacham (v. 29) = comfort.

64. NOACH.—The hero of the Flood derives his name from the Aryan story, where his name *No* was akin to *Naus*, a ship. The Hebrews, in adopting the foreign tradition, transliterated the name in two ways: Noach, which suited the allusions to sacrificing; and No'am, which accorded with the discovery of wine. The more religious derivation naturally survived, while traces of the other require to be sought for. Noah is the first real sacrificer, and his name is therefore associated with *minchah* = sacrifice, and *nichoach* = fragrant-smelling. It is remarkable that the only other place where the name Nochah occurs[1] it is by mistake for Na'aman (Genesis xxi. 46); compare also Numbers xxvi. 33, where No'ah suggests the elision of the *m* for No'amah. On the other hand, we have distinct evidence of the root No'am in Abino'am No'omi[2] and such combinations as " Father of No'am," " Daughter of No'am,"[3] by comparison with Abi-yah, Father of Yahveh, Achi-melek, brother of Molok, justify us in the belief that there was a god No'am, who, in accordance with the meaning of the root, would be viewed as a god of luck, good cheer, jollity;[4] in short a Phœnician Bacchus, which is very appropriate to the wine story of Noah. Ewald[5] alludes to interesting coins of the Flood, which, though

---

[1] 1 Chron. viii. 2.
[2] Judges v. 1.
[3] " Corp. Ins. Phœn.," p. 69.
[4] " Corp. Ins. Phœn." p. 95, &c.
[5] "Hist.," vol. i. p. 281.

"dating from the time of the Cæsars of the first half of the third century after Christ, can hardly have borrowed these signs exclusively from the Old Testament, since they represent one pair only as rescued, and, not like the Old Testament, the Father's sons and sons' wives as well. In a footnote he quotes Eckhel as reporting a letter missing after No: what if that missing letter were *m*?

65. CANA'AN.—The word Cana'an appears to have meant *low-lying* ground, and was originally applied to the shores of Palestine, whence later a Canaanite became synonymous with a merchant.[1] On account of the bitter hatred between the Israelites and Canaanites, the idea of *bowing down* (neuter) or *subdued* (passive),[2] is introduced here; and with historic reference to the servitude of many of the aboriginal races, especially in the reign of Solomon (Renan). The name, in the story, of the offending son of Noah (Ham = heat) did not lend itself to any suitable curse from the irate father; and consequently one of his innocent sons is subjected to a vicarious sentence of eternal bondage: "Cursed be Bowed-down, servant of servants shall he be."

It is interesting to observe how conveniently divines restored the curse to the original offender, and by interpreting Ham as Africa, discovered inspired authority and sanction for the slavery of the negro. Still, the story is consistent with itself so far, for it continues the interpretation thus: No'am = Bacchus, is intemperate; the *heat* of wine (Chemah) impels him to throw off his clothes, which gives occasion to the rude

[1] Job xl. 30.   [2] *Cf.* Judges iii. 30.

mockery of his son Cham. The connection between the words is the undoubted cause of the incident, otherwise Canaan could have played the part *in propriâ personâ*.

66. JAPHET.—Ewald (i. 279) shows, with great probability, that this was a god of the north, as Ham was of the south, once again in imitation of the Hindu mythology. Moreover, the fact, that in the Armenian legend, derived from "Assyrian or Babylonian documents," the three sons of Xisuthros, who corresponds to Noah, are Zervin, Titan, and Japetosthe, is very instructive, suggesting that the unknown foreign word was retained in its original form, *in this case*, because *without alteration* it afforded opportunity for a pun: "God shall enlarge (Yapt) Yaphet."[1] The reference to Japetos in Greek and Latin works is to be attributed to the Assyrian, not the Hebrew source, seeing that they have also preserved Titan.[2]

67. NIMROD.—The Hebrew derivation seems to have been from *Nimr*, a panther, employed metaphorically as wolf, raven, &c.,[3] for a great hero in fight, who hunted other nations; this metaphor has been taken literally,[4] and is used as a proverb to this day, as if Nimrod, instead of being some great conquering general, had been a mere celebrated huntsman. Later Jewish tradition derives his name from *Marad* = to rebel, and he is viewed as a sort of fallen angel; Abraham, too, is made his contemporary, and successfully to defy his tyranny; all which is instructive, as showing how some tradition is invented, not handed down. Nimrod is supposed to be really akin to

[1] Gen. ix. 27.
[2] *Cf.* Ovid, "Met.," l. 10, 82.
[3] Judg. vii. 25.
[4] Gen. ix. 10.

Merodak; but the original hero has not yet been found on the Assyrian inscriptions, as indeed can hardly be expected, considering the fabulous period (third generation after the Flood) assigned to him. The suggestion that the characters for Iz-du-bar can be read Namra-uddu has not been well received;[1] there is, however, a *race Namar*[2] to the south-west of Media, which may have been the aboriginal home of a conquering race that overran Babylonia and Assyria. In this case we must seek some explanation of the final *d* in Nimrod and above 'Irad,[3] which is at once suggested by the following sentence from the Appendix to the English translation of Schrader's "Cuneiform Inscriptions": "In Akkadian proper names, the word which appears for son or child is not this (*abal*), but another (*du*);" whence we deduce older forms—Nimrudn, 'Iradu.

68. BAB-EL = The Gate of God (Schrader).—The Hebrews regarded death, toil, and child-bearing as curses on mankind, instead of universal and beneficent laws. Whatever causes annoyance, inconvenience, and severance, with tendency to hostility, cannot by them be viewed as part of the original design, which was perfectly executed, but on account of man's sin was liable to the introduction of elements of imperfection; as a punishment to man, the negative act of withholding previous blessings assumed the positive form of a curse. The mixing of tongues suggested the root *balal*, and the opportunity of attributing the origin of a curse on mankind to their enemy Babylon was not to be lost; while the ruins in its neighbourhood

---

[1] Schrader, "Cuneiform Inscr.," Gen. x. 8.
[2] *Ibid.*, par. 415.   [3] Gen. v. 18.

gave some colour of truth to the narrative of a tower designed to reach to heaven. Thus arose the legend of the Tower of Babel and its attendant Babel of tongues, based on an impossible derivation, and intimately associated indeed with confusion, but of cause and effect, not of tongues. Separation of tribes and even of families produces a variety of dialect; the story in Genesis asserts that the dispersion of mankind was caused by the sudden occurrence of a variety of languages on one spot, where otherwise mankind would have been for ever congregated, speaking only one language. Inconsistent, too, with the historic truth of this narrative is its postulate, that all mankind was at that time centred at Babylon, and thence scattered by the difficulty of mutual intercourse, all of which is, moreover, absolutely at variance with the account in the preceding chapter, that Egypt and Palestine were already peopled before Babylon was built (Gen. x. 10). The note K (x. 25), that Eber's son was called Division (Peleg), "For in his days was the earth divided," must be viewed as an independent philological gloss, and even if correct, would throw the confusion of tongues two generations later, when the races of mankind were still more scattered. It is more probable that Peleg had the same meaning ("Stream.")

69. Thus in the opening chapters of Genesis we have in embryo the system of narration adopted through the first seven books of the Bible. Sometimes the story may exist first, being of foreign origin; but if so, it is altered to give it a fictitious appearance of Hebrew birth, by the use of words from that language skilfully employed as essential parts of the narrative.

Sometimes a whole story is compiled on the strength of an ingenious regard to a possible derivation of even the commonest words in everyday life. But whether indigenous or exotic, in no case is there any evidence of a simple natural story, where a pun irrepressibly bursts forth; on the contrary, the incidents are carefully arranged to bring in the play on words, however distorted and impossible. Now, we not unnaturally ask, Why are we required to suppose that this course of procedure suddenly ceased when the tale trenches on the more particular history of the Hebrew people? *

70. In the first place, the genealogies introducing the patriarch Abram bear all the characteristics of the antediluvian genealogies, the names being, many of them, foreign words, and though Ewald has identified many of these with various regions connected with them historically, we find here a principle of selection and arrangement the same as before, quite apart from their ethnographical value:

Shem.	A Phœnician god.
Arph-kesed.	District of Chaldæa (Kasdin).
Shelach.	Sent forth.
'Eber.	Crossed.
Peleg.	Stream.
Re'u.	Shepherds.
Serug.	Vineyards.
Nachor.	Euphrates = Nahar (ch for h).
Terach.	Caravan (cf. Arach).

Noah had three sons, whom we have seen to have been three gods or sections of humanity. Shem's five sons are clearly nations: Elam, Ashshur, Arphaxed (Chaldæans), Lud (Lydians), and Aram (Syria); again Terah had three sons, Abram, Nahor, and Haran. Now it has been shown that these names survive in the names of districts: Terach in Trachonitis, which is close to the Hauran (= Haran) which would be the older form. Is it not plain that we have here a steady adhesion to the same principles observed in what might be termed by some the prehistoric narrative? How far the methods are fairly applicable may be judged after perusal of the following instances.

71. LOT.—On the arrival of Abram in Palestine, he found in the south, in the neighbourhood of the Dead Sea, a Seirite family[1] called Lotan—*i.e.*, the race of Lot. That some descendants of Abram, or closely allied family, occupied the same region, which continued to be known by the same name, may be viewed as a fact; but his nephew, the so-called prophet Lot, whose family is represented as dispossessing the older Lot, must be regarded as a mere legendary character, introduced as supplying episodes for the novel, and welcome for the opportunity thus afforded of illustrating the eternal hatred between Israel and Moab and Ammon[2] by representing their ancestors as of incompatible temper. One important episode[3] is viewed by all modern critics as belonging to none of the various authors whose styles are recognisable in the Hexateuch. The names of the kings are doubtless historic, so far that they are derived from some tradition. Schrader[4] makes out a case for identifying Amraphel of Shinar with Hammurabi of Babylon: there is one thing certainly in its favour, it throws back the accepted date of Abram's life two hundred years—from 1900 to 2100 B.C.[5] It must not only be forgotten that, being a

---

[1] Gen. xxxvi. 20.   [2] Deut. xxiii. 3.   [3] Gen. xiv.   [4] Vol. ii. p. 299.
[5] See *ib.* p. 297: B.C. 2350, Sayce, "Verdict." p. 165.

very late addition, probably made in Babylon itself, its evidential authority on the value of the story of Lot is *nil*; whereas, on the contrary, it bears actual testimony to the progressive evolution of the story of Abram and Lot, and to the general principle that tradition, like scandal, "vires acquirit eundo." The anomalous introduction of a High Priest, Melchizedek, is a dramatic incident that betrays its origin by its anxiety to prove the antiquity of tithes and the quasi-papal supremacy of priest over king; it stands or falls with the amount of credence accorded to the existence of Lot generally, and the age of this particular pericope.

72. LOT'S WIFE.—A pillar to the south of the Dead Sea has been known by this name from remote antiquity. Some explanation of its possible origin may be expected. We have seen that the Lot tribes dwelt in this vicinity before Abram's time: is it improbable that some conspicuous basaltic pillar (40 ft. high)[1] may have been the landmark known as *Ashath* Lotan = the Pillar of the Lot tribe; and that on the circulation of the Sodom and Gomorrha legend, this name was modified, without change of consonants, into *Esheth* Lot = Lot's Wife?[2]

73. SODOM and GOMORRHA.—It is indeed remarkable that these two cities should have been proleptically known as "Conflagration" and "Submersion" long prior to their fate of being consumed by fire and obliterated by the waters of the Dead Sea. That

---

[1] "Dict. of the Bible."
[2] *Cf.* C.I.Ph. 86, A. 13, B. 5. Ashthath Mikal—*i.e.*; Hebrew, Shatboth, pillars, with Aleph prosthetic.

some cities may have been destroyed by natural agency is not impossible, and that vague recollection of the fact led to the assignment to them of names appropriate to their terrible fate is not lightly to be denied; but the details given all turn upon the historicity of Abram's nephew. Further, the tale of Lot's wife, together with the ridiculous pun extracted from a city whose name was " Little "—" Prithee let me flee unto it; is it not a *little* one ?"—(ridiculous, because Lot did not dwell there, preferring the safety of the mountains; who, then, was there to alter the existing name?) increases the degree of improbability which already exists. The narrative of the incestuous origin of Moab and Ammon was based on an *impossible* derivation of the former name, and invented in the days of the decline of Israel, sixth, or at the earliest seventh, century B.C., when Moab and Ammon were elated at the downfall of the younger race, who were naturally embittered against them. Allusion is clearly made to this story in Job xxx. 5–8: "Children of shame, yea nameless," dwelling in caves.[1] Comparing this tale with the similar one told of Gibeah of Benjamin (Judges ix.), we may note that the crime so heavily punished in each case was not the unnatural one, in neither case accomplished, but the breach of the laws of hospitality, held in such high reverence by all Hebrew and Arabic tribes—an interpretation confirmed by Job xxxi., xxxii., xxxiii.:

> " The stranger did not lodge in the street,
> I opened the gate to the wayfarer.
> If because I feared the great mob,
> And the scare of other families affrighted me.
> I was silent and went not forth to the door.

[1] *Cf.* Gen. xix. 30–38.

If the only evidence adduced by Ewald in support of Lot's having a "true historical existence,"[1] is Genesis xiv., itself open to grave suspicion, and concerning which he admits that "it is evidently only the Israelite modification of the legion that connected Abram with it;" there seems nothing to deter us from consigning the whole narrative of Lot to the limbo of instructive legend.

74. MORIAH.—The site of the attempted sacrifice of Isaac by Abram is reported to have been on a mountain in the *land* of Moriah (? Amorites).[2] Abram calls the place (in verse 14) Yahveh-yireh = Yahveh, will provide, referring to verse 8, and undoubtedly intended as the derivation of Moriah from the root Raah = to see, provide. Now, a note is added, quoting a common proverb, "God appears on a mountain," which is in accordance with the frequent practice of worshipping on high places, and here bears special reference to the appearance of the angel (11). By a slight alteration the abstract character of the proverb is contracted into a concrete saying that could not have been a proverb (14): "In the mount of Yahveh shall He appear." This note is of later date than the story itself, and is doubtless due to the following narrative—the *only other* place where the name Moriah occurs.

75. "Solomon began to build the house of Yahveh at Jerusalem .... in the second day of the second month."[3] This is surely the original reading, into which was introduced the following note: "In the mount of the Moriah, which was shown to David his father, which he set up in David's place, in

---

[1] "Hist.," i. 312.   [2] Gen. xxii. 2.   [3] 2 Chron. iii. 1.

the threshing-floor of Ornan the Jebusite; and he began to build," &c. The awkwardness of the construction and the repetition of "began to build" are sufficient indications of what must have been the original text. Note *en passant* that LXX. and Syriac both have Amoriah here; the Syriac has it also in Genesis, where the LXX. evidently also had it in the Hebrew text before, but translated it "lofty"; whence we conclude that the Aleph has been *omitted* from the earlier Hebrew text because the root of Amoriah was plainly at variance with the derivation suggested by the narrative in Genesis. We thus obtain inductive proof that the scribes themselves saw this derivation as the *purpose* of the story. The expression, "which was shown to David," is sufficiently consonant with 2 Samuel xxiv. 18, where the prophet Gad says to David, "Rear up an altar"; but the chronicler (xxi. 16, 20) makes David and Ornan *see the angel*, in accordance with which, by a slightly strained construction, the words "which was shown to David" were understood to mean "where he appeared to David." The association with the name Moriah led to the insertion in the Genesis narrative, "In the mount of Yahveh shall he appear." Thus the two stories act and react on one another, for we cannot suppose that the chronicler introduced the name Moriah without reference to the idea that the spot was (in his opinion) already consecrated by Abram's sacrifice of Isaac.

76. Tradition places the threshing-floor of Nachon[1] in a valley, and Ruth (iii.) is said to go "*down* to the threshing-floor"; we have therefore no grounds for believing that the site of Ornan's threshing-floor

[1] 2 Sam. vi.

was any hill, still less this particular hill. The chronicler (xxii. 1-4) makes David prepare to build the Temple, and then, recollecting chapter xvii., inserts verse 5 to transfer his preparations to Solomon; of all which we have no record in Samuel and Kings. The motive seems to have been, not to lose sight of a piece of ground consecrated by the erection of an altar by David.

77. The Temple hill had *no* distinctive name, Moriah or other. This is probably due to its summit having been cut off to form the square plateau on which the Temple was erected. Though separated from Mount Zion by the Tyropœan valley, it is, as Gesenius points out, *included* under that name whenever Zion is spoken of as the seat, the holy place, of Yahveh; for it is not conceivable that the royal palace should so completely have eclipsed the sacred edifice. If, as Ewald intimates, Zion and Jebus are synonymous, both meaning *drought*, it is surely reasonable to suppose that *all* the hills of Jerusalem may originally have been known as Mount Zion; and that the height on which David's palace stood retained the name κατ' ἐξοχήν, which was also employed in speaking of the hill without a summit, which had never known a distinctive name. The above application still holds good, even if we think it doubtful that David should continue a name only slightly disguised after his conquest, and if, accordingly, we prefer to adopt another derivation for Zion—viz., fortification, citadel—which appears more appropriate, and the claim of which is recognised by Gesenius.

78. The Moriah in Genesis could have been nowhere near Jerusalem, which, according to Genesis xiv., was a city ruled over in Abram's time by Melchizedek, and not of a suitable privacy for the occasion. The

Samaritans equally naturally identified Moriah with Gerizim, and with less difficulty, for the plain, or terebinth, of Moreh (a similar name) is spoken of as near Sichem [1] and near Gerizim.[2] Further, the place was seen "from afar" after three days' journey, which agrees better with the seventy-five miles from Beersheba to Gerizim than the forty-five miles to Jerusalem. In conclusion, the *silence* of Prophets and Psalmists to this name Moriah is final crushing evidence against the Temple hill having ever been known by this name, as their custom is to employ archaic names with freedom.

79. BEER-SHEBA.—In Genesis xxi. 30, 31, Abram and Abimelek confirm a treaty of peace by the sacrifice of seven ewe lambs: "For these seven ewe lambs shalt thou take. . . . Wherefore he called that place Beer-sheba = Well-of-*Seven*." Another account (xxvi. 28) proposes a new derivation—Well-of-*Oath*: "Let there now be an oath betwixt us." By combining these two narratives, we see an evident attempt, not only to explain Beer-sheba, but also to connect the Hebrew words for seven and oath, as if in ancient times the oath was not complete till a feast or sacrifice was held, at which a present of seven articles—here lambs—was made. Another derivation is hinted at at the end of this last story (xxvi. 32): "We have *found* water, therefore he called it Shebah," a play on Sib'ah, plenty, Well of *Plenty*. The phrase "found water" is quite inconsistent with re-opening wells formerly dug by Abram; we must see in verse 18 a harmonising gloss, just as there is a very manifest one in verse 1: "*Beside*

---

[1] 1 Gen. xii. 6.   [2] 2 Deut. xi. 30.

the *first* famine that was in the **days of Abraham.**" The real origin of Beer-sheba is lost, but should probably be sought in the name of some god (*cf.* Amos viii. 14); perhaps the seven planets. The other wells appear to have been called after different tribes—*e.g.*, 'Eseq = Esauites ; Rechoboth = Reubenites.

80. BEER-LACHAI-ROI.—This is a spot to the south of Judah, well known as Lechi, around which various traditions have clustered, with a view to offering explanation of the name.

(1) Genesis xvi. 14. After the angel had appeared to Hagar, she thought she had seen God himself; for she called the name of the "Yahveh who spake with her, thou art the God whom I saw," El Roi, "for she said, I continue to live (to *see* the light) (Job xxxiii. 28, 30) after my seeing God," wherefore the well was called Beer-lachal-roi = The well of my seeing and living.[1]

(2) Genesis xxi. 19. God shows her the well, a more probable conception than the one in the above narrative, where Hagar is represented as sitting by a well-known fountain ; and as the construction, according to the next derivation, takes *chai* as object to *roi*, there appears in this second story of Hagar to be a latent suggested derivation, Beer-lachai-roi = Well of my seeing living waters.[2]

(3) Genesis xxiv. 62–65. Another derivation. Beer-lachai-roi is a favourite dwelling-place of Isaac, and (or because) here first Rebecca beheld her future husband: thus it would mean "my seeing my family," chai = family.[3]

---

[1] Judges xiii. 22.   [2] *Cf.* Gen. xxvi. 19, &c.
[3] 1 Sam. xviii. 18 ; Ps. lxviii. 10, 11 (10).

(4) Judges xv. 17-19. Samson, after miraculously slaying a thousand Philistines, single-handed, with the jawbone (*lechi*) of an ass, finds a spring of water in the jawbone (*lechi*), and *its* name is henceforth 'En-lechi-haqqore unto this day. Many commentators understand 'En-lechi-haqqore and Beer-lachai-roi to be different names for the same well; and they are not so dissimilar as they appear, *Beer*, and *'en* being used interchangeably of this well or spring, even in Genesis xvi. 7. It is probable, therefore, that there was an almost effaced inscription on the well-stone, *lch-ra*, which in Genesis is read *lchi-ra(i)*, and in Judges, *lchi-(hq)ra*. As a solution of the problem in Judges, I would suggest the following: In this rocky neighbourhood—*cf.* Rock Etam (8)—there were several sharp, jagged rocks, known as the jaw (compare Devil-Teeth in Argyleshire); it only requires a family of the name of Ass = Chamor to have dwelt in this neighbourhood, to complete the source of the story of the ass's jawbone. Some countenance seems lent to the conjecture by Ishmael being called a wild-ass man, and the fact that names like Beth-Hagar are found in the vicinity to the present day; *Chamran*, Hagarenes, Nabatæans are mentioned together in Sennacherib's inscription of his victory over Merodak-Baladan.[1] The name is common enough amongst the descendants of Seir; the Hyena (Zibeon) family are ancestors of the ass (Chemran) tribe (Genesis xxxvi. 24. 26); also Chamor the Hittite (Genesis xxxiv). That Lechi itself was high ground is clear from its name Ramath-lechi; though, with the usual ready perversion, Ramath = High-place, from

---

[1] Schrader, p. 344. 16.

Rum, is taken as from Ramah = to throw, and understood of the *casting away* of the jawbone.

(5) 2 Samuel xxiii. 11. Shammah, the Hararite, won a victory over the Philistines at Lechi (E.V. into a troop). It is a remarkable coincidence that all the heroes connected with Lechi have the stem *shm* in their names—I*shm*ael, *Shim*shon, S*ham*mah. As regards the last, there is nothing extravagant in supposing him to have been of the Ishmaelite race; observe 1 Chronicles ii. 17-27, 30, 31, where Ishmaelites are in David's service. Among the sons of Ishmael, we find Hadar (Genesis xxv. 15,) Hadad (1 Chronicles i. 30); and below, in 2 Samuel xxiii. 25, Shamman is called Haradi, and in 1 Chronicles xi. 27, Harori. Whichever of the various forms may have been originally correct, there is little doubt that they all refer to one and the same race.

The above, with its five historic associations, is a highly interesting specimen of the manner in which stories grew around a place of even no great celebrity, but apparently of special significance to Ishmaelite and Iskite families. We may learn from this what degree of reliability may be attributed to the tales about the origin of more celebrated places, like Bethel, Gilead, &c.

81. GILEAD.—Such names as Gil-ed, Heap-Witness; Ger-Shom, Stranger-There; Ab-Ram, Father-High, afford *primâ facie* presumption of rough-and-ready root-finding; in every case the triliteral root is more probable, as elsewhere the roots are selected to provide material for episodes on which the reality of the names impresses a fictitious stamp of genuineness.

(1) Genesis xxxi. 48. Jacob and Laban are said to

pile up a heap of stones, beyond which neither of them was to pass; such a cairn, for a landmark, was probably of great antiquity, serving the purpose elsewhere played by natural features—brooks, hills, or the basaltic pillar of the Lotan. That the whole district of Gilead derived its name from this circumstance is highly improbable. Gesenius thinks Gilead means stony ground, from an Arabic quadriliteral root; but considering it was a field of *contention*, and that its ancient boundary was a stream—Jabboq = Quarrelsome, on account of frequent border disputes with the Ammonites (Deuteronomy iii. 16)—there is no strong reason for renouncing the Hebrew root *Gala*, the meaning of which is given above.

(2) Joshua xxii. 34. Reuben and Gad, on returning east of the Jordan to the land of Gilead, raised there an altar, a great altar to see (verse 10), "which they called" (34), "saying, It is a witness between us that Yahveh is God." The name is omitted. Rashi says, it is necessary to add one word, "Witness;" the Syriac add "Altar of witness." There can be little question that Gilead is the missing word; a second story, based in customary manner on the same interpretation.

82. BETHEL.—The anxiety to trace the sanctity of this place back to Jacob-Israel would be very natural among the northern people; its further association with the patriarch Abram must be attributed to antiquarian foibles, when the idea arose that Abram as the ancestor of the race must have visited every sacred place and shared in the history of the people by anticipation. Thus, for instance, he is made to go down into Egypt, though to describe the journey it is necessary to borrow wholesale from the life of Isaac, whose relations with Egypt are indisputable. The so-called Jacob's *ladder* remains a mystery; the word *sullam* might mean *highroad*, but more naturally should be taken as akin to *tselem*, pillar.

83. PENUEL. — Genesis xxxii. 30. An *eastern* boundary, *facing the sun*, near the river boundary Jabboq, suggested, in connection with the latter, the poetical allegory of Jacob's wrestling with God, and being face to face with him.

84. These must suffice as illustrations of the manner in which the stories of the Hexateuch are compiled. The facts thus brought to light cannot be lightly dismissed; they have to be reckoned with, and after consideration of other factors of Hebrew history—genealogies, festivals, customs, &c.—we shall be in a better condition to form a calm opinion on the Exodus from Egypt and the Conquest of Canaan, as reported to us by the same authorities.

CHAPTER IV.

GENEALOGIES

85. WHEN, in colloquial parlance, we speak of the Jews as "a peculiar people," we imagine that we have Scriptural authority[1] for the expression of what is an undoubted fact, the dissimilarity of the Hebrew race from all others. Unfortunately, however, the original idea is "special treasure,"[2] sealed and protected by Yahveh, a totally different conception. Nevertheless, the fact remains, that we are justified in calling the Israelites "peculiar," in the modern sense, in every point which suggests itself for comparison with other nations—history, laws, customs; but in no particular do we recognise their idiosyncracy more manifestly than in the importance attached by them to genealogies, which form so large a part of 1 Chronicles, Ezra, and Nehemiah.

86. The names of these books at once suggest the period when a natural reason can be assigned for special interest in pedigree. We can imagine that the Huguenots escaping from France would, in the haste of flight, not forget to take with them title-deeds and family trees, so as to be in a position on their return to establish their identity and re-claim

---
[1] Ex. xix. 5; Deut. xiv. 2.   [2] Cf. Mal. iii. 17; Eccles. ii. 8.

any property to which they might be entitled. So would the Israelites in the confusion after the destruction of Jerusalem, when they were driven forth as captives, endeavour to take with them similar evidences of personal identity and legal claims to property.

87. From that day the practice has been said to be very general among them; but its previous existence in their midst as a universal custom may well be doubted. If, as some assert, the genealogies in the first eight chapters of Chronicles are mainly fictitious, to supply a missing want, consistently with their general maxim, that what is now was also in the beginning, they are practically of no value. Some stray evidences, it is true, of fabrication force themselves upon our notice; but in view of the *manifest harmonising effort* of the Chronicler, his determination to assimilate the description of the past to his own idea of what is right and necessary, the discrepancies in the genealogies preserved by him—discrepancies which in some instances betray traces of a tradition incompatible with the story of the Hexateuch to which he was devoted—cannot with any semblance of convincing argument be ascribed to the wanton inventiveness of his brain. Rather is the Chronicler entitled to the highest praise for preserving tables containing matter contrary to his personal predilections.

88. The greater part of these genealogies being thus shown of earlier date than the era of the Babylonian Captivity, their claim to serious consideration is thereby so much the more enhanced. Paradoxical as it may seem, their value increases in direct

ratio to the evidence they bear of absence of all that is usually considered essential to genealogy. It will be found on examination that the older lists are not family trees of successive generations of father and son, but partake more of the nature of a Domesday Book, preserving the names of districts, towns, and villages, assigning them to certain nations, tribes, and families, and poetically recording priority of existence as paternity, exchange or absorption of property, as marriage; increase of area of townships, as birth; conquest and captivity, as death.

80. In 1 Chronicles i-viii., whatever its imperfections, we have the embryo of at least the first seven books of the Bible. Call them rough notes, mnemonics, what you will, I believe that this is the form nearest to the most original, left to us of what little Hebrew boys learned by heart, say in the days of David, and which was subsequently explained to them, enlivened with tales and narratives connected with the greatest men. Of the names of races and towns thus carefully selected for their importance and suitably grouped together, it was gradually assumed that there was an order, first, of historic priority, second, of family connection—both of which assumptions entail manifold difficulties in the history of the time prior to David; while it will be seen that with Kuenen, we must discard the latter *in toto*. The *form* of the lists in Chronicles must be considered as more ancient than that presented in Genesis. Several such lists, almost entirely free from annotation, were at the disposal of the Chronicler, and his merit is, as has already been observed, to have copied them down without prejudice, for it is not possible that their discrepancies

could have escaped his attention; as, for example, when in *one* chapter four or five different family trees are recorded by him for Judah alone.

90. The *same* lists had been available for the earlier compilers of Genesis and Numbers; but there the careful rejection of all names incompatible with the accepted hypothesis is conspicuous. Is there, then, any motive for this rejection? There surely must be, for, on the other hand, no reason can be assigned for the preservation of apparently dry, useless names, which have been laid on one side as so much rubbish. It will be granted that a sufficiently powerful motive has been found, if it can be shown that from the gloomy depths of this pile of refuse gleam gems of *lost tradition*, which throw new light on dark places of Israelite history, and shed bright colours of beauty on hard and plain fact. As the spectroscope tells us of the presence of metals in distant orbs as truly as if we handled them in the laboratory, so these genealogies reveal to us a history otherwise lost to us for ever, and quite at variance with the account in the Hexateuch, which has by many been already condemned on internal evidence. There we have the history of *Joseph* set before us as the history of *Jacob;* Joseph and Levi are the only leading characters—the parts played by Judah and Reuben are secondary and insignificant when not absolutely discreditable and degrading. The successful reception of such partial or perverted history will cease to cause astonishment when it is remembered that the chief literary activity of Israel prevailed in the north. The inquiry into the facts of the case is our main purpose, to which this cursory review of the principal features and motives of Hebrew historic composition is a necessary preliminary.

91. It is perfectly legitimate to apply to Hebrew genealogies all the methods of research employed in the study of modern history, and to avail ourselves of any principle suggested by parallel circumstances. Thus there is no objection to removing the discrepancy between the genealogies in Matthew and Luke, by assuming the one to give the list of regal names of those who actually sat on the throne, while the other records the line of royal descent. The probability of the truth of such an assumption is confirmed by observation of facts within our own reach, —*e.g.*, the descent of Victoria from Edward III., compared with the names of intermediate monarchs. So, too, the modern idea of regency during the declining years of any monarch has, with the attendant distinction of kings *de jure* and *de facto*, served to remove chronological difficulties—*e.g.*, as regards the duration of Amaziah's and Uzziah's reigns.

92. It is also equally true that fathers, sons and uncles often have the same name, but the application of this principle must be made with caution, for it is manifestly improper when tribes and towns are being dealt with. The presence of the *same* name in *different* lists, under the latter circumstances, is indicative of some historical fact (to be sought for), or of a variety of tradition, or indeed of an error. In this connection I must dwell on a point which I have not seen treated of elsewhere. The ethnographical value of genealogies is already recognised, but I believe we must also observe an *historico-geographical* import before we can understand the apparently conflicting statements in the genealogies. Take as specimens the Ardan assigned to both Canaan and Caleb; Qorach to Esau, Caleb, and Levi; Bilhan to Levi, Reuben, and Benjamin; Yithran to Se'ir and Caleb; Zerach to Esau and Judah; Ye'ush to Esau and Benjamin, &c. &c. The apparent confusion appears to me due to a natural survival of ancient race names, and to the absence of maps. If a series of maps were now published, representing, as far as possible, the tribes scattered over Canaan when the Hebrews first entered as strangers in the land; and then successively onwards, showing the same country occupied by Ishmaelites, Iskites (Isaac), and Esauites; subsequently again by Jacobeans and Josephites; we should see the same *tribal* names in small type; Ardan, Qorach, Yithran, Zerach, Bilhan, Ye'ush, &c., occupying the *same* places on the map; though the *district* names in larger type would be *changed*.

93. An important point, not to be overlooked, is, that names ending in *n* cannot have been originally the names of individual men, as this form is suggestive of the Arabic plural termination. Such tribal plurals are specially conspicuous in the Se'irite race [1]—Lotan, Zibe'on, Dishon, Dishan, Alvan, Chemran, Ishban, Yithran, Keran, Bilhan, Za'avan, Aqan, and Aran. Not only are many of these found elsewhere (see preceding paragraph), but other names conform to the same principle—Cana'an, Reuben, Sime'on, Zebulun, Yeshurun, Cherzron, &c. If we bear this rule in mind, we are distinct gainers, there is no longer any question of doubt that what are called the twelve patriarchs were really tribes, nor have we any hesitation in recognising the

---

[1] Gen. xxxvi. 20-30.

Names of Tribes and Men not Interchangeable 73

greater antiquity of such names wherever we may meet them.

94. There seems very little to support the prevalent theory that in ancient times men called land *after their own names*. Names of places and men seem to have been selected on different principles. Tribes were called after their tutelary deity, or some natural feature of the soil or configuration of the ground, or after some cherished animal. Men's names were chiefly formed from verbs, generally combined with the name of a deity as a terminating syllable—*e.g.*, -el -shaddai, -zur, -yah, -ba'al. It is to be noted that names of tribes and places do not appear till very late, and then in no numbers, as the names of men; the distinction thus drawn is, then, not arbitrary. If the usual position were correct it would be inexplicable to find names of ancestors not repeated in their posterity; but this fact is evidence that for centuries they were deemed *inapplicable* to men.

95. We now proceed to test the value of Hebrew genealogies in respect of certain vital particulars. We shall inquire how far they fulfil their natural function as aids to chronology; whether different tables are consistent or not with each other; what evidence there may be of intentional fabrication.

96. In Matthew i. 71, we are told that from Abraham to David, from David to destruction of Jerusalem, and from destruction of Jerusalem to the birth of Christ are three periods of fourteen (7×2) generations. The first period gives an average of sixty years to a generation, the second thirty, and the third forty years. As a matter of fact, Solomon to Jehoiakin[1] gives us seventeen, not fourteen, genera-

[1] Zedekiah, the last king, belonged to the preceding generation.

tions; taking this as a fairly reliable standard for computation, and roughly representing the three periods as 900, 400, and 600 years respectively, we should expect thirty-seven, seventeen, and twenty-five generations, instead of the symmetrical fourteen, fourteen, fourteen. It is not my purpose to digress into a dissertation on the comparison between the tables given by Luke and Matthew, but I cannot refrain from observing that, taking up Luke iii. after writing the above, I found that he reckons twenty-three generations from Neri to Jesus, which proves the accuracy of the above calculation, twenty-five. Further, when we find that with Matthew he gives fourteen generations from Abraham to David, instead of the required thirty-seven, the reason of their agreement here is that in that period they both have only the same authority, Chronicles; and we deduce the conclusion, that, owing to the absence of reliable genealogies, no less than twenty-three generations are missing; in other words, nearly *two-thirds* of the history from Abraham to David is a *blank page*. Thus the genealogies will prove of negative value in our research; they suggest what from other arguments we infer, that not only are generations missing in the days after Joshua, but also in the so-called patriarchal times from Abram to the Exodus.

97. The idea that the Hebrew historian reckoned forty years to a generation is based only on their suppositions with regard to doubtful history. From David to the Babylonian Captivity, a period of about 440 years, there are (not reckoning Jehoiakin, on account of his youth) seventeen generations of twenty-six years, which sufficiently accords with modern calculations. On the other hand, the average from

Abraham to David is sixty-four years, consistently maintained in the half-periods, Abraham to Moses and Moses to David, following the so-called royal line. There is nothing to support the bare statement of the great ages which men attained from Abraham to David, and which then suddenly gave place to more ordinary ages of half their duration. It is pretty manifest that the length of life is assigned to compensate the prolonged duration of a generation, owing to the absence of reliable information as to facts and names.

98. Now, we have no reason to believe that the author of the Gospel of Matthew, who was a special student of Old Testament literature, was himself the inventor of the device he employs. He simply availed himself of an existing system recognisable in the ancient writings, where we find:

Adam	to	Enoch	7		
Methuselah	to	Shelah	6	to	Cainan 7 (LXX.).
Eber	to	Terah	6		
Abraham	to	Ram	7	or	Moses.
Amminadab	to	David	7		

We have here a manifest attempt to obtain a multiple of 7 (7 × 5) generations from Adam to David, and, following the idea in Matthew, 7 × 2 to Babylonian Captivity, making a total of 7 × 7 generations from the Creation to the destruction of Jerusalem; which thus occurred in the fiftieth or jubilee generation. But the same figures are arrived at with greater accuracy by regarding the other favourite number of the Israelites (10), for then we have

	Adam	to	Noah	10
	Shem	to	Abraham	10
	Isaac	to	Jeconiah	30

and this is doubtless the scheme which the Old Testament author had in his mind: Creation to Flood, ten generations Flood to destruction of Jerusalem, forty generations, It was only natural that he should endeavour to break up this jubilee into periods of seven years each. The correctness of the figures proved the *object* of the author, and nothing more. It is, moreover, evidence that the present *selection* of names to form the permanent genealogies must have been finally made *after* the destruction of Jerusalem, which event occupies the prominent, if not proud, position of being the second great catastrophe in the history of the world.

99. The perfect symmetry of the figures is presumptive evidence of adaptation and absence of historic truth, in which opinion the study of the following six tables will confirm us:

TABLE A.	TABLE B.	TABLE C.	TABLE D.	TABLE E.	TABLE F.
		ABRAHAM.			
		ISAAC.			
		JACOB.			
JUDAH.	LEVI.	LEVI.	LEVI.	LEVI.	JOSEPH.
Pharez	Qehath	Qehath	Gershom	Merari	Ephraim
Hezron	'Amram	Yizhar	Shime'i	Machli	Beri'ah
...	...	...	...	...	Rephach
					Resheph
					Telach
					Tachan
...	...	...			La'adan
...	...	...			Ammihud
RAM	AARON	QORACH	...	...	ELISHAMA
Amminadab	Eleazar	Abiasaph	...		Nun
Nachshon	Phinehas	Assir			Joshua
16 Salmon	...	Chehath	...		•
...	...	Zephaniah	...		
		'Azariah	...		

Table A.	Table B.	Table C.	Table D.	Table E.	Table F.
JUDAH.	LEVI.	LEVI.	LEVI.	LEVI.	JOSEPH.
...	...	Yoel	...	...	
	...	Elqanah	Yechath	...	
	...	Amasai	Zimmah	...	
	...	Machath	Ethan	...	
	...	Elqanah	'Adaiah	Bani	
	Abishua	Ziph	Zerach	Amzi	
	Buqqi	Tuach	Ethni	Chaqaliah	
...	'Uzzi	Eliel	Malkiah	Amaziah	
...	Zerachiah	Yerocham	Ba'asiah	Chashabiah	
Bo'az	Maraioth	Elqanah	Mikael	Malluk	
'Obed	Amariah	Samuel	Shime'a	'Abdi	
Yishahi	Achitub	Yoel	Berakaah	Qishi	
David	Zadoq	Heman	Asaph	Ethan	

Refer for A to 1 Chron. ii. 3–12; B to vi. 1–8; C to vi. 33–38; D to vi. 39–43; E to vi. 44–47; and F to vii. 23, 25–27.

100. In the above tables we have, with the exception of transposing the order of Shime'i and Yehath (Table D), a palpable clerical error, strictly adhered to the lists as they are given. The total number of generations from Abraham to David is thus 31; with Joshua occupying the midway station, 15; but this is dependent upon the *bona fides* of Heman's and Joshua's family trees. At first sight, we might congratulate ourselves upon finding some trace of the missing links, the necessity for which we urged in a preceding paragraph; but there is need of the exercise of great caution, for we shall see hereafter that the Ephraim genealogy is in a sad state of confusion, while Heman's is suspicious from its tautology. The most that can be said is, that there is undeniable evidence of the discovery by some critical spirit among the scribes of the insufficiency of the usual genealogy to meet the requirements of chronology.

101. A very serious question for consideration is, whether Heman, Asaph, and Ethen were cotemporaries of David, or indeed actual individual men at all. The exaggerated importance attached to them as rivals, *longo sed proximi intervallo*, of Solomon (1 Kings v. 11); iv. 31) is suggestive of a latter legendary tradition, such as would be expected, if the musical classes of Levites, known as *sons* of Asaph, *sons* of Heman, *sons* of Ethan (Yeduthun), became anxious in later days to magnify their fabled ancestors, of which custom we have irrefragable evidence in the phrase *sons* of Machol = sons of Dance, whence an ancestor, Machli, was invented. The names "Kalkol and Darda" only occur in this passage in Kings, and from parallelism with the preceding verse should be probably taken as a textual error, some significant phrase, " more than *all* the *knowing* ones of the sons of Dance Music," having after corruption been taken as the names of men. Part of this verse is transcribed with the error in 1 Chronicles ii. 6, where Ethan and Hemán appear as sons of the *Judite* Zerach, owing to a mistaken idea, rashly conceived, that the style Ezrachite in the title of the Psalms lxxxviii. lxxxix. required this explanation. It would seem hardly necessary to dwell on the identity of the great Ethan and Heman of David's day, with two men of the same name in Solomon's reign, whose renown was at least equal, were it not for a stout denial of it by Keil, &c. The dedication to the sons of Qorach in Psalm lxxxviii. is a token of identity, worthy of some regard as upsetting the Judite claim of a separate pair of notable rivals.

102. If we take the date of the Exodus at 1320

(Kuenen) and 990 as the end of David's generation, which he survived, we require eleven generations for this period, with which Zadoq's and Asaph's lines sufficiently harmonise, while three generations are missing from the royal line: Admitting for the time, for the sake of argument, the accuracy of the lines, we note as remarkable that Aaron[1] married the *granddaughter* of his cotemporary Ram; practically, therefore, a lacuna should appear between Aaron and Eleazar, as the fruit of his late marriage would be coeval rather with grandchildren by an earlier connexion. For similar reasons, a space should be left after Judah, as Pharez was born to him when his third son Shelah had attained a marriageable age, forty years.[2] It also strikes us as strange that the cotemporary heads of Judah and Levi should be Serpent (Nachshon) and Serpent's Mouth (Phinehas); that Father of Asaph (Abiasaph) should be ancestor of Heman instead of Asaph; and that Ethan and Ethni should appear in the lines of Asaph instead of Ethan.

108. We cannot say whether the four generations from Levi to Exodus are the cause or effect of Genesis xv. 16, nor whether the dozen names from Joseph are meant to harmonise with the four hundred years of Genesis xv. 13, or not. Kuenen[3] notices the presence of two redactions, and remarks that four generations is the older tradition. It is impossible to settle the duration of the sojourn in Egypt from the data in the Bible. It is asserted in Genesis xlvi. 12 that Hezron was born before the arrival of Jacob at

---

[1] Exod. vi. 23.   [2] *Cf.* Esau, Gen. xxvi. 34.   [3] Hex. 325.

Goshen. Now, the Exodus occurred in the days of his son Ram (or his cotemporaries Aaron and Moses (fourth generation from Levi); the greatest lapse of time that could, under the most favourable circumstances, be permissible from above data, would be less than a hundred years; but it will be seen that two hundred and forty years are required from an independent calculation below. The words, "There arose a king in Egypt who knew not Joseph," are not by any means suggestive of a lapse of a couple of centuries or more, but in their natural sense seem to imply how soon the grateful memory of Joseph vanished.

104. Paul[1] following Exodus xii. 41, reckons 430 years from before the birth of Isaac, perhaps from the call of Abram, which is probable, as the LXX. and Samaritan Pentateuch insert in Exodus after "which they sojourned in the land of Egypt" the important addition "and in the land of Canaan." A comparison of Genesis xii. 4 and xxi. 5 makes the birth of Isaac occur in the twenty-fifth year of the sojourn in Canaan: Isaac was forty when he married Rebecca (xxv. 20), say sixty at the birth of Jacob (xxv. 21), who was 130 years of age when he went down into Egypt, making a total of 215 years for sojourn in Canaan. This leaves another 215 years for the sojourn in Egypt, of which some ninety years fell in the lifetime of Joseph (l. 26), so that 125 years would be left for the affliction and bondage. This calculation, based on an assumption of the truth of ages and dates given in Genesis, results in a conclusion hopelessly at variance with the prophecy,[2] "shall *afflict* them four hundred years." The exact equality of the sojourns in Canaan

---

[1] Gal. iii. 17.   [2] Gen. xv. 13.

and Egypt is surely more than suspicious, especially when we remember that a remarkably similar period of 480 years again elapses to the building of Solomon's Temple.

105. We have thus seen that not only does the genealogy disagree with the chronology, but that both of them share the same charge of convenient round numbers, yet neither so does their testimony agree. This would be sufficient to throw discredit on the details of the history built upon such a foundation in any other literature. The question of the chronological difficulty is fully dealt with by Kuenen,[1] but cannot advance to anything like certainty till more light is thrown from the Egyptian sources on the Hyksos and the Hebrew relations with Egypt.

106. Another important question bearing on chronology is the rate of propagation of the Hebrew race. In Genesis xlvi. 27 we read that seventy souls formed the household of Jacob on his arrival in Egypt; this *includes* two sons of Judah born in Egypt, two sons of Judah whose *graves* were in Palestine (xlvi. 12), and, according to Keil, several *unborn* grandsons and great-grandsons of Jacob. Here, again, we have the determination, in spite of difficulties, to arrive at a convenient number to fix in the memory; the rabbis find grave significance in the figures, for on it they rely for an interpretation of Deuteronomy xxxii. 8: "He set the bounds of the people according to the number of the children of Israel"—*i.e.*, seventy races of mankind (Genesis x) and seventy in Jacob's family (Genesis xlvi.). With or without the explanation, we cannot be expected to treat such a method of calculation very seriously. But

[1] "Rel. Israel."

let us accept the fifty-four grandchildren of Jacob as the descendants of Abram in the fifth generation, inclusive: how could these, with one intervening generation, multiply into the two millions, of whom 600,000 were warriors, that took part in the Exodus? Thus genealogy, chronology, and population statistics disagree among themselves, but agree in refuting all claim to the author of historic accuracy, without which foundation the history totters to its fall. Is it worth while to attempt to unravel so hopelessly entangled a skein? Shall we assume a larger immigration into Egypt, or a lengthening of their stay there by several generations, and, after all, reduce the exaggerated number of the host that wended its weary way from the land of bondage?

107. What, again, of Abram's other families? Were not the Ishmaelites and Midianites numerous tribes at the time when the youth Joseph and his twelve brothers are depicted as the only representatives of the promised seed? Are we not confronted once more with unhistorical incongruity? When the Hebrews came out of Egypt, were not the Moabites, Midianites, Ammonites, all of whom were of coeval parentage with them, important nations? In 400 years, even allowing a dozen generations, a score of powerful races, each some hundreds of thousands strong, has never yet sprung from the loins of one man. The history must in some manner be reconstructed; more time must be allowed; Abram, Isaac, Jacob, and the twelve patriarchs must, along with Ishmael, Edom, Moab, Midian, and Ammon resume their places as races, each of which requires some hundred years for its own development.

108. This subject will form matter for separate consideration in a subsequent chapter, where will also be investigated the serious contradictions between different genealogical tables, notably in regard to the royal house of David; for 1 Chronicles ii. 50-55 derives the Bethlehemites through Salma (Salmon) from Caleb, brother of Ram, the reputed ancestor of David. As this Caleb can be shown to be identical with Caleb the Qenizzite, there is a motive for assigning Salmon and Bo'az, the Bethlehemite family, to Ram—viz., to disguise the fact that the royal house was not of pure Jacobean descent, though this *national intermixture* is hinted at in the ordinary genealogy by the incestuous connection of Tamar and Judah, and [1] the marriage between Salmon and the harlot Rahab. Nor is evidence wanting of confusion in other lineages. The Libnite and Shim'ite sub-sections of the Levites are referred to both Gershom and Merari sections; the Machlites are both co-ordinate with and subordinate to the Mushite; Samuel is derived by two lines, differing in length and names, from Quorach, who is called in one case the son of Yizhar, and in the other of Amminadab. The Benjamite family tree is a hopeless enigma. Specially remarkable is the reference to Matri, an important section of the Benjamite family[2] not mentioned elsewhere. In connection with the story of Achar,[3] the descent of a Judite section is given, not found elsewhere; for 1 Chronicles ii. 7 is simply a note referring to Joshua, and has no independent value as corroborative evidence. In short, we shall find that, as genealogy, the lists from Moses to

---

[1] Matt. i. 5.   [2] 1 Sam. x. 21.   [3] Josh. vii. 1.

David are to be assessed at only a slightly higher value than the pre-Mosaic ones.

109. As we advance into the field of history proper, there is less reason to be on the alert against fabrication of family names; still, our suspicions are naturally excited by coincidences too curious to allow of explanation. Comparing 2 Chronicles xxix. 12 and 1 Chronicles vi. 35, 44, we discover that not only were Mahath, the son of the Qohathite, and Qish, the son of 'Abdi the Merarite, Levite officials together in the reign of Hezekiah, but they were contemporaries, father and son, in both lines, long previously, being eleventh and twelfth in descent from Levi. Again, 'Eden or 'Iddo, the son of Yoah, the son of Zimmah, in the same verse recalls the same three names in the same order,[1] in the Gershonite family. Who can blame the prompting thought that the Chronicler has employed the names of actual Levites in the days of Hezeqiah to fill in lacunæ in the genealogy of the days prior to David.

110. Are we wrong in expecting special care to be exhibited in the preservation of the high priests' pedigree? We know that Zadoq, the high priest, anointed Solomon, and was instrumental in making his nomination popular; it is with some feeling of surprise, then, that we read[2] that Azariah, the *fourth* in descent from this Zadoq, officiated at the dedication of Solomon's temple, for the words, "he it is that executed the priest's office in the house that Solomon built in Jerusalem," either mean that or nothing, being equally applicable otherwise to all the

---

[1] 1 Chron. vi. 5, 6 (xx. 21).   [2] 1 Chron. v. 36 (vi. 10).

high priests. The cause of the origin of this mistake is very instructive, as illustrating the complex manner in which mistakes act and re-act on each other, one naturally begetting another. The prime cause here is the careless insertion of Nehemiah xi. as 1 Chronicles ix., for there all the officers of post-exilic times are transplanted to swell the host of Davidic officials; it does not seem to have struck them as strange that 'Azariah, Hilqiah, Meshullam, Zadoq, Meraioth, Achitub, should be the order in v. 38-40 (vi. 12-40), testifying to the correctness of Nehemiah, where they appear as the high priests till the Captivity, and that the same should serve for the genealogy of the high priest in David's closing days. Having made this mistake, the next conclusion was that the high priest at the time of David's death also officiated at the consecration of the Temple, and a note to that effect was accordingly appended to an 'Azariah, unfortunately the wrong one. It is, of course, possible that the gloss was originally put in the margin against v. 35 (vi. 9), and slipped down, as that 'Azariah would be the grandson of Zadoq, and might be called his son.[1]

111. Much discussion has arisen over the relation between 1 Chronicles ix. and Nehemiah xi. Some insist that the names of officers, together with their pedigrees, *might* be identical in the days of David and Nehemiah; while others affirm that the two tables are intended to be the same, and infer that the Chronicler inserted it bodily from Nehemiah to provide a list of

---

[1] 1 Kings iv. 2. Azariah ('Uzziah) the *king*, took the priest's office upon himself. Has any confusion arisen, because the high priest's name also was Azariah.

Levites in David's reign. It is true that the opening verses, 1 Chronicles ix. 2, 3, are not quotations from Nehemiah; but the expressions are clearly inappropriate to the times of David, and smack of the period of return from exile: "Now the *first inhabitants* that dwelt in their *possessions* in their cities, were the *Israelites*, the priests, Levites, and the Nepinims; and in Jerusalem dwelt of the children of Judah, and of the children of Benjamin, and of the children of Ephraim and Manasseh." Further comment is unnecessary; the words speak for themselves. We may, however, conjecture that this was a stray leaf, belonging to another text of Nehemiah, which found its way by accident amongst the lists of names in Chronicles; was inserted here on account of the allusion in verse 1 to the carrying away to Babylon; and has since been subject to notes and glosses to accommodate it to the reign of David. Its late date is testified by the lineage in verse 11 (quoted above), where the names of the six last high priests previous to the Captivity are given, and by the reference to the grandson of Pashchur, the son of Malkiyah, cotemporary of Jeremiah.

112. The best way to judge of the possibility of the independence of these two tables is to see them side by side, and observe whether the identity of names and pedigrees does not outweigh the slight differences discernible.

NEH. XI.	1 CHRON. IX.	NEH. XI.	1 CHRON. IX.
4. Pharez	4. Bharez	'Uzziah	'Ammihud
Mahalalel	Bani	'Athaieh *	Uthai *
Shephatiah	...		
Amariah *	Imri *	5. Shiloni	5. Shiloni
Zekariah	'Ormi	Zekariah	...
		Yoyarik	

Comparison continued

NEH. XI.	1 CHRON. IX.	NEH. XI.	1 CHRON. IX.
'Adaiah	...	12. Malkiah	12. Malkiah
Chazaiah		Pashchur	Pashchur
Kol-choseh	...	Zekariah	...
Baruk	...	Amzi	..
Ma'aseiah *	'Asaiah *	Pelaliah	...
		Yerocham	Yerocham
7. Benjamin	7. Benjamin	'Adaiah	'Adaiah
Yesha'iah	...		
Ithiel	...	13. Immer	12. Immer
Ma'aseiah		Meshillemoth	Meshillemith
Qoliah		Asriqam	Meshullam
Pedaiah	...	Achzi *	Y-achzar-ah *
Yo'ed	...	'Azarel *	'Adiel *
Meshullam	Meshullam	'Amashsai *	Ma'asai *
Sallu	Sallu		
		15. Buni	14. Merari
9. Zikri *	6. Zerach *	Chashabiah	Chashabiah
Yoel *	Ye'uel *	'Azriqam	'Azriqam
Hassenuah	7. Hassenuah	Chashub	Chashub
Yehudhah *	Hodaviah *	Shema'iah	Shema'iah
10. Yoyarib	10. Yehoyarib	17. Asaph	15. Asaph
Yeda'iah	Yeda'iah	Zabdi *	Zikri *
Yakin	Yakin	Mika	Mika
		Mattaniah	Mattaniah
11. Achitub	11. Achitub	Baqbuqiah *	Baqbaqqar *
Meraioth	Meraioth	Yeduthun	Yeduthun
Zadoq	Zadoq	Galal	Galal
Meshullam	Meshullam	Shamma' *	Shama'iah
Chilqiah	Chilqiah	Abda*	'Obadiah *
Seraiah	'Azariah		

The names marked * have great similarity, the differences being only such as are found elsewhere[1] in cases of undoubted identity, and due to confusion of similar Hebrew letters. In verses 4, 5, 7, the Chronicler manifestly had originally the heading and only the

---

[1] For good examples, *vide* Driver's "Samuel."

last name or two; in verse 4, however, he apparently started with the ambition of supplying missing links, which he afterwards abandoned; whence the last names, 'Athaiah and 'Uthai, are to be identified, and the preceding discrepancy ignored. By reference to 1 Chronicles xxiv. 27 we find that *Buni*[1] was of the house of *Merari;* thus Nehemiah xi. 15 and 1 Chronicles ix. 14, allude to the same line, the former stopping at the cotemporary of Immer and Malkiah, the latter giving the chief Levite section.

113. In 1 Chronicles v. 27-41, vi. 1-15, there is what purports to be a complete list of high priests from Aaron to the Captivity; but, comparing it with the list of kings, we find at least half a dozen names missing, while certain high priests mentioned in the narratives are passed over. Here again a table is necessary to set the facts plainly:

King.	High Priest.	Narrative.
Solomon	Zadoq (1 Kings i. 39)	
	Achima'az (2 Sam. xv. 36)	
	'Azariah (1 King iv. 2)	
Rechobo'am		
Abijah		
Asa		
Jehoshaphat		Amariah (2 Chron. xix. 11)
Yehoram		
Azhaziah		
Yoash		Yehoiada' (2 Kings xi.)
Amaziah	Yochanan	
'Uzziah .	'Azariah	'Azariah (2 Chron. xxvi. 17)
Yotham	Amariah	
Achaz	Achitub	Uriah (2 Kings xvi. 15; Is. viii. 2)
Hezeqiah	Zadoq	'Azariah (2 Chron. xxxi. 10)
Manasseh	Shallum	

[1] Beno, doubtful form.

King.	High Priest.	Narrative.
Amon		
Josiah	Chilqiah	Chilqiah (2 Kings xxii. 4)
Yehoiaqim	'Azariah	
Yehoiakin		
Zedeqiah	Seraiah	Seraiah (2 Kings xxv. 18)

The incompleteness of a list which professes to be a genealogy is presumptive evidence against its authenticity, which is corroborated by the omission of names in the narratives. It appears very doubtful whether the names from Amariah, Achitub, &c., have not been copied direct from 1 Chronicles ix. 11, under the impression that they are names of high priests, whereas it is impossible that the corresponding name in Nehemiah xi. 11 can be so, seeing that there we have the genealogy of a certain Seraiah, who must not be confounded with Seraiah the high priest at the capture of Jerusalem, whose grandson Jeshua' accompanied Zerubbabel in the return.[1] A comparison with Ezra vii. 1–6 convinces us that these names really belong to his genealogy, the genealogy of a scribe, not of a high priest; we observe also that Ezra omits several names given by the Chronicler; in fact he appears to leap from Amariah, cotemporary of 'Obed, to Amariah, cotemporary of Yotham; but an actual clerical error of this kind presupposes the existence of a genealogy such as the Chronicler gives us, which is highly improbable in view of the principles of selection above noticed, which vitiate the claim of historic reality for his priestly genealogies.

114. This cursory review of some of the crucial genealogical questions results in sufficient testimony to

[1] Ezra iii. 8.

justify the assertion that, apart from the names of the kings, we have no ground to believe that careful pedigrees of the priests, certainly not of the people generally, were kept, or, if kept, not preserved, prior to the Captivity. We must therefore be very cautious in accepting conclusions based on the accuracy of genealogical tables.

CHAPTER V

HEBREW FEASTS AND CUSTOMS

115. In a preceding chapter (II.) we remarked that a noticeable feature in Hebrew history was the manner in which customs of later date were ascribed to greater antiquity, or (we should add) certain phases of them were so ascribed, for the purpose of conferring upon them fictitious authority, even when the historical and prophetical writings are silent concerning them, or reveal quite contrary practices, or when unmistakable signs of their gradual development give clear indication that the most perfect form could not possibly have existed first. We have already seen in the coincidence of an outburst of plague interrupting the census ordered by David, that the Levitical instructions on this head could not then have been in existence; the poll-tax was probably introduced to avert the repetition of a similar calamity, the religious aspect being conciliatory to the Deity. The expedient resorted to by Hezekiah on account of the ceremonial uncleanness of some of the people, suggested the insertion in the code of an alternative second Passover in the second month, which now appears as a keen anticipation of every possible difficulty, in a manner which excels the best modern legislation, where laws require re-editing as defects and omissions become practically evident. We will now proceed to inquire briefly into the historical evidence of the observance of the Sabbath, Circumcision, Passover, Sacrifice, Place of Worship, Ark, Priesthood, &c.

116. It is not necessary to premise that we do not assign to documents an antiquity corresponding to their position in the order of books in the Bible. The labours of Ewald, Graf, and Reuss, to discover the component parts of Hebrew literature, cataloguing peculiarities of vocabulary, indicating the presence of later explanatory glosses, and establishing evidence of characteristics of certain periods, have during the last thirty years been so amplified and systematised, especially by Wellhausen and Kuenen, that the following theory has received general acceptance.[1] During the period, say 850 to 700 B.C., a first definite attempt was made to reduce the history of Israel to a written system. Here two factors are observed; the earlier showing preference for the name Yahveh and the other for Elohim, but both together known as the Prophetical History; as their standpoint corresponds with that observable in Isaiah, Amos, Hosea, and Micah. Somewhere about 600 B.C. a new school of thought, of which Jeremiah was the chief exponent, produced the Book of Deuteronomy, and introduced glosses and annotations into the existing history. On the return from captivity, say 480 B.C., the new conditions of the people demanded fresh legislation: the Book of the Law was written definitely to meet this demand, the priests now became the chief rulers of the people, and as a consequence Ritual took a prominent place: in all this they were influenced by

[1] *Vide* Driver.

their newly acquired lore during the seventy years in Babylon. It was necessary, on account of the traditional veneration for the name of Moses, to represent the new code as nothing new, but of greater antiquity than existing histories; the Law was read (Nehemiah viii.) to the people as one that had been long forgotten and neglected, but had really been binding from time immemorial. As a natural sequence, the history had to be touched up afresh, and in part rewritten, to bring it into conformity with this assumption. This work is known as the Priestly Code. The author of Chronicles, Ezra, and Nehemiah lived in the *third* century B.C. We must bear this in mind in estimating the historical evidence adduced in the following paragraphs.

117. Sabbath.—The division of the month into equal parts seems to have been one of the original aims in the distribution of time. The Greeks had *ten* days (a third), the Romans *eight*, and the Babylonians and Semitics generally *seven* days (a quarter). This last seems to have been chosen as the nearest approach to combining an equal number of days with observation of the phases of the moon. As the sun and moon, with Mercury, Venus, Mars, Jupiter, and Saturn were called the seven planets, each day of the week was named after one of them, the seventh being dedicated to Saturn. It is to be noted that apparently[1] each month had four sabbaths—on the seventh, fourteenth, twenty-first, and twenty-eighth days; the remaining days not counting to the next week, as the next sabbath would fall on the seventh of the ensuing month. If this is a fact, it would be interesting to know when the weekly

---

[1] Sayce: 70, 71: Schrader: i. 19.

sabbath—independent of the month—came into vogue. On special occasions the Israelites also observed these monthly sabbaths irrespective of the days of the week, viz., the fourteenth and twenty-first days of the first month (Passover)[1]; the fifteenth and twenty-second days of the seventh month [2] (Tabernacles). This arrangement looks like a survival of some such ancient custom, otherwise, as the motive of the feasts was to celebrate the two equinoxes, they should have been movable as regards the day of the month, seeing that, like the Chinese, the Babylonians had recourse to an intercalary month every third year to bring the lunar year into conformity with the solar. It is of course possible that the Babylonian and Israelite custom of observing the seventh, fourteenth, &c., was in addition to the observance of the normal seventh day, as was the later Jewish custom. The point which is not clear to my mind is, whether this combined observation is of great antiquity, or indeed known to the Babylonians at all.

118. The Sabbath amongst the Israelites seems, in early times, to have been associated with *rest* from labour, and family *feasting*—in fact, a holiday rather than a holy day; which idea is confirmed by the marked manner in which it is coupled with the new moon,[3] which was an unmistakable feast.[4] After the Captivity, however, a further religious idea was added; the Sabbath was a day to be marked by "not doing thine own ways, nor finding thine own *pleasure*, nor speaking thine own words;"[5] a puritanical severity of which no

---

[1] Ex. 12. [2] Num. 29.
[3] 2 Kings iv. 23; Isa. i. 13; Amos viii. 5.
[4] 1 Sam. xx. 5; Hos. ii. 11. [5] Isa. lviii. 13.

earlier example is extant. It is strange that the Sabbath observed in Babylon seems to have had a double character—the Babylonian, "a day of rest for the heart," and the Accadian, "an unlawful day," "evil day."[1] It would appear, then, that the Hebrews preserved the ancient idea of the Sabbath which they brought with them from Mesopotamia, but adopted the Accadian practice during the Captivity. Christ as usual declared in favour of the old conception, before it was marred by innovations and hemmed in by restrictions. The Sabbath is a day of rest, not of self-denial : "The Sabbath was made for man, and not man for the Sabbath."

119. The Ten Words, not reckoning negatives, were originally—(1) I ; (2) Thou shalt not take ; (3) Remember ; (4) Honour ; (5) Not kill ; (6) Not commit adultery ; (7) Not steal ; (8) Not report ; (9) Not covet ; (10) Not desire. This is the form in which they are represented outside a Jewish synagogue in London. All other words are later necessary explanations ; but we are only concerned with the fortunes of the Fourth Commandment, the original form of which was Remember. Remember what ? The Deuteronomist in Josiah's day replied two things : (1) The Sabbath-day,[2] where, unlike the account in Exodus, he has "*Preserve* the Sabbath day ;" (2) Remember Egypt :[3] "Remember that thou wast a slave in the land of Egypt, and that Yahveh, thy God brought thee out thence with a mighty hand and stretched-out arm ; *therefore* Yahveh, thy God, commanded thee to keep the Sabbath day." At that time the Hebrews believed the observance of

---

[1] Schrader, rendered by Sayce "lucky day," evidently as a euphemism. [2] Deut. v. 12. [3] Deut. v. 15.

the Sabbath to be an institution *peculiar* to themselves, which they accordingly referred to the time of Moses, which even then was viewed as the *fons et origo* of their religion. In Babylon they found that others beside themselves reverenced the seventh day, and even surpassed them in its strict observance. They therefore came to the conclusion that it was *universally* binding on the human race. The Priestly Code therefore, adopting the more scientific story of Creation they found there, wrote Genesis i. 1-2, 4, in which God is represented as resting on the seventh day, which detail appears to be their own addition, as Schrader does not quote its equivalent in the Chaldæan account. Somewhat later, the moral of the Fourth Commandment was added to Exodus xx. 11 by a second redactor[1] where the reference to the Creation supersedes the allusion to Egypt: " For in six days Yahveh made heaven and earth .... and rested the seventh day: *therefore* Yahveh blessed the seventh day, and hallowed it." It is sometimes objected that the words in Deuteronomy v. 12, "as Yahveh thy God commanded thee," are positive proof of the previous existence of the narrative in Exodus. The fact is, that it is only evidence of the existence of the Ten Words, the hoary antiquity of which is disputed by none; while the liberty to which the writer considered himself entitled in interpreting the word "Remember" as referring to Egypt, shows that, though he was aware of the definite bearing on the institution of the Sabbath, he did not feel restricted by any authoritative explanation.

120. Two novelettes were added by way of illustra-

---

[1] Ewald, Kuenen.

tion.¹ Even the fall of manna respected the Sabbath, a double portion falling on the Friday to provide for the necessities of the people; and the stoning to death of a man who presumed to pick up sticks to light a fire on the Sabbath.² As these two stories are connected with food supply and cooking, they are plainly at variance with the former practice of holding family feasts on the Sabbath. The prohibition³ that no man shall go forth from his place on the Sabbath, does not accord with the pious Shunamite woman riding forth on an ass to visit Elisha, and her husband asking: "Wherefore wilt thou go to him to-day? It is neither new moon nor sabbath." All these notions of a strict Puritanical observation of the Sabbath are new, introduced after the Captivity, and clearly have for their model the later Babylonian custom, according to which "the ruler must *not* eat *cooked* meat, nor change his clothes, nor drive in his chariot on the sabbath, nor may medicine even be administered on that day."⁴

121. This should suffice to show that the Sabbath ordinance was of great antiquity amongst the Hebrews, probably brought from Mesopotamia with them;⁵ that when first inquiry was made into its origin, it was assigned to the period of the Exodus, but later investigations bringing tokens of greater antiquity to light, its observance was thrown back to the Creation. Most noteworthy of all, the custom of 500 B.C. was set forth as the constant practice from 1320 B.C.

122. CIRCUMCISION.—In the account of the great circumcision ceremony held by Joshua (chap. v.)

---

¹ Ex. xvi. 22–31.   ² Num. xv. 32–36.   ³ Ex. xvi. 29.
⁴ Schrader; Sayce, *loc. cit.*   ⁵ Schrader.

at Gilgal, there is much that suggests its being intended to represent the institution of that rite.

Yahveh tells Joshua to prepare "flint knives" for the purpose, of which no mention is made in the Ritual. The significance of this strange fact so impressed itself upon the LXX. that we find in the Alexandrine copy an addition to Joshua xxiv. 31: "There they laid with him in the tomb where they buried him, the stone knives with which he circumcised the sons of Israel in Gilgal, when he brought them out of Egypt, as the Lord commanded them, and there they are unto this very day." Considerable difference of opinion exists as to the extent to which circumcision was performed amongst the Egyptians, some asserting that it was confined to priests and some kings; others gather from Isaiah xix. 23-25, that Israel, Egypt, and Assyria were all considered as circumcised countries, otherwise they could not be eligible for the blessing of Yahveh; Jeremiah ix. 26 no more asserts that Egypt was an uncircumcised country than Judah—if that verse is to be taken strictly, the ten tribes *alone* practised circumcision. But whatever views may be elsewhere entertained, there can be no question that here [1] the Egyptians had taunted them with being uncircumcised, and that the author intended this to be, as we have said, the first institution of the rite. The words in italics in the following quotation from verse 2 are an undoubted gloss, inserted by some one who noted the inconsistency with later stories: "Circumcise *again* the children of Israel the *second* time." There is no allusion to a previous general circumcision of the nation, which is, moreover, inconsistent with the sup-

[1] Josh. v. 9.

posed existence of a law to the effect that every boy should be circumcised when eight days old.

123. The long involved parenthetical note, verses 4–7, was inserted by the Deuteronomist[1] when the manifest conclusion that the Israelites were previously uncircumcised was offensive. Such notes as these are exposed to the charge, *Qui s'excuse s'accuse*. The desire to remove the natural inference is evidence of its existence, while the futility of the explanation affords higher corroboration. Why was this simple rite on babes of eight days old neglected for forty years? No answer suggests itself. If, as is insinuated, all who ate the Passover in Egypt were circumcised, why were not their children, the very men who entered Canaan, circumcised at the prescribed time, as many of them must have been babes, or very young children, at the time of the Exodus. The inability to settle these difficulties attests the purpose of the original author to narrate the first known instance when circumcision became a national rite. I need only allude to the explanation offered by Keil and Delitzsch to show how generally the difficulty of reconciliation is recognised: "The sentence upon the fathers, that their bodies should fall in the desert, was unquestionably a rejection of them on the part of God, an abrogation of the covenant with them. This punishment was also to be borne by their sons; and hence the reason why those who were born in the desert by the way were not circumcised. As the covenant of the Lord with the fathers was abrogated, the sons of the rejected generation were not to receive the covenant sign of circumcision." Thus Innocent III. finds very ancient

[1] Driver, 99.

precedent for imposing an *interdict:* God himself for forty years denied the Israelite Church all religious privileges and consolations; and yet if this passage did not demand explanation, no one would have suggested the idea.

124. As to the historicity of the general circumcision, there are two points to be considered: 1st, what amount of ceremonial uncleanness would attach to the bodies of the men during the period of healing; 2nd, the serious danger to which the host was exposed by all the males being *hors de combat.* In Joshua iv. 19 we read that the people encamped in Gilgal on the *tenth* day of the first month; the Passover was duly kept on the fourteenth day of the same month (v. 10); thus three days are left for the act of circumcision with flint knives, and for the subsequent necessary healing (v. 8); the words, in the camp "till they were whole," recognises the impurity to which I refer, but the writer has overlooked the fact that two to three *weeks* are required for this purpose by an adult. They would also be physically incapable of killing the lambs for Passover, an imperative duty for the heads of households. In Genesis xxxiv. 25 we read: "And it came to pass on the *third* day (after circumcision), when they were yet sore, two of the sons of Jacob, Simeon and Levi, took each man his sword, and came upon the city boldly and slew all the males." A few hundred Canaanites could then have annihilated Joshua's army at Gilgal, for they would have been incapable of adequate resistance; we can only then marvel at the temerity of a general exposing his army to the risk of utter annihilation in a hostile country. On the other hand, as the keeping of the Passover is taken as a

natural occurrence, for which no special command of God is necessary, we must infer that it had been kept annually in the wilderness, and for this purpose the people must have been circumcised, "for no uncircumcised person shall eat thereof."[1]

125. The story is undoubtedly fiction: here again we have evidence that the desire to explain a name philologically results in the fabrication of narrative. No less than three stories are here given to account for the name Gilgal, which was probably an ancient name, like Gil'ead, and did *not* owe its origin to the *Hebrews* at all. Taking Gilgal as meaning *Rolling,* we find the waves of Jordan are rolled in a heap (iii. 16), while in a miraculous manner the waters above the ford thus created did not cause an immense inundation of the country, nor did those below leave the bed of the river dry for several miles; secondly, twelve huge stones are rolled up from the bed of the river to form an altar or landmark—both these derivations also suggest a combination like "Heap of Rolling"; thirdly, an ethical motive is introduced (v. 9), rolling away the reproach of Egypt.

126. In Exodus iv. 25, 26, circumcision is also represented as a novelty, exciting natural repulsion. Its position immediately after the words, "I will slay thy son, even thy first-born," is very significant, suggesting that the origin of circumcision was a commutation of the offering up in sacrifice of the first-born, to secure a blessing on the family, as here the recovery of a father from sickness. There can be but little doubt that the author intended this also to be an account of the original institution of the rite, and

---

[1] Exod. xii. 48.

here also a *flint knife* is employed. From a comparison of these two narratives we find trace of an ancient tradition, that at one time circumcision was performed on a large scale as a solemn function, and only observed in the family in the face of a pressing emergency; which differs very much from the private circumcision of an infant in each family, as a fixed national custom; and that stone knives were long used, as evidence of the great antiquity of the rite. Here, then, we have an excellent example of story, to be discredited in itself, and yet at the same time revealing an ancient tradition that would otherwise have been lost.

127. The spirit of research was not satisfied with thus attributing circumcision to Joshua and Moses. Reflection that this rite was also practised among other nations (Jerome says Edomites, Moabites, and Ammonites, though Josephus denies this [4]) who claimed the same great ancestor Abram, led the author of the Priestly Code to ascribe [2] its divine institution as a revelation to this Semitic hero. As the Arabs performed the ceremony in the thirteenth year, Ishmael is represented as that age when circumcised, but Isaac is circumcised at eight days, to provide authority for the later Hebrew custom. The absence of allusion to flint knives makes it clear that this was written later than the stories of Moses and Joshua, where they are mentioned. By assigning the institution in all its simplicity to the time of Abraham, authority is provided for the employment of any sharp instrument, knife or scissors: stone knives would otherwise have been *de rigueur*.

[1] Keil: Jer. ix. 25.   [2] Gen. xvii.

128. PASSOVER.—In the prophetical history we first hear of the Feast of Unleavened Bread;[1] the slaying of the Passover lamb is a separate incident recorded in Exodus xii. 21–28. The two are combined in Deuteronomy xvi.; but the allusion to the Passover is not emphasised; no mention is made of the lamb— apparently an ox would be equally acceptable; xvi. 2: "Thou shalt sacrifice the passover of the flock, and the *herd.*" This point is met by subsequent legislation;[2] which requires two *bullocks* and a ram to be slain on the first day of the feast. The Priestly Code[3] gives prominence to the Paschal lamb and the smearing of blood on the door-posts, a detail not given elsewhere; the unleavened bread is with him a mere accessory. Thus, so far from being irrevocably fixed in all its details at the Exodus, the feast of Passover passed through many stages, and did not assume a final form till after the Captivity.

129. We have but scanty information to go upon as to the observation of the Passover after its institution. If it were not for Numbers ix. 5, which records its observance in the second year after leaving Egypt, we should infer that, in spite of the solemn injunction to keep it annually for ever, it immediately fell into abeyance. Joshua v. mentions a solemn observance after the passage of the Jordan. The next time we hear of it is in Hezeqiah's reign:[4] such an observance would accord with Hezeqiah's pose as a reformer, but its omission by the author of Kings renders the account suspicious, and the Chronicler's statement that it was unequalled since Solomon's day increases the

---
[1] Exod. xxiii. 15, xxxiv. 18. [2] Num. xxviii. 19.
[3] Exod. xii. 1–20. [4] 2 Chron. xxx.

degree of suspicion, as no record of this important event has survived. In 2 Kings xxiii. we read that Josiah held a Passover, unrivalled since the times of the Judges, probably referring to Joshua's Passover. This was, of course, the result of the discovery of the Book of Deuteronomy;[1] the Chronicler *more suo*, out of consideration for the priestly caste, invents a great Passover in the day of Samuel. The fact doubtless is, that the Passover was observed as a family feast in each household,[2] till a later custom, based on the desirability to tighten the bonds of unity, after the destruction of the northern kingdom, found expression in Deuteronomy xvi. 2: "Thou shalt sacrifice the Passover in the place which Yahveh shall choose to place his name there," viz., Jerusalem. Hezeqiah may have been the first to see the advisability of this course. The simple utterance, "Three times in the year shalt thou keep a feast unto Me," leaving the place indefinite, shows the earlier custom[3] to "appear before Yahveh, God," is only equivalent to worship,[4] and is not restricted to any special holy place.

130. The Feast of Unleavened Bread has clearly for its origin the custom of abstaining from eating the new corn of the year[5] until it had been consecrated by waving a sheaf before God—*i.e.*, recognising God's right to the first-fruits, a custom that must have been ancient, though recorded in Leviticus xxiii. 9-14: "Ye shall eat neither bread nor *parched corn*, nor green ears until the self-same day that ye have brought an offering unto your God." That this ceremony took place on the day after the Passover, during the unleavened

---

[1] 2 Kings xxii. 8.   [2] Exod. xii. 2).   [3] Exod. xxiii. 14.
[4] Exod. xxiii. 17.   [5] Barley: Ewald, "Ant.," 352.

bread observance, is evident from the calculation of fifty days for Pentecost, reckoning also from this sheaf-waving.[1] An allusion to this practice is found in Joshua v. 11. "They did eat of the old corn of the land on the *morrow* after the Passover, unleavened cakes and *parched corn* in the selfsame day." Thus the Feast of Unleavened Bread is a most simple, natural act of recognition of the powers of Nature, as controlled by God, and its connexion with the commencement of the course of seasons attests its immense antiquity, and suggests a very general observance of it amongst Oriental nations. One of the Prophetical School of authors, however, to clinch its historical association with the Exodus, adds a note (Exodus xii. 39): "It was not leavened, *because* they were thrust out of Egypt, and *could not tarry*, neither had they prepared for themselves any victuals."

131. Pascha means *leaping;* its application to the feast is sought and found by the Prophetical School in the story that Yahveh would leap over [2] the doors smeared with blood, and only slay the Egyptians on each side. The objection to this story is, that it presupposes the intermixture of Hebrew and Egyptian dwellings, which is contrary to the repeated assertion that the Hebrews had a separate colony at Goshen, because the Egyptians objected to fraternise with them;[3] the meaning to *spare* is merely subsidiary both here and Isaiah xxxi. 5, the only other passage where the meaning "leap" is disregarded. It has been suggested that Pascha had original reference to the sun's *crossing* the line at the equinox, which heralds the renewal of

---

[1] Lev. xxiii. 15.   [2] Exod. xii. 23.
[3] Gen. xlvi. 34; Exod. ix. 26.

the earth at spring. There are many considerations in support of this conjecture, not the least of which is the fact that from this feast exactly six moons are reckoned to the second great feast, which thus occurred at the autumnal equinox, approximately. The history of Israel teems with allusions to some such ancient belief. At its very commencement Abram crosses the Euphrates, and his new career as a friend of God opens: in this connection it should be noted that a town on a ford of the Euphrates is still known as *Thapsachus*. Jacob crosses the ford Yabboq, and enters on a holier life, which is celebrated by the change of his name to Israel. Here, too, there is manifest regard paid to the root Pesach = to leap, to be lame, for Jacob halted on his thigh after his struggle with God. Israelites cross the Red Sea and commence a new life of freedom from Egyptian bondage; they cross the Jordan, and a new era in the promised land is marked. Elijah crosses the Jordan, and is translated to heaven; Elisha recrosses it, and his career as a great prophet opens. In imitation of this Old Testament thought, Christ enters the Jordan for baptism prior to the manifestation of his mission; from which we gather that the association of resurrection with baptism can be traced back to the original equinox festival. Paul's view on the subject is unmistakable; in Romans vi. 1–4 he says: "We were buried therefore with Him through baptism unto His death, that like as Christ was raised from the dead .... so we also might walk in *newness* of *life*." And in 1 Corinthians x. 2 he speaks of the Israelites being baptised unto Moses in the Red Sea. We believe then that the most ancient Paschal feast was celebrated at the equinoxes, but that the Hebrews, with their prefer-

The Sacrifice of the First-born

ence for observations of the moon, changed the solar dates to approximate lunar dates. Even Ewald admits that its usages betray a *pre-Mosaic* period.[1]

132. In connection with both these feasts, Unleavened Bread and Pascha, we find great stress laid on the redemption of the first-born of man and beast; but this is also a general custom, not necessarily restricted to this occasion:[2] "Thy fulness and thy *tear* thou shalt withhold, the first-born of thy sons shalt thou give to me; thus shalt thou do as regards thy ox and thy flock, seven days shall it be with its dam, on the eighth shalt thou give it me." The phraseology sufficiently attests the antiquity of this passage, the fulness and tear are generally understood, after the LXX. translation, as poetical equivalents for threshing-floor and *wine-vats;* but what is to hinder us from taking the words more literally: "Both that which thou canst part with without consciousness of loss, of thy plenty; and that which it will *break thy heart* to render up, thy tear, thou shalt not withhold." It has frequently been denied that the Hebrews ever, as a custom, offered human sacrifices; the passing children through the fire to Moloch is viewed as exceptional wickedness, part of the apostasy that led to the destruction of Jerusalem by Nebuchadrezzar. Ezeqiel xx. however, reveals to us an important tradition: after describing the supposed revolt of the Israelites in the wilderness, he makes God say (verse 18): "I said to their children in the wilderness, Walk not in the *statutes* of your *fathers;*" (verse 25) I, even I, gave them statutes not good, customs of death, and I defiled them with their gifts, when they passed through the fire *every* first-born, in order that

---

[1] "Ant.," 353. [2] Exod. xxii. 29, 30.

I might destroy them." The importance of this passage cannot be over-estimated; it not only distinctly asserts the general practice of heathen rites, which Joshua (xxiv. 2) distinctly hints at, but it harmonises that state of affairs with Yahveh's eternal control of the fortunes of Israel, by the explanation that such idolatry was permitted to hasten them to their destruction. What, however, requires explanation is, that this very expression of the bad customs, fatal to life, is found in Exodus xiii. 12, where the prophetical history records this order from Yahveh: "Thou shalt pass through the fire to Yahveh every first-born." Probably this last writer preserved the story of the divine command to Abram to offer up in sacrifice his son Isaac, as illustrative of the antiquity of the custom. We hold, then, that at the spring equinox, Phœnicians and Hebrews offered first-fruit of the corn and sacrificed first-born of men and cattle; this was the original Pascha, to which we consequently deny all claim to the meaning of sparing. For the sacrifice of the first-born son a lamb was substituted, tradition said by Abram, and it is to be noted that in this narrative the Rabbis see a reference to the Passover.[1] The connection between the Exodus and the Passover is thus summed up by Wellhausen (88): "What has led to it is evidently the coincidence of the spring festival with the Exodus, already accepted by the older tradition, the relation of cause and effect having become inverted in course of time. The only view sanctioned by the nature of the case is, that the Israelite custom of offering the firstlings gave rise to the narrative of the slaying of the first-born of Egypt; unless the custom be presupposed, the story is inexpli-

[1] Weber, 257.

cable, and the peculiar selection of the victims by the plague is left without a motive."

133. It will suffice to treat still more briefly of the other festivals. As the feast of the spring equinox combined two separate feasts—Unleavened Bread and Pascha—so at the autumnal equinox were celebrated both the Final Harvest and the Feast of Tabernacles. As a specimen of the curious determination to harmonise conflicting details, we may note 2 Chronicles vii. 9, where the feast spreads over a fortnight, which is carefully explained as being caused by one week's consecration of the altar, *beside* the ordinary week required for the feast; a gloss is appended to 1 Kings viii. 65, to confirm the truth of this statement, which simply arose from the double recital in Leviticus xxiii. 34 and 39, where also it appears to me that *the two verses have strangely changed places*. Solomon's dedication bears trace of being in accord with Leviticus xxiii. 34-36, Nehemiah's with Leviticus xxiii. 39-42; the Chronicler has blended the two accounts into one for Solomon's great feast. The ritual of this feast entails considerable slaughter of animals, as depicted in Numbers xxix.—two hundred animals of all sorts in eight days. Uniformly, then, in the history of the Sabbath, circumcision and their two chief annual feasts, we see how customs of the greatest antiquity are represented as institutions peculiar to the Hebrews, and their solemn binding nature persistently referred to the time of Moses; while stories are always fabricated in support of any position they may elect to adopt, or glosses later inserted to effect the same purpose.

134. **SACRIFICE.**—Seeing that very similar ideas

of sacrifice obtained among all nations,[1] we need not be detained long over this subject. The manner in which libations, offerings of fruit and vegetables, cakes, roast and boiled meat, are all referred to direct divine revelation to Moses, can only be attributed to the desire to stamp the commonest occurrences of every-day life with peculiarity and sacredness unknown to other nations. Some questions, however, naturally present themselves: what was the motive in disparaging fruit offerings by representing Cain's offering as rejected by God, seeing that such were actually ordered by the ritual? By the way, Cain and Abel seem together to have anticipated the spring festival observances, one offering the lamb, the other the corn and fruits. How is it that Abram was so acquainted with the ritual as to abstain from dividing the birds[2] in the manner required by Leviticus i. 17; and again, in Genesis xviii. 6, to employ three measures of flour for an offering to God in accordance with the three-tenths of fine flour so often commanded.[3] Have we not here once more evidence of determination not to permit the idea that ancient saints could have been ignorant of religious practices ordained long after their time. Our curiosity is also aroused by the sacrifice of seven bullocks and seven rams, which seems a perfect conception of sacrifice according to the notions of the Hebrew writers; yet this is only observed by the mythical Balaam, prescribed by Ezeqiel,[4] ordained by God,[5] and by the Chronicler described as observed by David[6] and by Hezeqiah.[7] Why is the ritual silent concerning this practice? Are Job and Balaam

---

[1] Especially cf. C.I.P. 165-167.   [2] Gen. xv. 10.
[3] Lev. xiv. 10, &c.   [4] Ezek. xiv. 23.   [5] Job xlii. 8.
[6] 1 Chron. xv. 26.   [7] 2 Chron. xxix. 21.

Methods of Igniting Sacrifices

indications of a foreign origin of this practice, a partial recognition of which was only granted during the Captivity.

135. A matter of some interest is the question as to how sacrifices were kindled. On ordinary occasions doubtless by the same rude means by which household fires were set alight; so we read [1] that after cleansing the Temple, sacrificial fire was procured by *friction of stones*. On solemn occasions recourse was doubtless had to some less manifest method to impress the congregation, the agent being the sun's rays concentrated through a species of lens. In Roman legend this was successfully accomplished by Numa Pompilius, though attended with fatal results when attempted by his successor. Such we may naturally conceive to have been the origin of the phrase, "fire came down from heaven and consumed the sacrifice," in the Jewish stories of the first sacrifice in the Tabernacle [2] and the Temple [3] also of David's sacrifice on the threshing-floor of Araunah; [4] this also gives a rational explanation of the death of Nadab and Abihu, attempting to sacrifice when they were intoxicated, [5] and the similar fate of Qorach and his brethren, unaccustomed to the service. [6] Ewald [7] cites Philo in his Life of Moses as alluding to the employment of solar rays in conjunction with heated stones. In the contest on Mount Carmel [8] both parties evidently relied on the sun's appearance for victory; and from 2 Macc. i. 31–36 we gather that some clear oil, like *naphtha*, was poured on the sacrifice, both to ensure ignition of the fuel and to enhance the effect,

[1] 2 Macc. x. 3.
[2] Lev. ix. 9, 24.
[3] 2 Chron. vii. 1.
[4] 1 Chron. xxi. 26.
[5] Lev. x. 2.
[6] Num. xvii. 35.
[7] "Ant." 29.
[8] 1 Kings xviii. 38.

the uninitiated supposing that water was poured on the sacrifice. The order[1] never to permit fire on the altar to go out, suggests that it was not considered advisable to repeat this ceremony too often; besides, in the nature of things, a morning and evening sacrifice at stated hours could not be dependent upon the chance of an obscure sky. Older narratives make such wonderful consumption of sacrifices beyond the reach of ordinary men, though it may be doubted whether the messengers of God in the stories[2] were anything else but prophets or wise men skilled in the mysteries of nature.

136. ARK.—When we consider the important part played by the Ark in the early history of Israel, it cannot fail to be a matter of surprise that we have so little information concerning it. In Deuteronomy x. 1–5 we have the simplest account of its origin. God tells Moses to hew two tables of stone, instead of those supplied by God himself the first time, and to make a chest to contain them—a mild satire on his previous destruction of the more valuable article; thus the size of the Ark depended on the measurement of the stones. When then we are told in the later narrative[3] that the dimensions of the Ark were 3 ft. 9 in. by 2 ft. 3 in. by 2 ft. 3 in., we can only conclude that the figures are an exaggeration, for no man unaided could carry such a bulk of stone (3 ft. by 2 ft. by 2 ft.) up and down a mountain; or it is possible we have here the recollection of a more magnificent chest manufactured for Solomon's Temple. The usual mode of conveying the box from place to place, appears, until the death of Uzza to have been

---

[1] Lev. vi. 12, 13. [2] Jud. vi. 12, xiii. 20. [3] Exod. xxv. 10.

by ox-cart. The Philistines in returning it[1] would, in their anxiety to find favour, naturally imitate the manner in which they had seen it brought on to the field of battle; and it is absolutely inconceivable that David[2] should abandon an existing custom in favour of a *foreign* precedent. It was *David* that *instituted* the bearing of the Ark on the shoulders[3] to avoid the recurrence of a similar catastrophe; therefore the elaborate provisions[4] for golden rings and staves for this purpose are further evidence of adjustment by the later author. As, then, Exodus is our only authority for the cherubim on the lid of the Ark, shall we accept this as a fact without inquiry? The cherubim, even according to Exodus,[5] were not on the Ark itself, but on the mercy-seat suspended over the Ark; at each end was a miniature cherub with two wings about a foot long, stretched over the mercy-seat, so that the four wings formed a canopy for it. We have a very different tradition in 1 Chronicles xxviii. 11-19, the mercy-seat (18), the chariot of the cherubim, is David's own device by direct revelation; he is not represented as indebted to Moses for either the idea or the pattern. The fact underlying this remarkable statement is that Solomon's Temple and Holy of Holies are quite independent of the Mosaic Tabernacle, the description of which by later writers is actually derived from Solomon's, and not *vice versâ*, as is usually believed. The Chronicler, in his regret that the Temple was not built by David, the saint of the Lord, instead of Solomon, with heathen proclivities, makes the former the important architect, the latter the mere clerk of works. Now, in 1 Kings vii.

---

[1] 1 Sam. vi. 7.   [2] 2 Sam. vi. 3.   [3] 2 Sam. vi. 13.
[4] Exod. xxv. 12-15.   [5] xxv. 18-21.

we are told that in the cubical sanctuary, measuring 30 ft. every way, two cherubim, 15 ft. high, were placed with their wings stretched in an unusual manner, one forward and the other backward, and as each wing was 7 ft. long, the backward wings touched the opposite walls, and the forward wings met in the middle of the room. Under these cherubim the box containing the revered stone was placed;[1] hence arose the phrase, applied to God, "Dwelling between the cherubim," and the inference, that these were, and always had been, an inseparable part of the Ark, though the expression could not have been coined till after the completion of Solomon's Temple. The peculiar attitude of the cherubim is distinctly Egyptian,[2] and it requires no argument to show that the probability of utilising Egyptian ritual ideas is more on the side of a Solomonic than a Mosaic origin. That Moses, however versed in Egyptian lore, should take these figures for a pattern for his sacred utensils, is repulsive to reason, and not less so, that he should one day cry, "Thou shalt not make to thyself the likeness of anything in heaven above or in the earth," &c., and the next make the image of fabulous monsters to grace the most sacred spot in his Holy of Holies. The Ark itself, then, was a strong chest, *without* cherubim or mercy-seat attached; its sanctity was confined to the contents, the table of stone, written by God himself[3]—*i.e.*, some ancient stone on which traces of undecipherable marks were still visible. There is nothing improbable in the notion that such a chest, made of acacia wood an inch or more thick;

---

[1] 1 Kings viii 6. [2] *Vide* first illustration *sub voce* "Dict. Bible."
[3] Deut. x. 2-4.

should survive for many generations; though the love of the marvellous in predicating durability renders us rather cautious in accepting the statement, that this box, made by Moses, was carried about freely in the days of the Judges and Samuel, and still survived to be deposited in Solomon's Temple. Of course, 400 years is not a tremendous age for a chest left unmoved and carefully protected, but, as I said, the bold expression of such ideas as the following makes one suspicious: "I have led you forty years in the wilderness: your clothes are not waxen old upon you, and thy shoe is not waxen old upon thy foot."[1] In spite of the assertion of the author of the Epistle to the Hebrews (ix. 4), the stone was the *only* contents of the Ark; in fact, as it was made to order, there would not appear room for anything else inside. The Philistines did not attempt to place their golden presents in the interior; also, *alongside* of it were placed the pot of manna and budding rod of Aaron—both of which are hardly to be viewed as historical—and probably the brazen serpent, the Nehushtan destroyed in the reign of Hezeqiah. It appears that in the days of Saul and David, the ephod, with its augural powers, was more highly prized than the Ark, while the fact that the little boy Samuel curled himself to sleep in its close proximity is once again distinct evidence that the idea of a mercy-seat, visited once a year by the high priest alone, is considerably antedated. In conclusion, it must always be borne in mind that the very detailed description of the Ark, and of the Ritual of Atonement peculiarly belonging to it, was written after

[1] Deut. xxix. 5.

the Captivity, when the Ark itself had been lost sight of for fully a century.

137. HOLY PLACE.—Places sacred to God were scattered all over Palestine; oaks and unhewn stone pillars were associated together in the worship of the ancient Hebrews, as well as of the Phœnicians and Druids. Of such sacred trees the following were the most noted: (1) the tree at Mamre, near Hebron,[1] under which Abraham sacrificed;[2] (2) the Teacher's Tree, Moreh, near Shechem, Abram's first recorded shrine,[3] afterwards a landmark.[4] Here Jacob buried his wives' strange gods[5] and Joshua set up a stone pillar in honour of the Book of the Law, appropriately compiled beneath the foliage of the Teacher's Tree; and here, according to the LXX., he buried his flint circumcision knives. (3) The Soothsayers' Tree, near Qadesh, a Qenite sanctuary; (4) a very celebrated tree near Ramah and Bethlehem; here Deborah, Rachel's nurse, is said to have been buried,[6] and Deborah, the prophetess to have dwelt.[7] It is also called the terebinth of Tabor,[8] which throws suspicion of conjecture in associating two women of the name of Deborah with a tree known as Tabor. Tradition assigns some great calamity to this spot; hence the tree is called the Tree of Weeping—surely excessive mourning for a nurse,[9] and the spot itself is called Weepers,[10] for here the whole nation lamented its backsliding. (5) One tree, probably east of Jordan,[11] where Gideon sacrificed to an

---

[1] Gen. xiii. 18.   [2] Gen. xviii. 5-8.   [3] Gen. xii. 6.
[4] Judges vii. 1, ix. 6; Deut. xi. 30.   [5] Gen. xxxv. 4.
[6] Gen. xxxv. 8.   [7] Judg. iv. 5.   [8] 1 Sam. x. 3
[9] Gen. xxxv. 8.   [10] Judg. ii. 5.   [11] Judg. vi. 11-24.

angel, as Abram had done at Mamre; (6) a tamarisk planted by Abram at Beer-sheba, under which he worshipped Yahveh.[1] The antiquity of these trees is beyond dispute—in fact, might well stretch back into pre-Abramite times; but there is an evident straining after providing a Hebrew hero for each which results in three or four tales concentrating on specially favoured trees. The worship of God being thus connected with the shelter of shady trees, Nature's tabernacles, it is not surprising to find that each neighbourhood had its tree where they performed some simple religious service, as Chinese women now do. It is only in later days, when the Prophetical Schools had purified the religious ideal, that the worship " under every green tree " is viewed as apostasy from God, and typified as adultery: the phrase is unknown, except to Jeremiah,[2] Ezeqiel, and Deutero-Isaiah.

138. Alongside many of these trees stone pillars were set up, large rough stones, called Matztzeboth, which, as Matztzub is a *station*, might, to preserve the assonance of the names, be rendered *statue*, were it not that the latter indicates a carved or graven figure, and would thus give rise to misapprehension. Jacob set up two Matztzeboth to God,[3] one as a landmark for Laban,[4] another as a tombstone to Rachel.[5] *Moses* himself erected twelve Matztzeboth at one place, at the foot of Sinai.[6] Absalom reared one in his own honour, to keep his memory green, as he had no sons;[7] the *double entendre* in the Hebrew nickname for it is an indication of the association of ideas between these pillars and parentage, to which Jeremiah and Deutero-Isaiah refer,

---

[1] Gen. xxi. 33. [2] Deut. xii. 2. [3] Gen. xxviii. 18, xxxv. 14.
[4] Gen. xxxi. 45. [5] Gen. xxxv. 20. [6] Exod. xxiv. 4. [7] 2 Sam. xviii. 18.

quoted below. Hosea (x. 1), speaks of these as thank-offerings, and foretells their discontinuance as a punishment, when there shall be a general interdict of all religious observances. Isaiah (vi. 13), in seeking an emblem for the future holiness of the Jews, after they had suffered humiliation, speaks of a tree lopped of all its boughs and branches, apparently destined for fuel, but elevated to the sacred purpose of becoming a Matztzebeth: this would seem to indicate the existence of *wooden* as well as stone Matztzeboth, the singular of which is Matztze*bah*. If the difference of form conveys the idea, then Absalom's pillar was of wood. The some prophet actually *promises* that hereafter a Matztzebah shall be set up in Egypt as a token of Yahveh's favour. In later times their erection was prohibited,[1] and Moses is further represented as ordering the destruction of those to be found in Canaan.[2]

139. The Asherah, a lopped tree, part of the Baal cult, does not appear to have been considered as innocent as the Matztzebah, with which it is frequently coupled; nor can I divest myself of the suspicion that some of the wooden Matztzeboth were carelessly called Asherah. There is no doubt that the worship of Baal had proceeded side by side with the worship of Yahveh; Hosea[3] distinctly alludes to this: "Thou shalt no longer call me Baal." Though more fully recognised in the north, on account of its proximity to Tyre, there is evidence of a hankering after Baal ritual in the south. It is strange, however, how seldom the prophets denounce the Asherah.[4] In Judges,[5] the episode of the hewing

---

[1] Deut. xvi. 22; Lev. xxvi. 1.
[2] Deut. xii. 3; Exod. xxxiv. 13.   [3] ii. 18 (16).
[4] Isa. xvii. 8; Mic. v. 14; Jer. xvii. 2, 11; Isa. xxvii. 9. [5] vi. 25–32.

down of the Asherah is inserted to provide an etymology of the two names Gide'on and Jerubbaal; it is a novelette on Deuteronomy vii. 5, where "wa-ashereihem tegadde'un" suggested an explanation of the name *Gide'on*.

140. The objection to the reverence paid to ancient trees and stones would appear to be, that, associated as they were with ancestral worship, the thing signified was forgotten in the sign; so that Jeremiah[1] complains that priests and kings say to a tree, "Thou art my father; and to a stone, Thou hast given me birth." Deutero-Isaiah,[2] on the other hand, employs without censure language based on the same idea, which is clearly intelligible to his hearers: "Look to the rock whence ye were hewn, and to the hole of the pit whence ye were dug; look to Abraham your father, and to Sarah that bare you."

141. Hills were considered peculiarly sacred because by their elevation they were so much nearer to the sky —the abode of God. It is not for nothing that tradition makes so many of its saints—Aarou, Moses, Joshua, and Eleazar—find a fitting tomb only on the hill-top. Bamoth, high places, were popular places for sacrificial feasts. Samuel observed this custom;[3] Solomon sacrificed at the high place at Gibeon,[4] and was vouchsafed a blessing in a dream; of the good kings—Asa, Jehoshaphat, Joash, Amaziah, Uzziah—it is expressly stated that the high places continued to be venerated in their reigns, though later historians view this as a slight blemish on their escutcheon. Hezeqiah, under the influence of Isaiah, was the first to enter on a general crusade[5] against Bamoth, Matztzeboth, &c.;

[1] Jer. ii. 27.   [2] li. 1. 2.   [3] 1 Sam. ix. and x.
[4] 1 Kings iii. 3.   [5] 2 Kings xviii. 4.

his iconoclastic zeal did not even spare the "brazen serpent" attributed by tradition to Moses. Invective against Bamoth is of still later date than the tirade against trees and stones;[1] the destruction of heathen Bamoth in Canaan is not ordered till so late as Numbers xxxiii. 52, who is anxious to supply what in his opinion was a serious oversight in the existing edition of the Torah; whence we gather that high places sacred before the arrival of the Hebrews continued to be venerated by them, and that, with the approval of the prophets, who in predicting the desolation of the high places refer to the utter *denudation* of the land by captivity, not the punishment of a form of worship distasteful to Yahveh :[2] "The Bamoth of Isaac shall be laid waste, and the sanctuaries of Israel rendered desolate."

142. Altars were scattered all over the land; Jeremiah complains that even every street of Jerusalem had an altar of its own. The patriarchs were represented as setting up altars in every place at which they sojourned. Before and after battle, in supplication and thanksgiving for victory, altars were erected by Moses, Gideon, Jephtha, Samuel, Saul; after a national calamity, like pestilence, by David; and for family worship, as by Micah[3] at Bethlehem,[4] &c. The general feeling of the populace is revealed by the words put into the mouth of Sennacherib's chief butler.[5] "Yahveh our God, is not that he whose high places and altars Hezeqiah hath taken away?" Remember, too, how the orthodox Elijah makes lamentation to God:[6] "The children of Israel have forsaken Thy covenant, thrown down Thine altars." A multiplicity of altars is then

---

[1] Ez. vi. 13; Lev. xxvi. 30.   [2] Amos vii. 9.   [3] Judg. xviii.
[4] 1 Sam. xvi. 5.   [5] 2 Kings xviii. 22.   [6] 1 Kings xix. 14.

quite *en règle*. Fuller information on this interesting subject can be found in Kuenen and Wellhausen; but enough has been said to show that the idea of one only sacred place, of sacrifice and worship confined to one sanctuary, is very modern, against the acceptance of which is arrayed a compact phalanx of historical facts.

143. Deuteronomy (xii.) is the source of this idea, that Yahveh could only be acceptably worshipped in one holy place, " the place which he shall choose to set his name there ": the phrase *Lasum shmo sham* is very artificial, and suggestive of mystery. The later historians saw in this a prophecy relative to Jerusalem; Solomon in his dedication prayer is *made* to say,[1] " The place of which thou hast said, My name shall be there;" though it is not till afterwards[2] that Yahveh gives the promise, "I have hallowed this house to *set my name there* for ever." In a note the historian cites this passage more definitely:[3] " Yahveh said, In Jerusalem will I set my name." It has been objected, and with considerable appearance of cogency, that the custom in prophecies *post eventum* is to insert the correct name, to enhance the value of the supposed prophecy;[4] as, then, we read,[5] " A child shall be born to the house of David, Josiah by name," so here we should expect " The place which he shall choose, Jerusalem by name." In the first place, the Deuteronomist could not ignore the four centuries or more, when Gilgal, Shiloh, &c., would, in his opinion, be the places where in turn God " set His name "; and secondly, the fact that this author had Jerusalem much

---
[1] 1 Kings viii. 29. [2] 1 Kings ix. 3. [3] 2 Kings xxi. 4.
[4] The allusion to Cyrus is to a contemporary (Isa. xliv. 28).
[5] 1 Kings xiii. 2.

in his mind while writing is attested by his preference for "inheritance" over the word "possession," even in this very chapter (xii. 9), though the word *nachalah* is used to disguise the reference instead of the rare word *Yerusha*,[1] which is distinctly assonant with *Yerusha*laim, Jerusalem. The words inherit, inheritance, disinherit are, as it were, the keynotes of Deuteronomy.

144. HIGH PRIEST.—The history of the rise of a priestly caste will be treated subsequently under the history of Levi; but we may collect again here some of the scattered hints we have already met with bearing on the position of the high priest. Under the head of Genealogies we have seen that, prior to the Captivity, the names of successive high priests have not been carefully preserved, even since the days of David, while the ancestors of Zadoq for several generations bear so suspicious a resemblance to, not to say identity with, the names of the high priests of the closing monarchy as to suggest fabrication. The office of high priest under David and Solomon is only that of a hierophant obeying the orders of the king; he has no independence, even in his own tent or temple. All the kings, judging from what we are told of David and Solomon, themselves performed the priestly office, offering sacrifice and burning incense; the Chronicler's fabulous account of the cause of Uzziah's leprosy really reveals the common practice of the kings.[2] It was not the high priest who was consulted by the king, but the prophet; even the relative positions of Moses and Aaron betray the same state of affairs. Whether the blending of the interests of the priests and prophets

---

[1] Deut. ii. and iii.   [2] *Cf.* 1 Kings. ix. 25.

was chiefly due to the prophet Jeremiah, himself of priestly family, cannot be said with certainty. The opinion of his cotemporary the Deuteronomist is expressed without reservation—the chief religious director of Israel is the prophet, not the priest:[1] "Yahveh will raise up a prophet from among thy brethren like unto me, to him shalt thou hearken." The allusion to "the priest that shall be in those days"[2] is indicative of an idea *strange* to the existing customs, and the position of the Levites as expounders of the Law[3] is an *equal novelty*. Hitherto prophets and seers rebuked the king when he went astray; priests were chiefly serviceable as oracles, and therefore indispensable, but still inferior to the prophets. When Gad the seer tells David of his guilt in numbering the people—or, in other words, attributes the coincidence of the pestilence and census to some sin, which he easily conjectures to be pride—David does *not* go to the high priest to offer a sin-offering, *nor* did he call upon him to sacrifice when the plague was stayed, *but* maintained his own right to the office of chief sacrificer for the nation.

145. That the king could make and unmake chief priests, is revealed in the story of Abiathar and Zadoq. When Saul massacred the priests at Nob, on account of assistance given to David on his false representation, Abiathar, the son of the chief priest, naturally fled to David, to whom he proved very useful with his divining ephod. Saul must either have nominated his successor, or been without an officiating priest for five and a half years. How Abiathar fell into disgrace with David is not related, but Zadoq suddenly appears in

---

[1] Deut. xviii. 18.   [2] xix. 17, xxi. 5.   [3] xvii. 12, xxxi. 11.

charge of the Ark,[1] Abiathar being treated as inferior
and ignored by the king; after the defeat of Absolom
they are spoken of together as priests,[2] reminding us
strongly of a similar confusion with regard to Annas
and Caiaphas in the Gospels. Solomon naturally sends
Abiathar into retirement for supporting Adonijah's
pretension to the crown; and Zadoq remains chief
priest without a rival. But when we read [3] that thus
was fulfilled the prophecy against Eli's house, we
require from our experience of genealogies to be
certified that Abiathar was descended from Eli, whose
functions seemed to have been discharged by Samuel;
and remembering another prophecy[4] promising the
eternal priesthood to Phinehas' family, to which a claim
is entered on behalf of Zadoq, we ask if both the
prophecies are capable of independent fulfilment, and
what was the occupation of Zadoq's ancestors during
the high priesthood of Eli's family. A more reliable tradition makes the hereditary priesthood *begin*
with Zadoq, and accordingly speaks of the house of
Zadoq.

146. Wellhausen's words are so weighty that I
cannot refrain from transcribing some passages wholesale on this point:[5] " In the Law the position of Aaron
is not only superior, but unique, like that of the Pope
in relation to the episcopate: his sons act under his
oversight; he alone is the one fully qualified priest,
the embodiment of all that is holy in Israel. He alone
bears the Urim and Thummim and the Ephod; the
Priestly Code, indeed, no longer knows what those
articles are for, and it confounds the ephod of gold with

---

[1] 2 Sam. xv. 25.   [2] 2 Sam. xx. 25.   [3] 1 Kings ii. 27.
[4] Num. xxv. 13.   [5] Pp. 149-152.

the ephod of linen, the plated image with the priestly robe; but the dim recollections of these serve to enhance the magical charm of Aaron's majestic adornment. He alone may enter into the Holy of Holies and there offer incense; the way, at other times inaccessible, is open to him on the great day of Atonement. .... His death makes an epoch; it is when the high priest, not the king, dies, that the fugitive slayer obtains his amnesty.[1] At his investiture he receives the chrism like a king, and is called accordingly the anointed priest; he is adorned with the tiara and diadem like a king, and like a king, too, he wears the purple, that most unpriestly of all raiment, of which he therefore must divest himself when he goes into the Holy of Holies.[2] What now can be the meaning of this fact, that he who is at the head of the worship, in this quality alone, and without any political attributes besides, or any share in the government, is at the same time at the head of the nation? What, but that civil power has been withdrawn from the nation, and is in the hands of foreigners; that Israel has now merely a spiritual and ecclesiastical existence? .... Foreign rulers had then relieved the Jews of all concern about secular affairs; they had it in their power, and indeed were compelled, to give themselves up wholly to sacred things, in which they were left completely unhampered. Thus the Temple became the sole centre of life; and the prince of the Temple, the head of the spiritual commonwealth, to which also the control of political affairs, so far as these were still left to the nation, naturally fell, there being no other head."

147. His genealogy and history being, then, uncertain

[1] Num. xxxv. 28.   [2] Lev. xvi. 4.

and unreliable, the evidence of the performance of his functions being conspicuous by its absence, the mercy-seat over the Ark having been seen to be a very modern invention, we have no hesitation in accepting the recent conclusion of critics, that the High Priest, with his regal rank and authority, his magnificent ritual, and his solemn entry once a year within the vail, to offer atonement for himself and the nation, are all the product of the period after the return from Captivity. The above quotations from Wellhausen provide a complete reply to the oft-raised objection, that such a ritual would be more fitting a period of national prosperity than one of depression. In fact, his arguments conclusively show that no other time in the history of the people provides all the necessary conditions for the conception of such an office.

CHAPTER VI

ELEMENTS OF IMPROBABILITY IN THE HEXATEUCH NARRATIVE

148. THE BIBLE, we are told, is unlike all other books, being the work of God; directly by revelation, and indirectly by inspiration. It is maintained that such things as were manifestly beyond the limits of human ken—as God himself, Creation, &c.; or of human memory—as the Fall of Man, the Flood, &c.—were in some undefined manner dictated by God to some favoured man, preferably to Moses; this is Revelation. Inspiration guided man in the choice of matter for eternal preservation, giving him an unparalleled sympathetic insight into the heart of man, and a unique sustained recognition of God's attributes of creation and preservation, and his prerogatives of selection and rejection. If there is such a thing as revelation, it may be only partially complete, but it cannot, consistently with our conception of God, contain any statement absolutely at variance with the laws of Nature. It is much safer, then, as a safeguard against misconception, and as a removal of a serious stumbling-block, to allow revelation to be absorbed in inspiration, as the latter term is not in its essence repugnant to the idea of imperfection. Frail man, even inspired by God, can err, without offence to the very first attribute we conceive of in relation to the Deity—viz., Truth.

149. Inspiration itself is, as its name indicates, an ethereal, intangible influence, whose presence we can recognise, but whose essence defies analysis. In fact, it differs but little from what is called Genius, which also eludes the cold precision of definition; we speak not of a steady, burning flame, but of "flashes of genius"; what evokes them, we know not; we feel in the presence of a power beyond the boundary-line of human intelligence. A genius is a man in the possession of a larger share of the divine afflatus than falls to the common lot of men, even of those we call clever. Inspiration is genius directed mainly in the channel of all that tends to the improvement and advancement of the human race. Thus, in the inspired books of the Bible we find laws relating to war, sanitation, husbandry, discussions on social and ethical problems, songs and proverbs bearing on the commonest experiences of everyday life, with its round of joy and grief, victories and defeats in conflict with sin. It is a mistake to suppose that the inspiration of the Bible consists merely in its function as a guide to heaven. The Old Testament knows nothing of immortality and a life beyond the grave; even the late Professor Mozley admits Daniel xii. 2, of the second century B.C., to be the first plain utterance on the subject. A perfect system for life on-earth was the aim of the inspired writers, with a vague idea that perhaps God's blessing and care might not terminate with death.

150. Degrees of inspiration are observed to vary with the genius of the author. Isaiah (xl.–lxvi.) thus takes a higher-rank than Jeremiah, who himself is superior to Ezeqiel; while the same author is found incapable of maintaining a level of excellence. It is a regard to this genius which was manifestly the criterion in the formation of the Canon both of the Jewish and Christian Church. Tobit is inferior to Daniel, the wisdom of the son of Sirach to Proverbs, Clement of Rome to Paul's Letters to the Corinthians, only in the lower tone of interest they evoke. They deal with very similar subjects taken from the same religious standpoint, but they are comparatively dull and flat. They are inspired with the same motive to benefit mankind and glorify God; the genius, however, is not of the same high order. We do not deny that holy men of old spake as they were moved by the Spirit of God, we increase indefinitely the number of men thus "God-breathed,"[1] and claim to judge them by the degree of genius stamped on their work.

151. If inspiration, then, is only a name given to a certain particular phase of genius, it may appropriately be applied to all the sacred books of the East and the philosophies of the West. God's glory is magnified, not diminished, by the modern study of the science of religions, which cannot be blamed for denying the monopoly of inspiration to the Hebrew nation. Holy Bible is simply one of many holy books of many nations, the term holy being applied to them on account of their great antiquity. Each nation believed in the superiority of its religion, the omnipotence of its own God; but the God and the religion were confined to that nation. The nobler view is, that the one only God was worshipped under many guises by various nations; that this worship was never perfect, being

---

[1] 2 Tim. iii. 16.

marred by conceptions more or less crude and grotesque, revealing ignorance more or less gross; but degrees of purity are here also manifest. In no nation has God "left himself without witness";[1] through nature, Hebrews and other nations alike groped after some unseen cause, the God of nature, "in whom we live and move and have our being."[2] In spite of this catholic recognition of the religions of other nations, Paul, as the manner of some Christians is to the present day, makes the astounding assertion[3] that morality is known to Judaism and Christianity alone; all outside their pale is a seething mass of moral corruption. The history of Israel refutes this careless assumption; the prophets with one voice proclaim its fallacy; Gibeah, Jezreel in contradiction shriek aloud their tales of crime. The writings of Horace and Juvenal no more conclusively prove the general licentiousness of their day, than the novels of Smollett and Richardson can be accepted as representing the average moral standard of a century ago, or Zola's pictures of depravity be admitted as witness to the normal conditions of modern French life. Tirades against vice, whether by ancient or modern prophets, always leave an exaggerated impression of its importance and the extent of its prevalence; the human race by a merciful provision does not appear to rot wholesale in this manner; with whatever force the waves of libertinism may break against social law and custom, the mass of mankind, by an instinct of self-preservation, seem to stand like a rock in favour of that virtue which is most necessary to the maintenance of public health and order. We have no reason to believe that Jews and

[1] Acts xiv. 17.   [2] Acts xvii. 27.   [3] Rom. i.

Christians are, as aggregates of men, freer from crime than Mohammedans, Buddhists, Confucianists, certainly not than Zoroastrians; while the former have one moral failing almost unknown to the others—hypocrisy, the subject of Christ's unceasing philippics, the natural result of living in an artificial moral atmosphere, too keen for the spiritual lungs of ordinary human beings.

152. GOD.—As the later writers delighted to represent the eternal existence of modern purified religion, it is not surprising that great difficulty is felt in tracing the development of the idea of God through the various stages of Hebrew history. We have already seen that the religion of the patriarchs was not of the purity which the authors would beguile us into believing it to have been. Could we have seen Abraham and Isaac bowing in worship, burning incense sticks and offering pieces of cooked meat to God, hard by the gnarled trunk of some branching tree, or muttering prayers, as oil was poured on the summit of a natural stone, we should involuntarily, with our modern sense of superiority, have exclaimed, "The heathen in his blindness bows down to wood and stone." These practices, carried on, as the prophets testify, late down to the fall of the kingdom, are manifest evidences of an ancient simple form of Nature-worship; and consistent with the belief that this was the earliest phase of Hebrew, as of all other religions, is their phraseology with regard to God himself.

153. We know so little (practically nothing) of Moses that we are not in a position to state with precision what form of religion he advocated. Tradition makes him the champion of Yahveh, and ascribes to him the later conceptions of the Deity entertained by the prophets and the post-exilic period. That he should be centuries ahead of his time is only what we should expect, from analogy with other national heroes and reformers. It is quite agreeable with his historical attitude of lawgiver and maker of the nation to assume that he first chose Yahveh as the national God of Israel; but that this worship continued alongside that of other deities previously worshipped, which it did not entirely supersede, is evident from the composition of names of men with those of what were afterwards viewed as strange gods; and above all, from the remarkable assertion in Amos v. 25, 26, that Saturn worship was the religion of the forty years' wandering in the wilderness :

> " Did ye offer sacrifices and offerings unto me
> In the wilderness forty years, O House of Israel!
> When ye bare your king Succuth,
> And your image Kaiwan,
> Star-gods ye made to worship?"

Schrader (ii. 142) states that Kaiwan is a name for Saturn, and Saccuth for Adar, which (i. 20) is also a name for Saturn; so that Amos employs two synonyms for Saturn, to emphasise his point.

164. Hard as it may be for us, with our ingrained prejudices, to suppose it possible for Moses to have permitted Saturn-worship to have continued side by side with the adoration of Yahveh, we cannot conceal from ourselves the fact that at some early period Saturn-worship must have prevailed, otherwise the choice of the Saturn day of the week for special observance as Sabbath is inexplicable. That moon-worship existed before Moses we have already seen; but his choice of the moon mountain, Mount Sinai, for the promulgation of his laws is subsidiary evidence of his relation to Nature-worship, quite incompatible with his supposed attitude of rigid hostility. The application of phrases directly borrowed from the ritual of sun-worship are not considered inappropriate in the mouth of Moses, as attributed to Yahveh:

Deut. xxxiii. 2. Yahveh came from Sinai,
Rose over Sair,
And shone from Mount Paran.

Other passages where Yahveh is addressed in the terminology of a sun ritual are Judges v. 4. 31; Psalm l. 2; lxviii. 2; xciv. 1; Habakkuk iii. 3, 4. In this connection we must not overlook the morning and evening prayer assigned by tradition to the high priest:[1]

"Arise, Yahveh, let Thine enemies be scattered,
And let them that hate Thee flee before thee."

Reference to Psalm lxviii. shows that originally this was an allusion to the dispersing of morning clouds and mists before the face of the rising sun; while at evening the prayer was that the earth might not be left in eternal darkness, that the sun would not fail to rise again next morning: *return*, Yahveh, to myriads of Israel. Here, too, naturally belongs the pregnant expression, Yahveh Zabhaoth (Yahveh of the Heavenly Host, the starry firmament), a term in much favour with the prophets and historical books, specially applied to him as God of Nature.[2] Though not found in the Hexateuch, this is without doubt the survival of a thought in keeping with the religious convictions of early times, when sun, moon and stars were worshipped,

[1] Num. x. 35, 36.   [2] Amos iv. 13.

either as distinct deities themselves, or, as in the time of Moses, different manifestations of the one true God.

155. The difference between the Nature-worship of Moses and that of the Phœnicians would then appear to have been not so much in the symbols and forms of worship, as in the superior purity of the conception of the Deity by the former, which he endeavoured to impress upon his people by his code of laws. That this ideal should become an *esoteric* doctrine, known only to seers and prophets, is precisely what we should expect, and provides a reasonable solution of the problem how the people continued for centuries practices which the prophets at length came to denounce as heathenish—not completely nor all at once, but slowly claiming more surrenders of old practices, which the later prophets denounce as wholly incompatible with the pure worship of Yahveh, while their predecessors by two or three centuries had alluded to the same without any token of disapprobation. It is because the whole history is written from the later standpoints of the Prophetical Schools, that those early forms of Nature-worship, shared in by Moses and Joshua and the Judges, came more and more to be represented as rebellion against the strict worship of Yahveh, which they supposed Moses to have taught. . . . . The fabled eternal purity of the Hebrew religion in patriarchal and Mosaic times, was the necessary fulcrum for the lever with which they attempted the upheaval of actually existing national prejudices. Their chance of success depended on their impressing their contemporaries with the conviction that their doctrines were not new, that, on the other hand, the worship of Baal had been an innovation. History shows that the people were slow to recognise the truth of assertions contrary to their own experience and the traditions of their forefathers. The writings of the prophets betray the instructive fact that they had not the old truth, fully formulated, to fall back upon, but that, on the contrary, they themselves were still evolving fresh phases of it. The fall of the northern kingdom and the captivity of the southern were the two eras that marked the triumph of prophetic Yahvism, for these catastrophes were interpreted not so much as the punishment for the national neglect to accept the reformation urged by the prophets, but as the natural consummation of a revolt, systematically sustained, with solitary intervals of triumphant piety, for a thousand years, against the Moral Law of Moses, which was fast approaching completion as a definite code.

156. When we remember that Moloch and Baal were sun-gods, though their names simply mean respectively King and Master, we can readily understand with what ease the sun-worship of Yahveh could be combined with them, how readily their names could be employed as synonyms of Yahveh. Thus it is that several towns scattered all over Palestine retained the name of Baal, and at one of these, Baaleh-Judah, known also as Kirjath-Jearim or Forest-town, the Ark of Yahveh dwelt for twenty years without raising any question of incongruity. Thus, too, Baal is compounded with the names of men, especially freely in the tribe of Benjamin, without causing any offence; though its non-employment later, and the substitution of the ignominious Boseth = Shame [1] prove that subsequently such epithets were considered disloyalty to Yahveh. Sayce

[1] *Cf.* Ishbosheth, Mephibosheth.

(p. 53) has shown very strong reasons for identifying David with Baal-hanan[1] or El-hanan,[2] the Bethlehemite hero who slew Goliath of Gath, the stem of whose spear was as a weaver's beam ; though in 2 Sam xxiii. 24 the simplest reading perhaps would be : " Asahel, the brother of Joab, among the thirty, the nephew (son) of his uncle Elnathan of Bethelem," for by a mere transposition we remove the difficulty of David's being one of his own mighty men. Note also that David's own son was called Baalyada.[3] The name Mephibosheth or Mephibaal for Jonathan's son, who was consequently David's *protégé*, must surely have been a metathesis for Phumi-baal = Mouth of Baal, recalling Phumi-yathon,[4] this was by accident, or possibly with intention, distorted into a form which defies derivation, and for which the Chronicler in despair substitutes Meribaal, no great improvement. This process of substituting Bosheth, or in more complimentary cases El, for Baal, prevents any reliable conclusion being arrived at as to the precise date when its employment in nomenclature ceased; for instance, its absence in the northern kingdom, especially in the house of Ahab, cannot but excite surprise. However, the significant fact remains, that in the houses of Saul and David, where Samuel's influence prevailed, no objection was felt or taken to this name, Baal, the curse of Israel. With regard to Moloch, the names of priests of Yahveh, like Abimelech and Achimelech, were modified into Abijah and Achijah ; in Malchijah of the later priestly days, its neutral meaning of king survives without any suggestion of idolatry.

---

[1] Gen. xxxvi. 38.
[2] 2 Sam. xxi. 19.
[3] 1 Chron. xiv. 7
[4] C.I.P. 10, 11, &c.

157. Other examples of names of deities, discoverable in the names of men assigned by the Priestly Code to the days of Moses, are 'Am, Zur, Yechud, Shaddai Yahveh, perhaps Nadab,[1] and of course the universal El. "Bela," the son of Beor, first king of Edom[2] is Bileam or Bola'am, son of Beor.[3] Dr. Neubaur has shown that Bala'am is Bil'am "Baal is *Ammi*," the supreme god of Ammon—as we have learned from the cuneiform inscriptions—whose name enters into those of Jerobo'am, Rechobo'am,"[4] as well as Ammi-el, Ammi-hud, doublets like Bil-'am, Eliyah, Eli-melek, &c. Of the Phœnician god Yechud more will be said below, under Judah; but Ach-ihud, Ammi-hud are commonly found in Numbers. The name Zur = Rock, applied to God,[5] was doubtless derived by Moses from the Midianites, whose chief,[6] in accordance with the custom generally prevailing among these nations, is called after the national god. We have seen under Matztzeboth that Moses gave his sanction to the use of stones in worship of God; on one occasion,[7] a victory was due to the timely aid of a stone, which was forthwith consecrated to Yahveh under the name of Yahveh, my banner, which a later note perverts into an allusion to Yaveh's *raising* his hand as he swore his eternal enmity against Amaleq; an impossible etymology. This story forcibly recalls another told of Samuel,[8] who, while sacrificing on a stone, was suddenly surprised by the Philistines, who however, were dispersed by a severe thunder-storm.

[1] = Nadhib, Prince. *Cf.* Adhon, Lord.   [2] Gen. xxxvi.
[3] Num. xxii.   [4] Sayce, 54, n.   [5] Deut. xxxii. 37; Is. xxx. 29, &c.
[6] Num. xxv. 15; xxxi. 8; Josh. xiii. 21.
[7] Ex. xvii. 12-15.   [8] 1 Sam. vii.

Samuel attributes the victory to the stone, which he calls Ebenezer, or Stone of Help. In Gen. xlix. 24, Eben, a stone, is used as a name for the God of Israel, instead of Zur, for the sake of assonance: Eben Israel and Abir Jacob. The later employment of Sela, a rock, in the Psalms, is probably a survival of Zur toned down to a neutral expression. The following list will give some idea of the extent to which the names of deities, later viewed as exclusively heathen, were freely compounded in Hebrew names:

Eli-zur or Zuri-el = Zur-shaddai = Eli-yah.
Amihud   = Ammi-shaddai = Ammi-nadab = Ammi-el.
Ach-ihud   = Achi-melek   = Achi-yah.
Pedah-zur   = Pedah-el.

I think it is Wellhausen who condemns all these names in Numbers as fabrications; if this is so, they still evince evidence of a careful system of research; but it appears more probable that, though their compilation into tribal lists is unhistoric, the names themselves are real and of great antiquity, as it is difficult to believe that the writers of the Priestly Code should deliberately compound names with those of heathen deities; thus providing evidence of the impurity of religion at the very period which they were labouring to depict as of unsullied purity—namely, the Mosaic age.

158. The name Shaddai is supposed to have been the orthodox patriarchal name for God. It is, however, unknown to the prophets, which is strange, and only occurs in the prophetical history three times.[1] On the other hand, it is very common in the post-exilic litera-

---

[1] Gen. xliii. 14, xlix. 25; Num. xxiv. 4. 16.

Shaddai of Doubtful Antiquity

ture [1] and in the Priestly Code.[2] The last passage is a little too pronounced in its assertion that Moses substituted Yahveh for the patriarchal Shaddai to be readily accepted as a reliable witness. It clearly makes the strongest case possible for the general view of the writers after the Captivity, which was shared by the authors of Job and Ruth, who employed this term to produce an effect of pseudo-antiquity. However, we must plead guilty to the weakness of believing this to be one of the many ancient ideas, recovered during the *captivity* in *Babylon*, with which the writers of the Priestly Code replenished the exhausted storehouse of Hebrew tradition and embellished the story of the Patriarchs. In Babylon they found, as a term "to denote those divinities which were represented on the monuments by colossal bulls, 'the word *sidu*'; the corresponding ideogram similarly designates in general the genius, good and bad."[3] And as Shedim in its evil sense was known to them,[4] they disguised Shedhi, in its good sense, as applied to God, by changing the vocalisation into Shaddai,[5] hence causing hopeless confusion for philologists. To a certain extent this also reveals a timid admission that the gods of the Patriarchs were of an inferior order, to which reference is made Joshua xxiv. 2. The translation Almighty, as an equivalent for Shaddai in our English version, is derived from the LXX., who made several attempts to render this word, and all of them are based on an impossible division of it into two separate parts. Renan[6] makes

---
[1] Joel i. 15; Ps. lxviii. 15, xci. 1; Job (thirty times), Ruth, Ezekiel, Is. xiii. 7.
[2] Gen. xvii. 1, xxviii. 3, xxxv. 11, xlviii. 3; Exod. vi. 3.
[3] Schrader i. 148. [4] Deut. xxxii. 17; Ps. cvi. 37; Gen. xlv. 7.
[5] So Noldeke in Schrader, ii. 307.   [6] i. 116.

an excellent suggestion, that the valley in the neighbourhood of the Dead Sea, called in Genesis xiv. (a late narrative) the Vale of Siddim, which the LXX., unable to cope with, render the Vale of the Salt Sea, was really known as the "Valley of Demons," Shedhim for Siddiim, without change of consonants.

159. The pointing Yahveh, in composition Yahu, is corroborated by the pausal Yishtachu = Yishtachveh, and is the form now generally adopted, with the meaning Life-giver, Causer of Being. This is the distinctive name of the God of Israel,[1] recognised even by foreigners.[2] In the Phœnician inscriptions (69), Yehubaal is found corresponding to Baal-yah,[3] and the Greek Yobel for Ebed.[4] In an Assyrian inscription[5] there is a king of Hamath called Yah-ubid, appearing elsewhere as Il-ubid. Thus Yahveh, though the peculiar property of Israel, is used by other nations; and was probably, like most other religious names, derived by them and the Hebrews from the same source, the Assyrian.[6]

160. To the prophets we owe the conception of Yahveh as a jealous God who would brook no rival; for we have seen that earlier saints, Moses and Samuel, did not scruple to recognise Nature-worship in one of its many forms, at least ascribing victory to a stone, which they still associate with Yahveh. The annotations of the Decalogue are of late date, probably Deuteronomic,[7] and here we may remark that it appears reasonable to conceive of what we call the Second Commandment as a note on the First, which

---

[1] Jud. xi. 11-23. [2] 2 Kings xviii. 25, and Mesha, stone, line 18.
[3] 1 Chron. xii. 5. [4] Jud. ix. 26; Kuenen i. 404, *n*.
[5] Schrader, i. 23. [6] Schrader, 25. [7] See 119.

could not well have been in vogue when Moses cast his brazen serpent and Micah his golden ephod, and Solomon erected his cherubim in the house of Yahveh. In that case, of course, we must adopt, with the Hebrew and the Catholic Church, the division of the Tenth Commandment into two parts, which is favoured by the employment of two separate words in Deuteronomy, "Do not covet thy neighbour's wife," "Do not desire thy neighbour's house," &c.; and by the observance of the sacred numbers, in this division, three commandments referring to God, seven to mankind. The Ninth Commandment does not thus become tautological of the Sixth, but denounces the sin of inception as well as of fruition, to which Job and Christ refer.[1]

161. The attribute of anger is commonly assigned to God by all nations, evidence of it being recognised in all calamities great and small, national or individual; but a wrath enduring for nearly 1000 years, from the first introduction of the Deity to the children of Israel until the Captivity, and never since removed, is surely unique, and as unnatural as unique. If we accept the Hebrew narrative as historical, the first generation of Israelites introduced to the worship of Yahveh were blotted out of existence as unworthy of the honour, a large number perishing within six weeks of that dread era. Barely do they arrive in the Promised Land when Yahveh's wrath is poured out on successive generations, and so on with mournful monotony through the history of the kingdom; gleams of sunshine are permitted in the reigns of David, Asa, Jehoshaphat, Uzziah, Hezekiah, Josiah; but none of these entirely escapes the glowering clouds that shroud the offended

---

[1] Job xxxi. 9*a*, 9*b*; Matt. v. 27, 28.

Yahveh. The only period of great national prosperity, depicted in exaggerated high colours, is a few years of Solomon's reign. To obviate the manifest anomaly of the marked success of a king whose religion was the most eclectic in his ready absorption of all manner of cults, ever known before or since, it became necessary to represent him as a renegade from former piety, to ascribe to him in his early youth the rare distinction of being favoured by visions of Yahveh, and to put into his mouth at the dedication service of the Temple a litany of unsurpassed beauty and piety, which betrays itself as a composition of so late a date as after the Exile; but even this Temple, the crowning act of his devotion to Yahveh, was designed and executed by foreigners after a foreign pattern. "The Temple of Jerusalem was built by Phœnician artists after the model of a Phœnician one. Even the two columns or cones at the entrance, the symbols of the sun-god, as well as the brazen sea or reservoir, with the twelve solar bulls on which it rested, were reproduced in the Jewish sanctuary."[1] Have we not here, once again, irrefragable evidence of history of the past written from a later standpoint? When in the very natural occurrence of the conquest of the puny kingdoms of Northern Joseph and Southern Judah by the gigantic Assyrio-Babylonian power, the prophets saw the outpoured vials of wrath on account of the prevalence of a religion of insufficient standard of purity, it cost little to take the next step, and, considering the antiquity of those objectionable religious ideas, to represent the frown of Yahveh as eternally bent on his chosen nation. Surely this is not history! The authors of the Prophetic History appear to have started

[1] Sayce: "Ancient Empires," 191.

No Evidence of a Self-revelation of God

the theory which was, as much else, developed by the Deuteronomist and fully matured by the writers of the Priestly Code.

162. Thus far we have seen nothing in the conception of God exhibited to us in the Hexateuch which in any way suggests a personal revelation of himself; on the other hand, we observe distinct evidence of human efforts—inspired, but still human efforts—to "find out the depths of God and to fathom the mind of Shaddai," which the author of Job (xi. 7) declares impossible. In fact, that writer in his protest against the orthodox view of his day, attacks this doctrine of unreasonable divine wrath, putting all the arguments in favour of it in the mouth of the three friends, who are finally discredited and disgraced by God.

163. It is true that an anthropomorphic and anthropopathic representation of God was necessary in the childhood of mankind, and indeed to a certain extent is still generally requisite; but if Christ could now speak, this representation would doubtless be one of the things he declares permitted on account of the hardness of our hearts, the dulness of our comprehensions. Allowing for a certain amount of advantage in thus describing God, lest by his etherealisation into a bare concept we should entirely lose the object of our love and reverence, there still remains much that is offensive to our natural sense of fitness and propriety. When we read of Yahveh's rage as the inflammation of his nostrils, and the description of his wrath assuaged when he smelled the sweet savour of cooked meat, are we not at once introduced into the presence of a Moloch, or indeed of some relentless Hindu deity? When we read of Yahveh's repenting of the creation of man,[1] of the deliverance of Israel from Egypt,[2] of the election of Saul,[3] of the effect of the pestilence,[4] we recognise the feebleness of the casuistry which endeavours to explain away the discrepancy between these explicit statements and the more exalted notion of the Deity which presents him as "not a man that he should lie, nor a mortal that he should repent."[5] When we read of Abram and Moses pleading and arguing with God against a premeditated wholesale destruction, there is no escape from the effect produced: the Deity is actually inferior to his own created saints. It is true that Abraham only ventures to remind God of his chief attribute, "Shall not the Judge of all the earth do right?" but Moses does not scruple to appeal to a fear of public opinion, "The Egyptians shall hear of it," and the Deuteronomist has no hesitation in making him mildly boast of his success in dissuading God from a determined course: "Yahveh hearkened to me this time also."[6] In the frequently recurring phrase, "I am Yahveh," in the Priestly Code, after every ordinance, small or great, we have the pretension to a royal signature as if proceeding from Yahveh; but, knowing what we do of its time and source, we cannot view it higher than what in mercantile parlance would be equivalent to "(*signed*) Moses *pro* Yahveh"; *i.e.*, it is a copy of a signature purported to be signed on behalf of an absent party. It served its purpose, but does not at the present day suggest sacred mysteries, more than " V.R." or "God save the Queen," at the end of Privy Council reports or an Act of Parliament.

[1] Gen. vi. 6.
[2] Ex. xxxii. 10; Num. xiv. 12.
[3] 1 Sam. xv. 11, 35.
[4] 2 Sam. xxiv. 16.
[5] Num. xxiii. 19.
[6] Num. ix. 19, x. 10.

164. In all this, again, we fail to see any sign of God's revealing Himself to man, but rather absolute evidence of man's assigning to God human passions and prejudices. Neither can we admit the ascription to divine revelation of the invention of clothes,[1] of shipbuilding,[2] of writing,[3] of architecture,[4] for the Tabernacle, as described, is a compact though portable building, *not* a tent; this does not hinder us from seeing a reverent acknowledgment of divine supervision of human inventions, provided that we do not deny the same when claimed by the Hindus for the miraculous denary scale of notation in arithmetic. If, then, the Hebrew writers groped in blindness after a gleam of God, if there is traceable a distinct evolution of their doctrine of God, can we accept as revelation the stories they proceed to tell of the origin of the world, of sin, of death? If God did not first reveal himself to man, how was it possible for man to identify the subject of these narratives as divine revelation? Such a position is untenable; it maintains the paradox, *ignotum per ignotius*.

165. CREATION. — Without direct revelation from God himself, it is not possible, without very advanced scientific knowledge, to frame any account of the creation of the world and the origin of the human race. To scientific knowledge there is not the least pretension in the Bible; and the former is impossible without a previous revelation of the Creator himself, which in the preceding paragraphs has been shown an untenable hypothesis. In the Hexateuch are two stories of Creation, mutually exclusive; if we hold to

---

[1] Gen. iii. 21.
[2] Gen. vi. 14.
[3] Exod. xxxii. 16; xxxiv. 1.
[4] Exod. 26.

the one, we must reject the other, we cannot at the same time accord full credence to two totally opposed narratives. In one we are told that clouds were created and afterwards plants[1] a reasonable idea ; in the other that plants were formed under a cloudless sky, and were supported by exhalations, that failed to mount high enough to mass into clouds.[2] In one we are told that man was the crowning success of animal creation,[3] in the other that animals were formed with the purpose (though unsuccessfully) of providing man with suitable companionship ;[4] in this connection, we may note, in passing, the strange conception, revealed by the LXX. translator of the Book of Job (xl. 19), that the hippopotamus was the *first* animal created, and with the special object of affording diversion for the angels. Once again, we are told in the one that God created a human pair,[5] in the other that man long sustained a solitary existence, till God compassionately created for him a woman from a rib taken from himself.[6] It is therefore evident that, though both of these narratives were penned by what we term inspired authors, only one, if either, can lay claim to be revelation, as the other seriously contradicts it. As regards the Prophetic Story[7] we have seen[8] that the details are derived from a study of philology combined with ancient legends of a beautiful garden and a fruit tree guarded by monsters, which are the common property of several nations. The Priestly Code[9] is here once again indebted to research in Babylon, as its story is an improvement on a Chaldean account of Creation, edited by George

[1] Gen. i. 6, 11.
[2] Gen. ii. 5, 6.
[3] Gen. i. 25, 26.
[4] Gen. ii. 18, 19.
[5] Gen. i. 27.
[6] Gen. ii. 7, 19, 22.
[7] Gen ii. and iii.
[8] Pars. 58, 59.
[9] Gen. i. 1, 2, 4.

Smith and referred to by Schrader. Professor Huxley has shown that the Revelation of Nature, as interpreted by means of geological research, gives the order of Creation very differently from the one supposed to be revealed by God himself. Without, however, the special scientific education required for the formation of a judgment on this argument, Macaulay's proverbial schoolboy can see that the fundamental principles of this story are absolutely wrong, arising from an arrogant and perverted view of Nature peculiar to the Hebrew mind. As the world was made and its populations arranged with a definite regard to the Hebrew race alone,[1] so the universe was made for and after the world.[2] That God created the sun and the stars subsequently to the earth, and simply with the object of providing light for this little spheroid, is contrary to the most elementary ideas of cosmography; and though harmonising with the ignorant conception of the sun as a small lamp travelling through the sky to illuminate the earth, is hopelessly incompatible with any claim for the story to the solemnity of Divine Revelation.

166. Two other stories in the Bible testify that the Hebrew conception of the sun was a portable lamp, which, though generally moving steadily in one course, could be held stationary or carried back again without inconvenient results. In the famous battle of Gibeon the old poet depicts the weary length of the contest, and the yearning of the exhausted victors for darkness to afford an excuse for staying the pursuit and slaughter of the vanquished, by the poetical turn:[3]

"The sun stood still in the midst of heaven,
And hasted not to go down, about a whole day"—

[1] Deut. xxxii. 8, 9.   [2] Gen. i. 14-19.   [3] Josh. x. 13.

i.e., the day seemed twice as long as usual. A later writer, wishing to improve the simple ancient record, makes Joshua order the sun and moon to be dumb (or stationary) with astonishment, to which a note is added: "So the sun did not set, nor the moon rise, till the victory was complete." This last is generally taken as the quotation from the Book of Jasher, but 2 Sam. i.–xviii. shows that the quotation *follows* the reference, yet precedes it, also in the first there is a system of scansion absent from the last, while the assonance of Shamam and Tamim is as conspicuous as of Yiddom and Yiqqom. It is singularly instructive to note here, as in par. 52, that where we have incontestible relics of antiquity, in Hebrew narrative the love of the miraculous is conspicuously absent. In 2 Kings xx. 10, 11, we read that the shadow of the dial went back ten degrees at the order of Isaiah, as a sign that fifteen years were added to Hezeqiah's life. As the prophets did not scruple to astound the populace by pouring naphtha on the sacrifice, when they would be surprised to see a liquid looking like water feed instead of quenching the fire, we must infer that Isaiah had contrived a mechanical appliance for turning the dial itself round either way, to meet the chance of the royal wish; but the story undoubtedly leaves the impression that the sun could travel back again without disastrous effects ensuing.

167. **THE FALL OF MAN**, if not the subject of Divine Revelation, necessarily resolves itself into a mere theory, which we may accept or reject according as the degree of probability in its favour prevails or not, after investigation. The author, as we saw in

paragraph 165, employs foreign legend to introduce this dogma. Whether he himself intended more than an allegory, combining the two truths, that sins against the healthy purposes of Nature hasten death, and that moral delinquencies are transmitted from father to son, neither of which propositions will be denied by modern science, we cannot say. But we have no hesitation in asserting that all Hebrew and Christian mankind accepted for two thousand years, as fact, that man was created perfect, and in one dire moment fell from a state of grace to danger of perdition, from immortality lapsed into a condition where death was possible and inevitable. To suppose that death was introduced into God's creation by the free-will of one of his creatures, is derogatory to Divine power. Sin must have been the slow outgrowth of the self-gratification of men, as the population of the world gradually increased; it could not have been let in like a flood upon humanity by the one act of a single pair. The original pair must have been sinless, or comparatively so, because no occasions of sin could present themselves: evil passions—anger, cruelty, lust—would arise as the field for them expanded.

168. The main feature in the Hebrew idea of perfection is the absence of change. The stars that twinkle, the moon, with its quarterly phases and final evanescence, are to the Hebrew mind lacking in this attribute, and therefore chargeable with sin:[1]

> " How should man be just with God?
> And how the woman-born be pure?
> He appoints the moon, when she is not to shine;
> And the stars are not pure in his sight."

[1] Job. xxv. 4, 5.

Compare also Psalm cii. 25, 26, where the perfection of God, as contrasted with the imperfection of the earth, consists in his immunity from the changes produced by increasing age. Religious views based on such conceptions are not of a practical nature, but of a pronounced transcendental type. Change is the law of Nature, observable in the universe and in the world itself, both in animate and inanimate creation; not revelation, but ignorance alone, could see in change a token of God's displeasure. The author of the later story of Creation[1] recounts a series of six metamorphoses, successively aiding in the final result of Creation, each in turn being very good, but, inasmuch as progressive so far imperfect. The earlier writer[2] is so convinced that change was the result of sin, that he reports the Creation as a sudden and complete occurrence; he leaves one to infer[3] that the perpetual cycling change of evaporation, formation of clouds, condensation into rain, did not exist at the first, but was the consequence of man's fall. He is, however, slightly inconsistent in admitting the change produced by the later creation of man, beasts, and woman.

169. Modern science teaches us our ignorance of the real facts underlying the terms destruction and construction, death and life. John Mitchell (*Jail Journal*): "Is not the destruction, then, as needful as the construction? Rather tell me, I pray you, which is construction, which destruction? This destruction is creation, death is birth, and

"' The quick spring like weeds out of the dead.'"

[1] Gen. i.   [2] Gen. ii. and iii.   [3] Gen. ii. 5.

Dr. James Hinton, an eminent physician—whose devout attitude to the Scriptures at once forestalls the charge of any approximation to what is stigmatised as free-thought —thus expresses in his " Life in Nature " the answer of modern science to the important question, What is Life? (Chap. i.): " It is *resistance* to death which causes us to live." (Chap. ii.) "We are continually dying. In all our actions force is given off, the very same force by which the body lives, and portions of our frame accordingly waste and are cast off. . . . . Life ever growing old, and yet ever young, ever dying, ever being born. . . . . Life is an action *produced* by its opposite. It has its root in death, and is nourished by decay." The principles discovered by science are eternal. At his creation, then, man had no life other than that which in its constant struggles for maintenance, was a silent witness to the existence of death. The first man and woman, in their every action must have given off force, the very same force by which their bodies lived. In short, in accordance with God's laws of nature, man was not created immortal. The assertion, then, that death was contrived by God as the punishment of sin, cannot be a divine revelation, being contrary to God's revelation in Nature, but is merely the imagination of the inspired writers. Had no seeds dropped into the soil, died and sprouted into life; how without death of the blossom was formed the fruit on which Adam and Eve lived ? How, without annual death of their leaves, did the trees effect the change necessary to their life ? Continual death has been the eternal law, eternal as regards the history of the earth, of life for vegetable and animal kingdoms alike. It is not truth and poetry that charms us in the vivid description :

> "She ate,
> Earth felt the wound, and Nature from her seat,
> Sighing through all her works, gave signs of woe
> That all was lost.
> Beast now with beast 'gan war, and fowl with fowl.

This is Milton's inspired portrayal of what is alluded to by Paul as "the earnest expectation of the creation for redemption" from the curse brought upon its innocent self by man's sin; and is, moreover, only the logical conclusion from the premises, that the world was created perfect, that death and corruption were unknown till "her rash hand, in evil hour forth reaching to the fruit, Eve plucked," that they were not the ordinary course of nature, but the evil consequences of man's wanton marring of God's perfect work by disobedience.

170. The horizon of the author betrays itself elsewhere in the narrative. It is what is repulsive to man, not to God, that is related as the punishments attendant upon the Fall, and not one of these but is either a necessary or beneficent law. Oppression from superiors, or in its most modern form competition among compeers, has rendered the necessary occupation of man's life unpalatable, and converted labour into slavery; but toil in itself is a blessing, not a curse; the sweat of man's brow sweetens, not embitters, his daily bread, and without toil its blessed counterpart, rest, could not be enjoyed. The pangs of childbirth appear to be a natural law, from which the brute creation is not exempt. The observation of Lady Brassey and other travellers prove that among less civilised people the inconvenience is slight and remarkably transient; as a curse on primeval woman, it would not, then, have been a severe punishment. Were there no worms, going on their bellies and eating dust, before the temptation of man, that the curse of the serpent should justify us in the belief that this subtlest of the beasts of the field had previously

> "Addressed his way, not with indented wave,
> Prone on the ground as since; but on his rear
> Circular base of rising folds that towered
> Fold above fold, a surging maze, his head
> Crested aloft."

The author takes the facts of Nature as he finds them, and here once more sees the curse of God, which can only be supported by fabulous conjecture. But also observing the instinctive mutual methods of assault, how the serpent attacks the heels of horses and other animals beside men, while these beasts as well as men by instinct aim their defensive blows at the serpent's head, he proceeds to place in the mouth of God a prophecy connected with a secondary curse: "I will put enmity between thee and the woman, and between future generations of serpents and men: they shall aim at thy head, while thy descendants shall aim at their heels." The Hebrew word *shuph* means to desire, long for, nothing of the nature of bruising, which is, moreover, inappropriate to the bite of a serpent. We follow Kuenen, and most moderns, whose view is admitted defensible by Gesenius.

171. In the curse of the serpent, in his doom from a proud erect attitude to a sinuous grovelling course, we have an allusion to some occult Hebrew legend of fallen greatness, which reveals itself in some passages of the Book of Job—*e.g.*, where of the crocodile it is said xli. 26 (34):

"He hath no ruler upon earth;
He is king of all the reptiles"—

literally sons of pride, where *shachats* is used as a play on *sherets*, reptiles; elsewhere, too,[1] the same theory is hinted at in astronomical myths of conquest of pride, all associated with dragons and serpents. This is indication of the same logical mind at work which recognised the difficulty of a human race emanating from a solitary male, and which here sees that the fall of man cannot have been a spontaneous moral illness, but an inoculation on a healthy subject from a previously fallen intelligence, who is purposely referred to, with becoming vagueness, lest the inquisitive mind, satisfied that evil could not have originated in a perfect, immortal being, should still presume to ask for an explanation of the creation of evil in the pure and spotless heaven itself. Satan, the god of evil, in conflict with Yahveh, the God of Good, was not in the author's mind, but an angel or intelligence fallen through pride,[2] still, however, perforce subservient to God, as in Job and the New Testament. Deutero-Isaiah, in his opposition to the dual power of the Persian or Babylonian religion,[3] recognises God as the author of evil. Evil is only the correlative of right, as darkness is of light, and death of life. Without evil, darkness, and death, we should not be in a position to understand the terms, right, light, and life. Nay, more, as death is the actual cause of animal life, so opposition to evil is not only the test but the very mainspring of the existence of right.[4] Here, again, we notice that the Yahvist, consistently with his standpoint, supposes a complete and perfect

[1] Job ix. 13; xxvi. 13. [2] Isa. xiv. 12. [3] Isa. xlv. 7. See Cheyne.
[4] Doussen's "Elements of Metaphysics," 276.

creation from the very first; while the Priestly Code, with his more natural supposition derived from Babylonian sources of pre-existent Chaos, represents God as evolving a beautiful creation from previous disorder, which is consistent with the philosophic doctrine that evil precedes right, and death life. The two views of creation differ, then, more materially than at first catches the eye. We reject the story of the Fall of man, not merely because of its conspicuous legendary character, but because its assumptions with regard to the origin and nature of death and evil are at variance with the revealed works of God; and because the rise of man, not his fall, is the state of affairs with which history acquaints us; a truth which is even attested by the Biblical history itself, with its progressively developed characters of Abraham, Moses, Deutero-Isaiah, and Christ.

172. THE FLOOD.—The two accounts of Creation have been kept separate; an attempt has been made, however, to blend the narratives of the Flood into one, which has naturally resulted in repetition and contradiction. The older, the Yahvist, gives a week's warning to Noah (Gen. vii .10), forty days' rain (vii. 12). It is doubtful whether this includes the forty days' prevalence of the flood (vii. 17), and another forty days' abatement (viii. 6), and three weeks before Noah ventured out; making a total of 68, 108, or 148 days, according as we view the forty days as concurrent or not. The later Priestly Code is very exact: God gives Noah minute instructions how to build his large ship (vi. 13-22); the flood lasted a year and ten days, beginning on the seventeenth day of the second month of the 600th year of Noah's life, and ending on the twenty-seventh day of the second month of his 601st year; in five months, or 150 days, the waters culminated, and the Ark, whose draught exceeded twenty-two feet, stranded on Mount Ararat. In two months thirteen days, the surface of Ararat appeared; whence we gather by aid of vii. 20, that twenty-two *feet* of water in depth had subsided; in another three months the remaining three *miles* of water had disappeared, and the face of the earth was dry. The only detail in which any harmony can be observed between the two accounts is in the 40+21 days of the Yahvist, and the sixty-one days from the tenth moon first day to first moon first day of the Priestly Code. It is remarkable that the Yahvist is more anxious about the distinction between clean and unclean animals (vii. 2) than the Priestly Code (vii. 15); the only explanation that seems to suggest itself is, that, having gone into details as to the measurement of the Ark, this author had scruples about the accommodation of seven pairs of clean animals in addition to the ordinary couples of unclean. However this may be, we find that the two stories of the Flood, as of the Creation, are irreconcilable: we must take our choice of which, if either, is to be revelation.

173. In the different stories of a flood by different nations, each of which describes the destruction as universal, we have varied accounts of separate experiences of great floods caused by excessively heavy rains, and which, befalling the occupants of a valley, were remarkably fatal. The loss of life in the particular neighbourhood produced a lasting impression, and a never-dying tradition arose, which greatly magnified the deluge to such proportions that in each case the whole human race was represented as swept out of existence, with the exception of some favoured few: two according to the Greek, eight in the Hebrew, and several in the Chaldee narrative. The duration assigned to the Flood by profane authors agrees so far that a week is assigned in each case, though the seven *days* of Chaldæa require to be increased to nine to suit the Greek reckoning (par. 117) in the story of Deucalion; in these there is nothing of the grossly improbable. The Yahvist, however, extends the term to ten or more *weeks*, while the priestly author, to magnify the occurrence, is satisfied with nothing less than a *year*. Above (par. 64), we observed that the Yahvist author endeavoured to identify Noah with the Phœnician Bacchus No'am, but that the name itself is really Aryan, and indicative of a Hindu source. All these considerations sufficiently betray ordinary human agency, without regarding the miraculous element required by the small size of the Ark and its enormous freight of animals. There remains, moreover, the consideration of the mass of water thus superimposed upon the earth. Take the diameter of the earth as 8000 miles, and the height of Ararat as 3 miles; in addition to the existing supplies of water on the face of the earth, 603 *millions* of *cubic miles* of water would be required to float the Ark to the summit of Ararat. Now, *one cubic mile*, or 5451 million cubic yards of water weighs, 4360 *million tons;* it follows, therefore, that the extra weight thrown on the earth's surface by the flood was 2,629,080 billions of tons, or by Continental reckoning, in excess of two-and-a-half trillions; while the whole mass of the earth is given as 6067 million billions. The figures are enormous, and merely because the ratio of the mass of the earth to the bulk of water is 2307, cannot, I fancy, be disposed of lightly, as by Keil, who quaintly remarks that the proportion is no greater than that of a profuse perspiration to the body of a man. I have not seen the question treated of by a scientific man, but it must strike one as a matter of some interest to be informed whence such an enormous body of water came and whither it retired, to say nothing of other questions of interest—such as, what effect would be produced upon the earth's orbit and speed by such an accession of mass. In conclusion, no amount of sophistry can remove the impression, that in the author's view the rainbow did not exist before the flood, being devised by God as a sign of His protection. This is of course simply due to the ignorance of its physical causes, but is corroborative evidence of human fallibility, not of divine revelation.

174. THE CALL OF ABRAM.—Let any one read carefully Genesis xxxi. 1–16, and he will observe first the singular coincidence of the divine command to return to Canaan immediately ensuing upon the narrative: "And Jacob beheld the countenance of Laban, and behold it was not unto him as heretofore"—surely enough in itself to prompt departure without a divine revelation; more especially as he had not left the Promised Land under direct orders from God. He will observe, secondly, that the curious device employed by Jacob[1] is here related by him to his wives as pursued under angelic instruction; and it must not be

[1] Chap. xxx.

overlooked that the Samaritan Pentateuch is so apprehensive of this vision being attributed by anybody to Jacob's own fertile imagination, that they insert between verses 36 and 37 of chapter xxx. an historical (?) account of this circumstance. Jacob, however, betrays himself (xxxi. 12, 13) by making one and the *same* vision dictate to him his pastoral trick and his return home; events, supposing them to have been real, sundered by many months, if not years. In Jacob's speech we recognise the shifts to which a man of his disposition would be driven in suggesting to his wives a plan which he was doubtful would meet with their approval, and in confessing a trick (highly improbable in itself) employed successfully against their own father. The episode, unworthy in itself of serious consideration, still inculcates a lesson of grave importance; for it reveals to us how naturally these writers attributed to direct revelation every human impulse, and further suggests what value may be accorded to other narratives of angelic visitation, when they do not shrink from employing heavenly messengers on the basest errands. When, then, in Genesis xii. 1, we read, "And Yahveh said to Abraham, Get thee out from thy country and thy kindred and thy father's house, unto a land that I will show thee," we at once recognise the spontaneous act of the Hebrew race, reverently referred by the author to providential guidance of a more distinct character than is vouchsafed to the generality of mankind. It is also to be noted that the migration was commenced by Terah, and had proceeded as far as Charran before the Call of Abram, who severed himself from his family, not in Ur of the Chaldees, but at Charran. Tradition disapproved of the more ordinary occurrence

recounted in Genesis xi. 31, where Terah took Abram
his son, &c.; and represents Abram as a sort of "pious
Æneas" conveying his father from a doomed district;
like Anchises, Terah also dies almost on the border of
the future home of the race. Of the very modern
tradition we hear nothing till Acts vii. 2; the story in
Genesis supports the more natural account, for Abram[1]
sends Eliezer to his own country, to his kindred at
Charran. Other traces of late tradition present in the
New Testament are the marriage of Rachab and Nachshon,[2] and the statement that Melchizedeq was "without
father, without mother, without descent." We can
hardly believe that these and other small details, like
the beauty of the infant Moses and his Egyptian scho-
larship, were really preserved for 600 or 800 years
after having been set aside as unworthy of a place in
the history. The discovery by Sayce[3] in the Tel-el-
Amarna correspondence of a similar mysterious person,
Ebed-tob, priest, and King of Jerusalem, who describes
himself in language nearly identical with that employed
by the author of the Epistle to the Hebrews, is interesting as a literary coincidence of expression, but can
have no bearing as evidence of the historicity of the
Melchizedeq episode. It is more probable that these
extra touches were due to the labours of the schools of
learned research which existed at the time of Christ
and in the preceding century. The minute discussions
that took place over every detail of the history and
ritual would lead to the prevalence of ideas not always
preserved in the Rabbinical writings, but accepted as
authoritative sequels to the sacred Scriptures. It is
well known that the life of Abraham has been subjected

[1] Gen. xxiv. 4.   [2] Matt. i. 5.   [3] "Verdict," p. 175.

to enlargement by means of legend, much of which is of considerably later date than the Exile in Babylon, but what antiquity should be assigned to them appears impossible to determine.

175. I do not propose to deal with the narratives of the patriarchs at length. The manner in which stories have arisen through derivation of names of places has already been demonstrated (chap. iii.), and later on we shall investigate the doubtful etymology of the names of the men themselves. With the rejection of the tales founded on philological derivations, a large part of the patriarchal history is at once discredited. But there are other events, stated to be facts, which are suspicious; for instance, the remarkable circumstances attending the births of successive generations, a series of miracles, which, by its frequent appearance and imitation in later narratives, leads one to the inevitable conclusion that the birth of children from aged or sterile parents was for the Israelite race the rule and not the exception. It is true that other nations share this weakness for representing the birth of their heroes as attended with prodigies of various kinds, but these are at once admitted to be legend, and not accepted as history: why should the Hebrew stories be more readily accredited, especially when, from quite independent reasons, other tales of the same men and women are shown to be fiction? The offering up of Isaac by Abram is simply the ascription to him of a Phœnician legend with Assyrian improvements; the moral of the episode, which strikes even children as incompatible with the notion of God, is distinctly at variance with the true principle enunciated:[1] " God cannot be tempted

[1] James i. 13.

with evil, neither tempteth he any man." The Israelites were haunted with the fear that the purity of their ancestry might be called in question; it is not surprising therefore to find particulars given of the careful choice of wives for Isaac and Jacob. But as the strength of a chain is its weakest link, we regret to find that the twelve sons of the latter patriarch are left to find their own wives, perhaps, like Esau, from kindred tribes, Ishmaelites, &c. Unless the history of Lot can be established, chaps. xiii. xiv. xviii. and xix. can only be viewed as romance, as they stand or fall with the existence or not of the *man* Lot. The visit of Abram to Gerar is clearly added in imitation of Isaac's sojurn there, while his journey into Egypt is introduced to make the father of the race experience its later vicissitudes, very much as, with an inverse motive, the baby Christ is made in a doubtful story to go down into Egypt.

176. JOSEPH.—Several details of the life of Joseph are manifestly derived from the story of Samuel, as the following facts in common to both sufficiently indicate. Each was the son of the barren favourite of two wives; for each a miniature ephod was made; each had dreams in his youth; Samuel was a seer, and performed priestly functions; Joseph divined with a cup, and prophesied by his own visions and the interpretation of the dreams of others; Samuel was a Nazarite— the term Nazir is applied to Joseph in Jacob's song; Samuel was an Ephrathite, the tribe of Joseph is often called Ephraim; .the mother of Samuel lived at Ramah-Ephratah; the mother of Joseph died at Ramah,[1] near to

[1] Jer. xxxi. 15.

Bethlehem-Ephratah.[1] A seven years' famine in early Egyptian history is referred to as a typical calamity in a very late inscription;[2] a reference to it therefore in the story of Joseph is neither proof of its historicity, nor a criterion for establishing its antiquity. The episode in connection with Potiphar's wife is found elsewhere, being in fact a favourite subject of Eastern romance. The remaining points of the narrative are an idyllised representation of the experience of the later Josephite race successfully asserting its superiority over the older Judaite race ; while the protection shown by Judah to Benjamin in Genesis is a touch suggested by the absorption of the latter tribe, at the secession of the Ten Tribes. The life of Joseph, then, as we have it, must have been begun to be written after Samuel, B.C. 1040, and could not have been finished before the days of Rehoboam B.C. 920. There is no evidence of a pre-existing tradition of a hero, who should have lived 500 or 600 years before.

177. MOSES.—If we accept the narrative in Exodus as history, there is poetic justice in the universal slaughter of the Egyptian first-born, which appears as an atonement for the wholesale massacre of the Hebrew male infants. But above (132) we have seen that a mistaken notion of the age and origin of the Passover is the source of the tale of the firstborn, so that thereby some ground is afforded for doubting the earlier story, which is intimately bound up with it. Independently, however, it would appear strange policy to destroy a race of useful slaves by permitting the survival only of the female infants. It must be

---
[1] Gen. xxxv. 19.   [2] Sayce, "Verdict."

remembered, too, that Moses is represented as a solitary instance of providential escape. Whence, then, eighty years later, sprang the generation of males that accompanied Moses in the Exodus? Were the 600,000 fighting men all over the age of eighty? The common story of exposure of water and miraculous preservation of an infant destined to become a mighty hero,[1] is here introduced to provide a mistaken derivation for the name; Pharaoh's daughter calling him "Moshe, because from the water I *drew* him"(*mashithi*). Observe, the Egyptian princess gives a *Hebrew* derivation to a word that may be of Egyptian or Assyrian etymology. We shall see below, under Levi, that there are traces of a tradition that this tribe is of Qenite origin; in the Book of Exodus, Moses is made to flee to Midian, where he dwelt for forty years, and intermarried with a leading Qenite family, and we must bear in mind that marriages of this sort are, in early tradition, the common expression for the actual historical association between different races. Thus, at the outset the story of Moses is based, *not* on traditional facts, *but* on traditional theories.

178. The story of the Ten Plagues is in itself highly improbable. Quite apart from the fact that the majority of them have been of frequent occurrence in Egypt, we cannot but marvel at the forbearance of Pharaoh, in not slaying the runaway slave who forced his obnoxious presence on the despot. It is, however, of more importance to note that these ten plagues are not all

---

[1] Sayce, "Ancient Empires," p. 62, gives the legend of Osiris, who was imprisoned in an ark and flung into the sacred Nile. "The ark was borne across the sea to the holy city of Phœnicia, ... but Osiris had died only to rise again."

sprung from traditions of equal antiquity. On the contrary, there is evidence of a gradual access in number, *four* in the Prophetical Writings being assigned to Yahvist, and *two* to the Elohist; while it is not till after the Captivity that *ten* plagues are known. The Priestly Code has a tendency to round off the number of events, for by it the blessings of Abram are raised to *seven*; similarly, here they add four plagues, two of which, lice and boils, are ill-disguised duplicates of two already recorded, flies and murrain. We have seen above, under the inquiry into the age and origin of the Passover institution, that it was pre-Mosaic. What foundation is there for the story of the Exodus as we have it in the book of that name? In this composite setting how can we expect to find a pure gem of the first water? Because the Israelites boasted of their glorious departure from a land of slavery, an event, on their own showing, accomplished only by the direct miraculous intervention of the Deity himself, are we justified, in the absence of specific information on the Egyptian monuments, in ignoring the Egyptian tradition, preserved by Manetho, that the Hebrews were driven out of Egypt as a pestilential nuisance? The two stories agree so far, that in both the Hebrews are in full flight; in both there is an army of Egyptians, in one case content with merely driving the Hebrews well out of their territory, in the other vainly pursuing, with a view to bring them back into slavery. Sayce[1] tells us that the Egyptians had a great cycle of 1460 years; the end of one Sothic fell in A.D. 139; the previous one, therefore, allowing for an error of four years in the calculation of the

[1] "Ancient Empires," p. 77.

birth of Christ, must have fallen B.C. 1325. This year fell in the reign of Manephtha, son of Ramses IL,[1] who is accepted by the majority of scholars as the Pharaoh of the Exodus. It would then appear probable that, for the celebration of the close of the cycle, the Egyptians wished to purify the land, and all foreigners were driven out as ceremonially unclean. As the cycle was completed on the 28th of July, it would seem reasonable that Hebrews should be cast out in the spring at the equinox, which, to a certain extent, agrees with the Hebrew version of the story, while the improbable statement of Manetho, that the Hebrews were a race of lepers, must be taken as a metaphor for ritual impurity, not unknown to the Hebrew Scriptures.

179. Of the forty years' wandering in the wilderness we know nothing except for some incidents recorded of the first and last couple of years. As the motive of many of these is to aggrandise the claims of the high priest, a dignitary not known for several centuries later, we cannot accord them much credence, especially when in one instance the additional motive of the irrepressible derivation is manifest—viz., Num. xvii. 16-28 —where the story of the twelve rods is to account for the use of the word *rod* for *tribe;* and again in the kindred story of the revolt of Qorach, probably an instructive lesson for the suppression of discontent,[2] where we notice serious discrepancies and additions in the accounts in Deuteronomy and Numbers, showing how the tale assumed shape. The appointment of the seventy elders is assigned at one time to the direct revelation of God, at another to the sagacious advice of

---

[1] Kuenen, i. 121.   [2] See below under "Levi."

Jethro, Moses' father-in-law; and yet, again, to the express wish of the people. Here we certainly have not preserved tradition, but varied theories of the rise of the quasi-parliament. The interviews related to have taken place between Moses and God are, as we have already seen, inconsistent with the most elementary idea of a holy, perfect, and unapproachable Being; Moses is God's superior in wisdom and justice on more than one occasion. Wherever Mount Sinai may have been, whether in the site favoured by tradition or in Edom, as Sayce suggests, its name is connected with moon-worship; all we can believe is, that Moses, to impress the people with the divine origin of his law, ascended this peak in the midst of a storm, and represented himself as having there had an interview with the Almighty; later tradition expanded this simple and legitimate device. Not Moses only, but Aaron and his sons and the seventy elders, ate and drank in the presence of God, whose form they beheld without paying the usually attached penalty of death. It is strange to read of Moses' reminding God that the people could not ascend the mountain, because, in accordance with the divine command, the mountain had been fenced round; and not less strange to note that, though previously told by God that the people had rebelled and were committing idolatry, Moses descended the Mount with the intention of handing over to these unworthy recipients the tables of stone inscribed by the finger of God, till suddenly, turning a corner, the sight of their apostasy burst on his view, when,

"Because things seen are mightier than things heard,"

he cast down the tables and broke them into a thousand

pieces, as the nation in his opinion was unworthy of so signal an honour. Observe that, after being informed of the apostasy, he was commanded to take the tables of stone down; this would appear to be an unnoticed instance of disobedience and display of temper from the meekest of men. Apparently Moses fasted for 160 days out of the 730 elapsing between the Exodus and the repulse from Canaan. Now, all these incredible points are not found in one connected, carefully compiled history of one date, but are found scattered over pages of narrative, for the most part written 500 to 900 years after the days of Moses. Of the Ark and high priest, and ritual in his days, we know nothing but that they were not as described in the Hexateuch, for that description is based on subsequent experience.[1] What, then, is left which we can accept as the really ancient tradition of Moses? Only, that he led a Hebrew race out of Egypt, gave them some moral and social laws, and died before the Hebrews had returned to Canaan; we know nothing of his parentage or brethren—later tradition has supplied particulars, but they are so manifestly fabricated that we cannot accept them as carefully preserved tradition.

180. JOSHUA.—We are not told how he escaped Pharaoh's ruthless edict. His father is called Nun— *i.e.*, Fish; whether this has any connection with his twice leading the Hebrews across the fords it is impossible to say. Like Moses, he is probably a personified idea, his name Victor being specially suggestive. Of his early days we are provided by tradition with scant information: at one time he is already a

---

[1] See chap. v.

military hero, leading the hosts to battle at Rephidim; at another he is an attendant on Moses. By comparing Exodus xxiv. 13-14 and xxxii. 17, we find that Joshua went up the Mount higher than any one else but Moses, and tarried for him, thus fasting forty days and nights, though he does not usually get the credit of it; and in xxxiii. 11 we again find Joshua left in an ambiguous position for an indefinite time, for he, who had no business in the Tabernacle, departed not out of it. His association with Caleb as one of the twelve spies, as well as the subject position of the latter to him in the conquest of the land, is highly improbable; for in the consideration of Caleb, under the heading of "Judah," we shall find reason to doubt that they were even contemporaries, while the independence of Caleb as a southern general is asserted in the Book of Judges. The Circumcision and the Passover at Gilgal have been already seen to be unhistoric; the battle of Gibeon has been glorified by the gradual introduction of a miraculous occurrence; how, then, can we accept the story of the capture of Jericho, the seven-fold march round its walls on the seventh day by the whole host being a physical impossibility (Kuenen); and the continued marching for seven consecutive days necessitating the *breaking* of the *Sabbath*. The story of Achan introduces us to an important family of Judah, not elsewhere met with. Towns besieged by Caleb and his party are reported as conquests of Joshua. What, then, is left of the historic life and victories of Joshua? We have in him merely an Ephramite hero of great antiquity, whom subsequent tradition has supplied with an *entourage* of a very composite character. If we could accept the statements as facts, we should find in them trace of a tradition that Joshua, like Moses, performed the priestly office, the prerogative, according to other accounts, of Aaron ; but it is more probable that these touches are merely intended to aggrandise Joshua, making the successor of Moses his former companion on the most solemn occasions, without any regard to the significance of the details.

CHAPTER VII

ENQUIRY INTO THE ORIGIN OF THE NAMES OF THE PATRIARCHS

181. In the preceding chapters we have endeavoured to consider the principles on which Hebrew writers compiled their genealogical tables and composed narratives, the details of which were suggested to them either by a transparent, though erroneous, derivation, or were the result of some effort at research. Apart from this important question of philology, we observed a disregard for historic truth, or, if that term is offensive, let us say historic propriety. The present chapter will be a sort of Onomasticon, in which the ordinarily accepted derivations of the ancestors of the Israelites and some adjacent tribes will be considered; and, where possible, other derivations based on more reliable philological and historical principles will be suggested. Of these, some will commend themselves more readily, while others are confessedly experiments, and rather hint at the direction in which solution may be expected, than providing a solution itself.

182. ABRAM.—Remove the stories connected with Lot and Hagar, the incidents at Shechem, Bethel, and Hebron, which are only inserted to illustrate the antiquity of the reverence attached to these places, and which do not tally with the subsequent allusions to them in the times of the later tribes, Iskites and Jacobeans; strike out the sacrifice of Isaac, as a modification of a Phœnician legend, and the inauguration of the rite of Circumcision, as of priestly origin; condemn the tales of the visits to Egypt and Philistia, as derived from the history of the Iskites who had historic association with both places; and we have nothing left but the Call of Abram on which we can rely as an actual fact; for the burial of Sarah at Macpelah is a tradition incorporated by the priestly author at a late date. Now, this wholesale rejection is not a predetermined conclusion, but follows naturally from the arguments given above, when considering the claims of the Lot and Sodom narratives to historic acceptance; and from those given below under the heading of Sara, Isaac, and Judah, &c. Tradition has preserved the name Abram as that of the leader of the Hebrew immigration into Palestine and Arabia; but as the story of his life was not committed to writing till over one thousand years after his death, we cannot expect to have reliable details of his life, still less can we hope for the careful preservation of the minute family particulars that postulate the existence of a diary rather than of a memoir.

183. No derivation of this name is attempted in Genesis. Ewald[1] strangely inverts the statement[2] by proposing that Abram was only contracted from Abraham, which is of course no change of name at all. I say *strangely*, not because the suggestion is not worthy of all respect and consideration coming from

---

[1] "Hist.," i. 324, note [2] Gen. xvii. 5.

such a master, but because it is *inconsistent* with his frequent assumption that the story in Genesis is to be accepted as history. In the same place, however, he admitted that it may have had a segholate etymology— Abr-m, compare 'Amr-m, Gersh-m; and as the usual derivation Ab-ram = Abi-ram, " Exalted Father," is too palpable a pun to be accepted as real, and as no other names of such hoary antiquity partake of this simplicity and preference for personal allusion, we must consider what root would provide such a segholate noun. Analogy with the forms G'bhir, Gibr, Gibbor, at once suggests A'bhir, Abr, Abbir. Now, why is God called the Hero of Jacob five times (of Israel, once)[1]? The word Hero = Abhir is very rare, and is taken as the exact equivalent of Abbir, in its sense of warrior, hero; but wherefore the different pointing, when applied to God? This form is older; why should we not suppose it to have been used of God in earlier times, and appropriated by the divine hero, Abram, the *deified* ancestor of the vast Hebrew race, including Israelites, Ishmaelites, Midianites, &c.—the hero of the East? Further, seeing that tradition associates Abram largely with Babylon, and remembering that *winged bulls* represented to the Babylonians divine beings, the gods or genii of the household,[1] should we be justified in obtaining thus a connection between Ebher = wing and Abhir = Hero, which are usually assigned to different roots. It would then be, because this root was forgotten, or more probably because it was offensively suggestive both of idolatry and a hated Babylonian origin, that we are told that God *changed* his older name Abram into Abraham. If the above proposition is considered too

[1] Sayce, "Hibbert Lectures," 290.

fanciful, we must either doubt that he was ever known by the shorter name, especially as the longer one has entirely superseded it; or fall back on the simple expedient of assuming Abram to be the preservation of an older form of the word 'Ebrews, since in Assyrian Aleph is found for 'Ain. Gesenius does not attempt to derive this name.

184. ABRAHAM.—Is the Pater Orchamus of Ovid:[1] Renan says, "Pater is undoubtedly used in a more restricted sense in Ovid's text"—her father, *i.e.*, Leucothoe's, who buried her alive, from which peril she was rescued by Apollo, a female version of Isaac's story; "but the expression Pater Orchamus none the less appears to have been imposed on Ovid by tradition"—yes, and Jewish tradition too, for Ovid, Horace, and Juvenal seem to have had considerable intercourse with Jews and acquaintance with Hebrew literature; *cf.* also Martial, xi. 24: "Swear you circumcised fellow by Anchialum" (?) Anoki-El, or as a substitute for the Temple of Jupiter, perhaps = Heikal. Renan further quotes Menant[2] as authority for the statement that the *kings* of *Ur* are frequently represented in a manner agreeable to the traditional conception of Father Orcham (Abraham), whose chief claim to this title (? Merciful) was his having substituted the sacrifice of a *kid* for *human* sacrifice. If this can be supported more fully in detail, we have the Abraham of Scripture further clearly connected with the Assyrian heroes. Unfortunately, in neither Schrader nor Sayce can I find any allusion to a name bearing the least similarity to Orcham, or even Racham, the *seventh*

[1] Met. iv. 202.   [2] Cyl de la Chaldée.

from Bel (? or Nimrod). I suppose, therefore, that M. Renan means, not that this name itself is found on Assyrian cylinders, but that the description of the aboriginal Assyrian monarchs accords with the peaceful, merciful type of sheikh who came from Ur of the Chaldees.

186. It must not, however, be overlooked that Ewald and others view Ur as a common noun (so LXX.) = territory of the Chaldees; in which case further research into the etymology of Orchamus is necessary, as Ur-Cham would suggest a root Cham, instead of Racham. The derivation in Genesis xvii. 5, Ab-hamon, may be intended to agree with this root Cham; it, however, does not account for the *r* in Abraham, which difficulty is evaded by Gesenius, who suggests that *rehom* might have been a prior form of *leum* = nations, which is merely translated by *hamon*. Against this, on the other hand, is the evident intention of the Hebrew authors to derive, *not* translate, words; and this difficulty is here caused by their determination to discover a root, where reference to number may suggest a prophetical or proleptical origin for the name, on strength of which they insert a solemn divine prophecy of the vast numbers of peoples to be descended from Abraham. Abu-racham, Merciful Father, read by Greek or Roman authors, Ab-urachman, would of course be a Semitic derivation, but in harmony with the conception of the merciful kings described above, and was probably in Renan's thoughts when he penned the sentence quoted. Some centuries later, we find two important sections (called sons) of the tribe of Judah named respectively Ram and Ye-rachme-el, which strangely recall Ab-ram and Ab-raham, their remoter ancestor.

186. HAGAR.— The Hagarites, or Fugitives, according to Strabo, a race near the Persian Gulf, neighbours of the Nebataeans and Chaulotœi, the Nebaioth and Havilah of the Bible. The Hagarites are mentioned in the Scriptures.[1] In the Genesis narrative they are identified with the Ishmaelites, and the name Hagar taken as that of their mother, who is represented as Abram's concubine. The fugitive nature of the tribe is turned into the act of their progenitrix; and occasion is taken for a double account of that event. See also under Beer-lachai-roi.

187. SARAH is, in like manner, the ancestress of the Israelites—*i.e.*, I-sara-elites. Though in each case the connection is concealed for the better development of the story of the individual, the *generic* origin of both is equally manifest. Her earlier name, Sarai—Tsarai= rival — is inappropriate, since, in accordance with common usage, it was more applicable to Hagar.[2] In Isaiah li. 1, Tsur, a rock, is employed in connection with the ancestry of the people from Abram and Sarai. Have we here a trace of a tradition of a blending of the Hebrews and Phœnicians in remote antiquity, described as a marriage between Pater Orchamus and Tyre? Pains would naturally be taken to efface this objectionable theory as much as possible. There must have been some strong motive for recording the change of name of both the fabled parents of the Hebrew race.

188. ISCAH is considered by the Rabbis to be another name for Sarah. As Abram's niece and grand-

---

[1] Chron. v. 10, 19, 20, xxvii. 31 ; Psa. lxxxiii. 7.
[2] *Cf.* 1 Sam. i. 6 ; Lev. xviii. 18.

daughter of his father, she could, after the manner of the East, be well described by himself as his *sister*, the daughter of his father; it is surprising that Keil should suppose it possible for Abram to have married his halfsister by his own father. On the other hand, being the daughter of Haran, she could not (with Ewald) be assigned as wife to her own brother, Lot; this supposition seems to arise from determination to avoid the identification with Sarah, which is all the more probable seeing that Nahor married the other sister, Milcah, also his niece. Despite the fabled nature of these relationships, we cannot conceive of the authors deliberately manufacturing incestuous marriages for their heroes, seeing that such are reserved for occasions when a covert insult is intended to be conveyed. Just as Sarah was taken for the name of Abram's imaginary wife, because the Yi-sara-el-ites were descended from her, so also the name Iscah was adopted as an alternative with reference to the race of the Isaacites (Yiskites).

189. ISAAC (Yshch-Aq).—Recalls his mother's name, Iscah; the final -q seems to bear some ethnic generic force; compare 'Amal-q, 'Ana-q, and possibly Darrumesh-q = southern = Damascus.[1] In conformity

---

[1] Darrum-mesheq. That this was the ancient form, from which Dammesheq is contracted, appears from 1 Chron. xviii. 5-6, where the form Darmesheq occurs; see also 2 Kings xvi. 10, Dmmesheq; and from the form Darmsuq in the Peschite. Its meaning is evidently *Southern Mash*ites. See Gesenius *sub* Mash. The Northern Mashites dwelt in the neighbourhood of the mountain Mash or Mesha, which separates Armenia from Mesopotamia; in Gen. x. 30 Mesha is the mountain, *not* Saphir, which is a town. Observe the Mash of Gen. x. 23, an Aramæan tribe appears as Meshek in 1 Chron. i. 17. The root Mesheq suggested in Gen. xv. 2 is an intolerable pun.

with the distinct ethnological motive of the Genesis history, we must look for some race Iskites, connected with the Abrahamides. "In Isaac shall a seed or race be called for thee, after his name." How is this fulfilled since the Israelites are not in the Bible known as Iskites? Is there any allusion outside the Bible which throws light on this? Ewald[1] says: "Manetho's list contains no single proof that Israel, at least that people alone, was understood by the name Hyksos;" but adds (393): "I have always recognised that the Hyksos must stand in some close relation to Israelites." He shows the Semitic origin of several words in connection with the Hyksos monuments: Zoan = Wanderers, First Hyksos king Salatis = Shallit,[2] Avaris (Monument Havar) = Hebrew *camp* (396); and adds: "It cannot have been for nothing that the oldest tradition assigns to Ishmael an *Egyptian* mother, and makes him dwell on the very borders of Egypt." But the same tradition places Isaac in the same district, and associates him intimately with Ishmael; and the fact that Hebron was his usual dwelling-place harmonises with the Hyksos origin of that city. The Hyksos were a Semitic race, some say related to the Hittite Empire, who came south, built Hebron, and seven years later[3] set up Zoan as their capital in Egypt. M. Maspero is of opinion that the *non*-Semitic type of the men portrayed on the San monuments represents a population *prior* to the Hyksos; so that the old objection that Hyksos were not Semites need not be considered. M. Renan (i. 138) speaks of the Josephites as "favourably received by the Hyksos and inviting the Jacobeans to join them," also on the following page he states that

---

[1] "Hist.," i. 392.   [2] Gen. xlii. 6.   [3] Num. xiii. 22.

identified with Hyksos

"the incoherent recital which Josephus borrows from Manetho implies at least the connection between the Hyksos and the Hebrews." The race afterwards known as the Israelites must have had some intimate connection with Egypt during this period, as there is no other way of accounting for their habit, in later times, of calling Egypt the Field of Zoan, long after San had ceased to be the capital. If in the Hyksos we may see the Iskites, descendants of Abram, who went into Egypt, and, after 500 years of sovereign power, represented as the rule of Joseph, were driven out, rejoining their congeners, the Jacobeans, who had remained in Palestine, when they assumed the name of Josephites, either because of their leader Osor-siph, or as a large *addition* to the Jacobeans; after which conjunction they became known as Israelites; we find at least a fulfilment of the tradition, embodied in the form of a prophecy, "in Isaac shall a seed be called for thee "—*i.e.*, as the Ishmaelites were called after Ishmael, so a race descended from Abram shall be called after Isaac. No great weight need be attached to the slight want of similarity between Hyksos and Iskites (Yischaq). That this mighty race, whose history blended strangely with that of the "peculiar people," should have failed to be assigned to the family of Father Orchamus, while Israelites, Edomites, Midianites, Ishmaelites, &c. &c., all claimed his parentage, would be more remarkable than the metathesis, which is easily explained by the word being foreign to either Egyptian or Hebrew, which it must have been, and altered by one or the other to convey a meaning. The Egyptian signification *Shepherds* is sensible, the Hebrew one is as ridiculous as its meaning implies, and under any circumstance is not worthy of grave consideration. As usual, the Hebrew author takes the most self-evident derivation, and associating it with the common word Tsacheq, to *laugh*, discovers no less than four occasions for its application in stories connected with him : Abram (xvii. 17) and Sarah (xviii. 12) laughed at the improbability of his birth ; while its other meaning, to *play* with, is found in connection with Isaac and Ishmael (xxi. 9, where the idea of *teasing* is only arrived at by a strained interpretation) and Isaac and Rebecca (xxvi. 8). The question arises, Why was Isaac introduced at all, if he played no important part in the history of the race ? While the assumption that his *rôle* was played out of Palestine, and so loses its place in the subsequent history, accords well with the silence of the prophets with regard to him. It is an actual labour on their part to bring in casual reference to him ; or, as in Amos vii. 9-16, the name Isaac is only employed in the interests of parallelism as a synonym of Israel—*i.e.*, the Josephites—which is very instructive.

190. REBECCA.—In accordance with the scheme observable in these writings, we ought to find some race or town intimately connected with the Iskites Hebron was a Hyksos town, but its early name was City of Arba', which suggests a root Rebha, the inhabitants of which would be known as Ribh'ites, or by the interchange of 'Ain and Qoph, which is quite *en règle*, as Ribhqites, whence the name for Isaac's wife, Rebecca or Ribhqah, was selected. Hence the ancient name for Hebron affords confirmation of the hypothesis advanced in the preceding paragraph ; for the city whose origin is closely allied to the capital of the Hyksos Empire

was known by a name manifestly assonant to the name of a tribe very intimately connected with the tribe of Isaac, whatever that may have been. After the Hyksos migrated into Egypt, the Rechobon (Reubenites) occupied this very district, which was subsequently the territory of Judah and the Calebites. The confusion between the similar names, Ribh'ite and Rechbite, of two races on the same spot, resulted in the suggestion that the word Reuben was derived from Rebha'.[1] Further, the stories of Reuben's relation with Joseph and Egypt are doubtless the consequence of this same confusion, as well as evidence of a tradition of the migration into Egypt of the Ribhqite section of the Hyksos.

191. ISHMAEL.—This name is derived on two occasions from the evident idea, "God hears," for God heard Hagar's affliction and Ishmael's cry.[2] In Phoenician inscriptions we frequently have this phrase applied to various deities, " because he heard their (his or her) voice." It is, then, difficult to credit the assertion that one nation took for its distinctive name "God hears his voice," which was too common a conception to serve that purpose. Races took their names chiefly— (*a*) from physical features of their countries, as Cana'an, Edom, Amorites, Naphthali, &c.; (*b*) from names of tribal gods, as Judah, Gad, Asher, Assur, &c.; (*c*) from names of animals (totemism), as Se'ir, Zibe'on, Chamron, &c. When we consider that the Ishmaelites occupied the *northern* parts of Arabia, and that Semele, Left-hand = North,[3] was a Phoenician goddess, the thought not unnaturally occurs to one, whether it is

[1] See Reuben. [2] Gen. xvi. 11. [3] *Cf.* Teman, Right-hand = South.

Is it conceivable that a man, however infirm and blind, could stroke a kid's skin, and mistake it for the back of the hand of the most hirsute monster that ever lived. Tuch (quoted by Keil) draws attention to the *long silky* hair of the Eastern goat, though how that increases the possibility of the deception is far from evident. Tuch's words are: "It is the camel-goat of the East, whose black silky hair was used even by the Romans, as a substitute for human hair."[1] Reference to the epigram does not confirm the allusion, as the following translation testifies: "He who spoke of your head as being shod, alluded, O festive Phœbus! to your covering your temples and crown with kid *leather*." These fables about Esau's goaty attributes can only be understood if we suppose that the Hebrew author derived his name from Se'ir by metathesis. Another example of an ancient name so transformed is Senir—Mount Hermon, which is also known as Sirion, and even further disguised as Sion.[2] Unless we see in Eseq[3] an allusion to the dwelling of Esauites in the vicinity of the well, we do not find much reason for believing that the territory of Edom was ever known by any other name than Se'ir, of which 'Esau was only a dialectic variety.

194. EDOM, or IDUMÆA, means *red*, and the district is so called from the red sandstone of which its hills are formed.[4] As usual, however, a twofold derivation of the name is discovered, as applicable to the imaginary hero from whom the race descended. Accordingly, we are told that "Esau was red at his birth, a not unusual occurrence (xxv. 25); and again that he was

[1] Martial, xii. 45.
[3] Gen. xxvi. 20.
[2] Deut. iv. 48.
[4] "Dict. Bible."

so called for selling his birthright for "a pottage of lentils." We note in passing that these vegetables are credited with the power of promoting the growth of hair, a rather superfluous quality for Esau to seek. To connect this incident with the required root, Esau is represented as being ignorant of this common form of food, and saying (xxv. 30); "Pray, feed me with some of that red, red (stuff) . . . therefore was his name called Edom." Dr. Kitto says that lentil pottage has a *reddish* hue, but the narrative demands something at least as red as a beet to be properly spoken of as red stuff. The historic basis that forms the nucleus of the story, the details of which are due to the novelist, are these: The Edomite race was known by tradition to be older than the Jacobean, and from the genealogical tables evidence remains that Edomites dwelt in the country afterwards occupied by Judah, Simeon, and Benjamin. Thus arose the idea of a man, an elder brother, Edom losing his birthright to his crafty younger brother, Jacob.

195. JACOB (YA'AQOBH).—A triple account of this name is given with two roots. (1) Genesis xxv. 26, quoted Hosea xii. 4: Jacob at his birth catches hold of his twin-brother's *heel*. (2) Genesis xxvii. referred to Jeremiah ix 3: "Does not one rightly call his name Jacob, for he has *outwitted* me these two times. My birthright he took, and lo, now he has taken my blessing." The connection between *heel* and *outwitting* does not appear to me to lie in the stealthy tracking of game by the spoor (Gesenius), but in the insidious attack of a snake (Gen. iii. 35; xl. 37) which lies hidden, and in a cowardly manner attacks the heel of the passer-by, who is unaware of its proximity. It is not the clever, skilful pursuit of prey which would disgust the sportsman Esau, but cowardly, underhand plotting his ruin.[1] There is a further allusion to the idea of outwitting[2] when in an impossible manner Jacob becomes owner of vast herds of sheep, all speckled and streaked, derived from his uncle Laban's flocks. In Genesis xxvii. 11 there seems trace in the words Se'ar and Cheleq of an allusion to "hills and valleys" [3]—Esau, the hairy man dwelling in the hill district of Se'ir, and Jacob the smooth man in the fields (Gen. xxvii. 27).[4] Of all the patriarchs, Jacob is represented as the greatest wanderer; it is doubtless to him that the pious Israelite, in reciting his ritual,[5] referred when he said, "A nomad Syrian was my father." Note the strange expression, suggestive of weariness and disinclination.[6] "And Jacob lifted up his feet and went." The Jacobean tribe then may well have been called, after their unsettled life, perpetually on the move, *Foot-print* makers.[7] The name Jacob is not in the Old Testament applied to ordinary men; in 1 Chronicles iv. 36, we find Jacobah a descendant of Simeon; but this probably is in post-exilic times, and would mark the transition to the common later use of the name.

196. ISRAEL.—As might be expected, several derivations of this late and favourite name for the Bney Ya'qobh are found.

---

[1] 2 Kings x. 19.   [2] xxx. 37–41.   [3] Deut. viii. 7; xi. 11.
[4] Cheleq, smooth, is an easy anagram on Chequel, Aramaic for field, and suggests another latent pun: Biq'ah valley, on Ya'aqobh.
[5] Deut. xxvi. 5.   [6] Gen. xxix. 1.
[7] *Cf.* Ps. lxxvii. 20 (19); lxxxix. 52 (51).

(1) Prince or warrior of God. The narratives allude to this derivation in assigning to the chief ancestress of the people the name of Sarah; and in the life of Jacob (xxxii. 28) he is said to have been so called, because he succeeded in wrestling with God at the ford Yabboq, the boundary between the Moabites and Ammonites,[1] and the scene of frequent struggles between those nations, which would quite sufficiently account for the name of the ford. The name Yabboq is somewhat of the nature of an anagram on Ya'aqob; this, together with its meaning, rendered it specially appropriate for introduction into the glorious and vivid allegory of successful, importunate prayer, which is represented as a physical struggle between man and God—Ya'aqobh and Yahveh. The later Seraiah, warrior of Yahveh, apparently name of Caleb, Othniel's brother, is confirmatory of this derivation, which certainly accords with the historical conception advanced further on, that the name of Israel was assumed by a religious league of Jacobeans and Josephites.

(2) Man sees God, Ish-raah-el, also found in the same context (xxxii. 30): "For I have seen God face to face," referred to by Christ (Matt. v. 8): "Blessed are the pure in heart, for they shall see God." This is the only derivation applicable to the second account of the change of name (xxxv. 9, 10), when "God *appeared* unto Jacob and called his name Israel."

(3) Yasharites = the Upright or Righteous, which is the most generally accepted derivation in modern times. The grounds in support of this root are mainly the following:

[1] Num. xxi. 24.

(a) Yeshurun, used of the Israelites.[1] It is usually considered a diminutive; but analogy with names like Zibe'on, Dishon, Sime'on, Reuben, &c., would make one infer that these late writers employed it in imitation of these old race names with the Arabic plural termination.

(b) Book of Yasher—viz., of Israelites. This is an ancient history or poetical chronicle of the people of Israel, only referred to by name, in Josh. x. 13 and 2 Sam. i. 18; but to which belong several other ancient fragments, in the opinion of Ewald. The Syriac translator renders Book of *Praises* in Joshua, and *Songs* in Samuel. The two ancient songs, Ex. xv. 1 and Num. xxi. 17, are introduced by a remarkable use of the frequentitive imperfect "Az Yashir," then *sang* Moses, &c.; both of them are considered parts of this book. Is the Syriac due merely to an association of ideas, or are they right, and the LXX. "Book of Upright" in Samuel, wrong? In Joshua the LXX. omit.

(c) Num. xxiii. 10. In the poetical effusion put into the mouth of Balaam, son of Beor, king of Edom,[2] we find a distinct allusion to this root for the name Israel:

> Who hath counted the dust of Jacob,
> Or the number of the quarter of Israel?
> Let me die the death of the Yesharim (upright),
> And may my posterity be like his.

This is again quoted in Ps. xxxvii. 37 and 38.

> Mark the honest (tam) and observe the upright (yashar),
> For the peaceful man hath a posterity;
> But transgressors shall be utterly destroyed,
> And the posterity of the wicked shall be cut off.

---

[1] Deut. xxxii. 15; xxxiii. 5, 26; Is. xliv. 2.
[2] Gen. xxxvi. 22; *cf.* Sayce 54.

The reference is the more evident when we compare Num. xxiv. 20, where, speaking of Amaleq in contrast to Israel, Bala'am says, "his posterity (is doomed) to utter annihilation"; and further, remember Gen. xxv. 27: "Jacob was an honest (tam) man." We have thus in Ps. xxxvii. an expression apparently only conveying the idea of Horace, "*Integer* vitæ scelerisque *purus*," but actually a cryptogram equivalent to "mark Jacob and observe Israel." The author of Job, who is well acquainted with this psalm, is the only other who uses this combination, Tam and Yashar, in his description of his hero.[1] There is great difficulty in seeing any appropriateness in the application of the term "honest" as an attribute to a man who throughout the early narrative is depicted as "wily." The rabbinical idea of youthful innocence is quaintly out of place in referring to a man over forty years of age.

(*d*) Christ recognises this derivation when, in speaking of Nathanael, he says,[2] "Behold a true Israelite, in whom is no guile."

In favour of this root we have, then, a fourfold testimony. There is no difficulty in admitting the softening of Yashar into Yasar, but some explanation seems to be required of the vocalisation, as we should expect Yishre-el not, Yishra-el.

(4) Direct = God directs (his way).[3] This late author had doubtless the name Israel in his mind, and was mindful of God's leading his people from Egypt when he made use of this expression with regard to the return from Babylon.

After all, have we any real derivation of Israel? These evident experiments, to discover one, seem

[1] Job i. 1, 8; ii. 3.   [2] John i. 47.   [3] *Cf.* Isa. xl. 3; xlv. 13.

the LXX., is the result of an ancient error in transcription, for the difference in Syriac between final *l* and *'Ain* is merely the matter of a slight extension of the double stroke; and if this be so, we must gather that they based their form on the double narrative alluded to above (par. 198). Ewald, in his " Lehrbuch," surely meant Josephus or Syriac, and suggests that they may have wished to employ -El with reference to " *Yahveh* hath looked, &c." Kohler in his blessing of Jacob is quoted by Kuenen (i. 408) as suggesting Reu-Ba'al which he translates " Face of Baal," and compares with Penuel. He would thus combine the 'Ain of the Hebrew and the *-l* of the Syriac. In the Moabite inscription which he quotes, Ruth is a *spectacle*, not a *face*; and in volume i. of the " Semitic Inscriptions " I cannot find a form supporting this suggestion.

200. In an Assyrian inscription given by Schrader [1] we read that " one hundred soldiers of Ba'sa "[2] " son of *Ruchubi*, of the land of Ammon, &c.," joined the twelve allies, one of whom was Ahab of Israel, against Shalmanezer. On " Son of Ruchubi "[3] who says: " These rulers are not represented as the actual sons of the individuals who are called their fathers, but simply as the governors of the territories named after the *founder* of the dynasty." Here, therefore, we must be on our guard against taking Ruchubi as an ally of Ammon, or as anything else than a *district* in Ammon, which a certain Ruchubi some time before had as a separate government. The association of the names Ruchubi and Ammon naturally reveals the fact that Reuben occupied the southern part of the district between

---

[1] P. 426, n. 2.
[2] I. 184, on 1 Kings xvi. 29.
[3] Bailis, cf. Jer. xl. 14.
[4] See Schrader, ii. 27.

Arnon and Yabboq, which was claimed by Moab, but was formerly taken and retaken by Ammon. Ewald[1] admits that the final א in Reuben is not radical, any more than in more common words, but he does not suggest any root for this ancient race-name. As no other words of the form Raab have survived, we are at once, by the "common interchange"[2] of Aleph and He, led to think of Rahab, to *excite, trouble*, and it is doubtless this derivation that suggested the allusion,[3] "*bubbling* like water" as applicable to Reuben, at the beginning of Jacob's blessing, which abounds in puns on supposed derivations of the names of the twelve tribes. As, however, this root is only employed metaphorically of "proud Egypt," it does not afford any ground for providing a derivation for the name of a Hebrew race. It is true that Aleph and Cheth are not so frequently interchanged, of חנק.אנק and Assyrian ראם for[4] רחם and very probably Genesis xxxvi. 21, 27, אצרן for חצרן and xxxvi. 26 אשבן for חשבן. Still the confusion of He and Cheth in ancient names is a matter of notoriety; we might then be justified in considering ראב to be for רחב a mollification of רחב. Gesenius is of opinion that a tribe Rechoboth[5] lived in the south near Edom, separate from the more northerly family in the direction of Lebanon, with whom the Ammonites were allied against David.[6] In case it might be supposed that this last is evidence against the hypothesis advanced above, it will be well to note, first, that the Syrians could not be properly spoken of as a district of Ammon; and, secondly, that in the Inscrip-

---

[1] Lehrbuch, p. 426.   [2] Gesenius.   [3] Gen. xlix. 4.
[4] Schrader.   [5] Gen. xxxvi. 37.   [6] 2 Sam. x. 6.

tion,[1] the Syrians are quite separated in position, being mentioned first in the catalogue.

201. The idyllised story of Jacob, given in Genesis, relates what, in more matter-of-fact history, would assume rather the following shape. Long after Abram had left Northern Syria, two tribes closely related in descent from him, the Edomites and Jacobeans, found it impossible to continue to live in close proximity. The Jacobeans, being less warlike than the Edomites, in their fear of them, returned to the Harran district, whence *two centuries or more* previously their forefathers had come. Here they induced some kindred tribes, described as sons, the offspring of marriage with their relations, to join their league and return with them. With such increased forces, the Jacobeans were less apprehensive of successful incursions from their more powerful congeners, who, in their turn respecting their grown might, accepted terms of reconciliation. One of these tribes consisted of families belonging to the Rechoboth—Reubenites, who, in the course of their wanderings southwards, left traces of their halting-places in the names of various spots, which survived long after they had migrated elsewhere—viz.: Beth-Rechob in Naphthali,[2] Beth-Rechob in Asher,[3] and in the neighbourhood of the well of Rechoboth in the south.[4] The main body settled down in the country afterwards known as Judah and Benjamin, before their final migration eastward, beyond Jordan. If, with Professor Sayce, we see in Samlah, Shaul and Baal-hanan[5] reference by foreigners to Samuel, Saul, and David, we observe that Saul of Benjamin is known to

---

[1] Schrader, i. 186.   [2] Jud. xviii. 28.   [3] Josh. xix. 28.
[4] Gen. xxvi. 22.   [5] Gen. xxxvi. 36–38.

aliens as *Saul of Rechoboth* or Reuben, which is further confirmation of the hypothesis, especially in view of the remarks made above upon the Bilhites and the Stone of Bohan.

202. It is very remarkable that Judah and Reuben have both two large subdivisions, known as Chezron and Carmi=Carmel; described as sons of each, but in later times only recognisable as districts in Judah. Chezron and Carmi are referred to Reuben;[1] while Chezron alone is referred to Judah.[2] The important vine-growing district of Carmel[3] is to be taken as the origin of the man Carmi attributed to both Reuben and Judah as a son, because the district was occupied by both successively. We have seen already a trace of the presence of Reuben on Judite territory, in the name for the well of Rechoboth; but here we have less conjectural testimony. Now such a blending of two tribes, or rather the absorption of part of one in the other, would in the style of the authors be expressed as a marriage of Judah with Reuben; and this is precisely what we find; for according to an ancient tradition, of which only a vestige survives in the Genealogy in Matthew i. 5, Judah marries Rachab. Apparently to continue the insults heaped upon Reuben, and strictly in accordance with similar tales about Judah and the origin of Moab and Ammon, Rachab, in the novelette about the fanciful taking of Jericho, is introduced as a heathen and a harlot. By the statement that Rachab dwelleth in Israel even unto this day, the author [4]

---

[1] Gen. xlvi. 9.; 1 Chron. v. 3; Num. xxvi. 6; and to Judah, 1 Chron. ii. 5, 7, iv. 1.
[2] Gen. xlvi. 12; Num. xxvi. 21; and Carmi, Josh. vii. 1.
[3] Josh. xv. 55;. 1 Sam. xv. 12, xxv. 5, 40.   [4] Josh. vi. 25.

betrays his knowledge that he is really dealing with a district or family, and not an individual woman. The phrase "unto this day" is always an evidence of a fact which has surprisingly endured for a long time;[1] but Keil strangely takes it as proof that the Book of Joshua was written in the lifetime of the characters, whose actions are recorded. Here then by an "undesigned coincidence," we get corroborative evidence that *Rechobon* is the original form of Reuben.

203. SIME'ON.—This tribe, which was subsequently lost, chiefly by absorption amongst Judah and Benjamin, embraces[2] in a remarkable manner two conspicuous families of Ishmaelites,[3] viz., Mibsam and Mishma', which are utterly unlike ordinary names of men, and are manifestly derived from the names of Ishmael himself and his daughter Basmath.[4] This again must be taken as geographical history, the Jacobeans who dispossessed some Ishmaelites, not only preserved the names of the districts, but themselves took a name very much akin to Ishmaelites. It is to be noted here that the two eldest sons of Jacob have so much greater an antiquity than the rest, that they have no real existence in the history of the people; Reuben alone of these two being barely alluded to in the Song of Deborah, while in the later Blessing of Moses grave fears are entertained of the extinction of Reuben, perhaps originally including Simeon.[5] In the allegory of Joseph, there may be some historic fact hinted at in the captivity of Simeon, such as his complete surrender

---

[1] *Cf.* Josh. iv. 9; 1 Sam. xxx. 25; 2 Sam. iv. 3.
[2] Chron. iv. xxv. [3] Gen. xxv. 13, 14.
[4] Gen. xxxvi. 3. [5] Deut. xxxiii. 6.

to the Philistines. The tale of his conquest of Shechem, in conjunction with Levi, points to a period when the *tribe* had a warlike reputation, and the event must be put during the (Iskite) Hyksos sojourn in Egypt, as well as many other instances of individual action, such as that related in 1 Chronicles vii. 21.

204. LEVI.—Several instances are given as the occasions on which this religiously important tribe received the name of Levi or Bond.

(1) Gen. xxix. 34. The birth of a third son shall be a bond between the husband and the unloved wife.

(2) Gen. xxxiv. 26. Simeon and Levi in holy bond of righteous indignation at the wrong done their sister, enter into a secret compact,[1] and together, unaided, slay all the males in the city of Shechem. This, and the next may both convey rather the idea of *allies*.[2]

(3) Ex. xxxii. 26. The tribe of Levi, righteously indignant at idolatry, go forth at Moses' command and massacre the unarmed dancing throng;[3] though it must surprise any thoughtful reader, if it were right and necessary for every man in this crusade to slay his brother,[4] why Moses did not set the example, and hew the ringleader, his own brother Aaron, before the Lord. This is the consecration of the tribe.[5] In precisely the same way the priesthood was secured to the sons of Aaron, by the act of Phinehas, grandson of Aaron,[6] in executing some criminals, although the everlasting priesthood had already been secured to Aaron and his family by the Divine promise.[7]

[1] Gen. xlix. 6. [2] *Cf.* Ps. lxxxiii. 9 (8); Dan. xi. 34.
[3] Ex. xxxii. 25. [4] Ex. xxxii. 27. [5] Deut. x. 8; xxxiii. 9.
[6] Num. xxv. 13. [7] Ex. xl. 15.

(4) The tribe is again consecrated to the service of God, as a substitute for the first-born of Israel, spared in the midnight slaughter of the Egyptian first-born;[1] they were a bond of the covenant thus formed between God and Israel.[2] There seems, however, in this derivation to be a reference to *exchange*,[3] borrowing and lending, as is more patent after perusing the following figures. It is strange that the total of the male Levites should be 22,300,[4] which is a little more than the sum of the first-born[5] of all the other tribes of Israel, which they were intended to ransom. Still stranger is the determination[6] to change the total 22,300 to 22,000, in order that ten per cent. of the people, 273, should remain unredeemed, who were bought off at five shekels each, of the *tenth*, *i.e.*, a half-shekel for each of the grand total, the *ordinary* tax at a census.[7] But these figures will not stand investigation. The total[8] of men from twenty years old and upwards, able to go forth to war, is 603,550, and the first-born of the same are 22,273; if we *ignore*, as they seem to have done, that the Levites[9] are counted from thirty (instead of twenty) to fifty, we obtain, by proportion, 317 as the number of first-born among the Levites, suspiciously intended to be excluded, as the Rabbis saw from the redemption of the other tribes, and so accounting for the 300 Levites more than were needed for that purpose (see above). Such exact figures in distribution of a population for a religious object, are manifestly indications of intentional manipulation. On the other

---
[1] Ex. xiii. 12.   [2] Num. iii. 13; viii. 16.
[3] *Cf.* Deut. xxviii. 12; Ps. xxxvii. 21.
[4] 7,500+8,600+6,200, Num. iii. 22, 28, 34.
[5] 22,273, Num. iii. 43.   [6] Num. iii. 49.
[7] Ex. xxx. 13.   [8] Num. i. 46.   [9] Num. iv. 43

hand, if we subtract from the total, 22,300 male Levites, the 8580 of the lustiest age, we find that eight-thirteenths of the tribe were under thirty or over fifty, which seems a large proportion even allowing for a higher rate of mortality at those periods of life, viz., the beginning and the end. Nor should we overlook the curious fact that while Moses and Joshua reach ages over 100, and are in full vigour, their contemporaries are *unfit* for work at fifty, showing a strange mixture of tradition and of regard to more natural events within the author's own experience.

(5) Instead of being bound to God, the Levites are said [1] to be attached to Aaron as his assistants.

205. These conflicting accounts of how the Levites acquired their name, throw grave doubts on the reliable information at the disposal of the ancients, the absence of which resulted in their composing stories agreeable to their own customs, or to the actual historical fact of the early fighting characteristics of the people known later as Levites. We are then justified in investigating the history of this tribe for ourselves, and considering what source is the most probable for their name, which as a synonym of priests [2] must be sought in that direction. Some few years ago, Professor Sayce found in Arabia an ancient inscription, where the word *Lewan* occurs for priests. This is precisely in accord with what we discover from the history of the Levites as given in the Bible. The priestly character of the tribe is associated with Moses, who is described as son-in-law to a (Lewan) priest of Midian. Though he delegates the priestly

---

[1] Num. xviii. 2.
[2] *Cf.* the expression, "The priests, the Levites."

functions to Aaron, he himself remains a priest, higher than the highest, for it is he that admits Aaron to the solemn initiation or consecration; and afterwards, though Aaron might enter the Holy of Holies only once a year, at the Feast of Atonement,[1] Moses had free access to the lid of the Ark, the seat of the cloud, the visible emblem of the presence of God. Later tradition depicts Moses in the threefold capacity of prophet, priest, and king; but the high importance attached to the details of ritual and religious customs, and the prominence assigned to the Levites in four out of five books of the Pentateuch, are evidence that early tradition viewed him as the father of the Levites— *i.e.*, of the priestly caste. The priesthood actually remained in his family at the sacred shrine in the north at Dan until the captivity,[2] for the *n* in Ma*n*asseh is a scribe's emendation to remove the apparent stain on the family name of *Moses*, which thus in his opinion was guilty of idolatry. The selection of the name Manasseh for this purpose, seems also to have reference to the renegade priest of that name who seceded to Samaritan schism.

206. It is not merely the *name* Levite which, as has been shown above, was a puzzle to later authors, resulting in the combination of conflicting traditions; but the *history* of the tribe itself is inconsistent with other facts observable, and was composed after the formation of the priestly tribe, which at first was not a tribe in the true sense of the word, but a guild of men chosen out of any tribe, and consecrated to the priestly office; though, as I shall endeavour to show, evidence exists that Qenites were preferred for the purpose.

[1] Heb. ix. 7.   [2] Jud. xviii. 30.

The distinction, being well paid [1] was in many cases hereditary, and so Lewan were found in all tribes. As a matter of fact the tribe of Levi was not scattered in Israel,[2] but on the other hand arose or sprouted in various parts of Israel. It is well known that at a later date religious services were restricted to the Levites, and believed to have always been thus restricted; but the assumption that this monopoly was enjoyed by them in ancient times has been conclusively demonstrated baseless, by Wellhausen and Kuenen. As represented, the Levites alone were to perform the religious offices at the *one* sacred place, where the Tabernacle or Temple might happen to be. The narratives, however, are plainly at variance with this theory. Not only were sacred shrines scattered all over the land, while hallowed spots were found "under every green tree and upon every high hill"; but those who sacrificed there, were *chiefs* of families or *hired* priests very different from the State-supported hierarchy.

307. Even so important a personage as the High Priest is shrouded in the mists of obscurity, if not in an impenetrable fog.[3] Aaron is described with every detail of his life and dress, as though he had been a contemporary of Jaddua; but his family tree, on which the apostolical succession (Aaron = Apostle) depended, is in a very dilapidated condition.[4] Later scribes have, too, attributed this high honour to those, whose claim even to birth in the so-called tribe of Levi is of the shallowest. Eli and his sons appear as important priests at Shiloh,[5] but the unsupported statement of 1 Chron. xxiv. 3 is not sufficient ground for the belief

---

[1] Jud. xvii. 10.   [2] Gen. xlix. 7.   [3] See 144. &c.
[4] See chap. iv.   [5] 1 Sam. l.

that Eli was descended from Ithamar, son Aaron, or in fact belonged more to the tribe of Levi than to that of Ephraim where Shiloh was situated. The episode[1] was written long after the events recorded, as the first opportunity, for the fulfilment of the prophecy in verse 36, would be in the reign of Solomon, when the Shiloh priesthood was for political reasons superseded by the Zadoqite. Thus verse 27 cannot be adduced as an independent argument in favour of Eli's descent from Aaron, which is merely hinted at in this passage of late date. If, however, we accept as fact, that Eli was the descendant of Ithamar, and occupied the High-priesthood, then for five generations, the promise to Phinehas, son of Eleazar,[2] was held in abeyance, or for at least 100 years, and the "covenant of an everlasting priesthood" was disregarded. In Ps. lxxviii., "But he despised the tent of Joseph, and chose not the tribe of Ephraim," we observe that the tent of Joseph is chiastically parallel to the Temple on Mount Zion, in the following verse; and this affords strong evidence in favour of the existence of a priestly family of Ephraim, while the oracle was at Shiloh.

208. When Samuel is introduced, his family is said to be from Zuph. It is not to be overlooked that in the families descended from Esau, we find Zuph along with such names as the following: Raguel,[3] Qenaz,[4] and Qorach.[5] If then Samuel was a Qenite, and Salma the father of Bethlehem a Qenizzite descended from Caleb,[6] we find an adequate reason for Samuel's search for a king in the little Bethlehem, viz., among his sympathis-

---

[1] 1 Sam. ii. 27–36.
[2] Num. xxv. 13.
[3] Qenite, cf. father-in-law of Moses.
[4] Qenizzite.
[5] Qenizzite and Levite.
[6] 1 Chron. ii. 51.

ing relatives. This also would account for Jeroboam's being reported to have discarded the Qenites (Levite) as priests, because of their relation with the Davidic house. It is worthy of regard as bearing on the fabled origin of Eli from the Aaronite family that Samuel also of the tribe of Ephraim,[1] performs all the functions of the priestly office; and that in his case, too, the chronicler is able to provide a priestly genealogy from Yizhar the uncle of Aaron.[2] The chronicler, in both these instances pursues consistently the course he has laid down for himself, which is to state, and insist upon, the existence from the most remote ages of sacred rites and official distinctions and regulations, which obtained in his own time. It does not disturb his view of the question, that Saul, David, and Solomon were at liberty to offer sacrifices, and even wear the priestly ephod[3] which are manifestly crimes of the deepest dye from the later standpoint, but in the earlier narratives are simple natural occurrences, which meet with divine approval and blessing. Instructive in this connection is the consideration of the following. Solomon offers incense upon the special altar appointed in the Holy Place[4] with immunity, but the same act on the part of Uzziah is punished as a wanton transgression.[5] Now the absence of this episode in the earlier authority,[6] indicates the motive that actuates the chronicler and considerably discounts the value of his testimony on such questions.

209. Not only do we observe good men of all tribes performing the priestly offices, but the Levites themselves are described as pursuing very secular avocations,

---

[1] 1 Sam. l.
[2] 1 Chron. vi. 18–23 (33–38).
[3] 2 Sam. vi. 14.
[4] 1 Kings ix. 29.
[5] 2 Chron vi. 19.
[6] 2 Kings xv. v.

for a large part of the army that flocked to David's standard at Hebron were Levites 4500, Aaronites 3700 under Jehoiada and Zadoq, with 22 captains of his father's house, evidently warriors by birth and training.[1] Also in 1 Chron. xxvi. we find the expression "men of valour" frequently applied to the Levite, notably to the Hebronites; 1700 of whom under Hashabiah, and 2700 under Yeriyah ruled west and east of the Jordan respectively, "in all the business of Yahveh and the service of the king." A strange combination, suggestive of days when the military service of the king was the real duty, and the business of Yahveh a secondary ideal; any way inconsistent with the Mosaic arrangement of Levites dwelling in cities, where their maintenance was secured during the intervals between their terms of duty at the Tabernacle or Temple. The absence of allusion to any military system, to which the Levites were specifically bound, betrays the conditions of the time of the writer, who is unaware of the fact. In this connection, we cannot but he surprised at the *search* for Levites (Hebronites) being crowned with success, by their discovery, in the fortieth year of the reign of King David in the city of Jazer of Gilead,[2] the very place where Levites should be expected, as 300 years previously, according to Joshua xxi. 39, this city had been assigned to them as a residence. The prominence thus given to the Chebronites cannot be entirely due to a natural preference shown by David to the city that first espoused his cause, for these Chebronites are already in every part of the twelve tribes; why otherwise the search for them in Gad, just alluded to?

[1] 1 Chron. xii. 25, 28.   [2] 1 Chron. xxvi. 31.

Levites are Qenites

210. Here we have the clue to who the Levites really were; for the Levites, Qohathites and Chehronites are all interchangeable with one another, being all derivable from synonyms, Levi = Qoath = Chehron = Bond, *i.e.*, a society bound together for religious purposes, at first carried out by the aid of the sword, of which the first symptom is in the story of the Taking of Shechem by two *men* Simeon and Levi. In the tales of the Forty Years' Wanderings the Levites are the military guardians and avengers of religious purity; and the deposition and execution of Athaliah by the Levite bodyguard of the Temple were instigated by religious zeal rather than political loyalty to the house of David. Now Cheber is the name of a family of Qenites[1] who settled in the north of Palestine, probably in the tribe of Asher, whose descendant he is represented as being.[2] A larger section of this family known as the Chebron = Chebrites, in remote times settled in the south, afterwards claimed by Judah; this section occupied the city Qirjath-Arba', and called it after their own name. But we are distinctly told that Caleb was the captor of Qirjath-Arba'. Now the Qenites and Qenizzites, who may be viewed as ancient races very near of kin, if not in later ages practically identical[3] are mentioned together[4] in Genesis xv. 19; and the author of the Book of Judges,[4] immediately after recounting the prowess of Caleb the Qenizzite, finds it the most natural thing, in that connection, to allude to the Qenite dwelling among the Children of Israel. We have then a Qenizzite family of Chebrites in company with Qenites in the south and a Qenite family of Chebrites in the north. Further, the Qenite family is intimately connected with the house of Levi, so much so, that Moses the great law-giver is represented as dwelling amongst them and intermarrying with them, such intermarriages being indication of ancient blending of two separate races, here the aboriginal race of Qenites and the section of the Abrahamites. The Qenizzite family is also nearly related, Chehron being assigned to the sons of Aaron, and, as we have seen, they hold the leading place among the Levites in the reign of David.

211. 1 Chron. ii. 55. "These are the Qenites, that came of Hemath, the father of the house of Rechab," appears to refer to all the descendants of the Qenizzite Caleb (50), for the construction is continued throughout and conjecture is confirmed by the fact that the *Sucathites* in verse 55, which are here called Qenites are elsewhere[1] described as *Socho* the children of Sheber, a descendant of Caleb the son of Jephunneh the Qenizzite. Sons of Socho or Sucathites, = Tabernacle-men, is a singularly appropriate name, for the sons of Rechab dwelt in tents.[2] The episode in Jeremiah shows, to say the least of it, a friendly relation between himself, a Levite of Anathoth, and these Qenites from the north. 1 Chron. ii. 55, moreover, tells us that the Rechabites were formerly sprung from Hemath, which is a Levitical town in Naphthali, and in close proximity to the neighbourhood, where the Qenites are elsewhere described as dwelling.[3] The above remarks may throw some light on the following quotation from the Dictionary of the Bible.[4] "While James the Just was being

---

[1] 1 Chron. iv. 18.
[2] Jer. xxxv. 8, 10.
[3] Jud. iv. 11.
[4] *Sub voce* Rechabites.

stoned [1] one of the priests, of the sons of Rechab the son of Rechabim, who are mentioned by Jeremiah, cried out protesting against the crime." Dean Stanley was struck with the anomaly of a *priest*, not only *not* of *Levitical*, but *not* even of *Jewish* descent.

212. Surely, then, even if we look on the Qenizzites as a diminutive, representing a younger though ancient branch of the Qenites, who could boast a more hoary antiquity, we cannot fail to see that Qenites, Qenizzites, and Levites are strangely intermingled. It is most highly improbable that there should have been scattered all over Israel a religious family known as the Qenites, and *also* another religious family called by the name of the Levites; and that, in many cases, they should have occupied the same towns. It is a significant fact, that the word for the reception of proselytes, is they shall be *bound* to Yahveh (Hebrew, *Levitised*); also, that in conjunction with the word Levites, we frequently find the expression added, "the *stranger* that is within thy gates." Have we not here indications of a lost tradition that the Levites were not originally of pure Jacobean descent? The Qenizzites were absorbed into Judah, and, but for the genealogical tables, we should have no evidence of the fact; why should not the Qenites, originally known from their religious cult as Lewan or priests, have come at last to be viewed as having always been a distinct, separate tribe, instead of mingled with the other tribes? The apportionment of forty-eight cities to the Levites in Joshua xxi. has long been viewed with distrust as an anachronism and must be dismissed; such mathematical precision, an average of four cities to each tribe is in itself questionable,

[1] Eus. H. E. ii. 23.

especially in the unsettled times that ensued through three or four centuries; we have also seen that in David's days nothing was known of this and similar authoritative distributions of the Levites. If the Levites were really of Qenite origin, an aboriginal race, their peaceful tactics, apart from religious fanaticism, and homely lives preserved their small settlements, when war was raging around them; as, in the case of Jabin, King of Canaan, and Saul's slaughter of the Amalekites. They may be described as religious oases several of which were scattered over the land amidst the less religious and even distinctly idolatrous families of other tribes. The more northerly were peaceable, and accordingly left in peace. The southern branch was more warlike, as we observe from the conquest of Qirjath-'Arba, and from David's employment of them as garrisons to keep order and administer justice throughout his realm.[1] It was, doubtless, the ancestors of those who joined the tribe of Simeon in attacking Shechem, which they must have occupied, as we find it later described as Levitical town. The religious character of this crusade is disguised[2] in a simple narrative suitable to the times of the Patriarchs, to which it is transferred.[3]

213. It is remarkable that the Chebronites, who were so numerous, powerful and influential,[4] are as a family dismissed with the barest allusion.[5] We can only account for this by assuming that, on account of their chief position, they were identical with the Aaronites, who were really the Qenite occupants of the city Chehron, though the author describes them as *sent* thither to dwell along with the Qenizzite conquerors of

---

[1] 1 Chron. xxvi. 29–32. [2] Gen. xxxiv. [3] See par. 203.
[4] 1 Chron. xii. 26–28. [5] 1 Chron. xxiii. 19; xxiv. 23.

Qirjath-Arba'. The Aaronites are represented as descended from the brother of Moses, *i.e.*, they were in some way closely connected with this hero, who in his turn was so intimately connected with the Qenites as to be reported to have married into their tribe, whence he learned the rite of circumcision (par. 126). The name Aaron does not appear to be of Semitic origin; the best derivation is *sent* (apostle),[1] which agrees with the story of his being sent by God as his brother's mouthpiece, as well as with the mission of the Levites to Hebron above alluded to.

214. The organisation of the Levites, that we find in Exodus and Numbers is *primâ facie* highly improbable, especially Numbers iii.; for we must not forget that David is described as the first to restrict the carrying of the Ark to Levites,[2] on account of the sudden death of Uzzah for touching that sacred vessel, and as subsequently appointing them to their various duties and stations.[3] The stories of the divine vindication of the sacred election of Aaron to the high-priesthood in Numbers xvi. and xvii. are incredible, for they include the total extinction of the Qerachites, who are still in existence in David's reign; the story of the budding rod, *matteh*, is an instance of a narrative devised to illustrate the derivation of a word, explaining how *matteh* came to be used as a synonym for *Shebhet*. The subsequent history of Judges and Samuel is not in accordance with this description of an established monopoly in favour of Aaronites, as we have already seen. Though Phinehas in the one, and Abiathar in the other (admitting, for the sake of argument, his

---

[1] Sayce. "Hibbert Lectures," 47 n. [2] 1 Chron. xv. 2.
[3] 1 Chron. xxiv.

claim to descent from Ithamar), seem to be preferred for consulting the Urim and Thummim; others also performed the priestly office. Jonathan, the grandson of Moses, a Levite of Bethlehem-Judah, a Qenizzite town[1] first established himself as a priest in Ephraim, and thence was promoted to Dan,[2] where the priesthood remained in his family till the Captivity. There is also another nameless Levite connected likewise with both Ephraim and Bethlehem-Judah. The wandering nature of the life of these earlier Levites is quite in keeping with what we know of the life of the Qenites.

215. The following theory appears to suit the scattered and somewhat conflicting data in the various authorities. A family of Qenites called Qohath (the roots *Qin* and *Qehath* are naturally akin) joined the Jacobeans, when they were settled after their return from Syria—*i.e.*, after they were strengthened by the sons of Rechob (Reuben) and had received into their federation certain of the Ishmaelites (Simeon). Thus we have the order Reuben, Simeon, Levi, which is represented as the birth to Jacob of three sons, in the same order. After Moses's time the Qenites, who accompanied the Josephites from Egypt under his leadership, fraternised readily with the Qohathites, and afterwards with the Chebronites. As they all performed the priestly rites they were all called Lewan, priests; hence the expression 'the Priests, the Levites,' *i.e.*, the priests, viz., the Levites. When Qohathites, Chebronites and other Qenites were all combined in one religious caste, they began to be viewed as a tribe of Israel, and it became necessary to find a son of Jacob from whom they could have sprung; and the

[1] 1 Chron. ii. 51.   [2] Jud. xvii. 11; xviii. 30.

general term Levites suggested the suitable name Levi, whence some one has proposed the name Leach, wife of Jacob and mother of Levi, to have been selected. The calling of the early Qenites Levi can only be understood as a proleptic use, like Hebron in the days of Abram.

216. When we come to consider the family of Levi as so often recorded we find it consists of three families, Qohath, Gershom, and Merari; it is passing strange that in the two last names we recognise the *son* and *sister* of Moses, Gershom and Miriam. To Qohath are assigned four sons, 'Amram, Yizhar, Chehron, and 'Uzziel. 'Amram (= immersion [1]) is a name selected with prominent reference to the story of the escape of his infant son from drowning; as only a fragment of Moses' line is preserved, the Aaronites are the only important race of this stock, unless indeed, as Aaron is more mythical than Moses, the pedigree should be assigned to Moses himself. Prominent as was the part played by the Chebronites, we find them without a genealogy; which can only be accounted for by a dislike to betraying their manifest connection with Caleb and the Qenizzites. In short, the word Qohathites seems to have been taken as equivalent to Levites, so that Aaronites and Chebronites, the chief branches of the Qenite race can be called indifferently by the common title. Yizhar's genealogy is a pure fabrication; its purpose is twofold—to provide Samuel with a pure priestly origin;[2] and to disguise the Qenizzite descent of the door-keeping Levites, the Qorachites (= Shornpates), who in ii. 42, 43 are said to be sons of Chehron the son of Caleb the Qenizzite. In 1 Chronicles vi.

[1] *Cf.* Gomorrha. [2] 1 Chron. vi. 18-23 (33-38).

7, 13 (vi. 22, 28) Samuel is traced through the *same* ancestors, up to Aminadab, a prince of Judah;[1] which device, apparently suggestive of intermarriage, sufficiently attests the difficult position in which the author found himself. Uzziel has no genealogy.

217. So little is known of the Gershonites, that his two sons Libni—*i.e.*, the Libnites, the inhabitants of the town Libnah in *Simeon*[2]—and Shimei, *i.e.*, Simeonite Levites, have an identical family tree;[3] while in xxiii. 8 La'adan, a son of *Ephraim* (vii. 26) is substituted for Libni, but he is confused (xxiii. 9) with Shimei also. Gershom, the son of Moses had descendants acting as priests in Ephraim (214); thus we have pretty conclusive proof that the Gershonites are not really anterior but subsequent to Moses; and Gershom son of Levi remains a fabrication to enhance the antiquity of this branch, and if so, in the interests of the north. The name Gershom is segholate like Adam, 'Amram, &c., and is derived from Garesh (= to expel), not two bi-literal words, Ger-sham, "stranger there," which is only after the nature of a pun. Moses' father's name referring to the history of the welfare of the nation, when the males were drowned, it is only reasonable to understand Moses' son named after an event in the fortunes of Israel, viz., their *expulsion* from Egypt, which has been transmuted into a triumphant departure.

218. Of the two sons of Marari, Machli and Mushi, we know very little. In 1 Chron. vi. 14 (29) the Libni and Shimei families ascribed to Gershom are fathered on Machli. Further evidence of the want of reliability in these genealogies is that while in 1 Kings v. 11

---

[1] 1 Chron. ii. 10. [2] 1 Chron. vi. 5. 6 (xx. 21).
[3] 1 Chron. vi. 26-28 (41-43).

(iv. 31) Ethan, Heman, Calcol, and Darda are *all* said to be sons of Machol = Machli ; we have in 1 Chron. iv. 29 (44) Ethan *alone* traced to Machli, and in verse 18 (33) Heman has quite a different genealogy, being son of Yizhar. A further complication with regard to these same men is observable (101) in 1 Chron. ii. 6, where the same four men are attributed to Zerah son of Judah. Though it is true that this might be cited as another proof of the Qenizzite origin of some of the Levites, it is rather to be considered as evidence of the manner in which their ideas, not the information at their disposal, assisted in or influenced the formation of Family Tables. "Mihi res, non me rebus, subiungere conor" was their motto. The identification of Merari with Miriam is strengthened by the consideration that the Machlites or *Dance*-Music Levites are assigned to the former, while tradition represents the latter as the introducer of sacred dance accompanied by song.[1]

219. The Mushi or Mosites (Mosheh is the Hebrew form of Moses) are also said to be a branch of the Merari ; but in 1 Chron. vi. 32 (47) the Machli are subordinated to them instead of being co-ordinated—*i.e.*, Machol is son of Mushi, not brother. Now, this Mosite Machli had a son Eleazar,[2] who had no male offspring; and a very similar statement is made of Eleazar, son of Moses, who had only one son Rechabiah, who again has a son Yishiah.[3] The other Eleazar had a brother Qish called Qishiah,[4] and mentioned as if an important branch. There would appear to be reasons for believing Yishiah and Qishiah to be interchangeable, both

---

[1] Exod. xvi.
[2] 1 Chron. xxiii, 22 ; xxiv. 28.
[3] 1 Chron. xxiii. 17.
[4] 1 Chron. xv. 17.

meaning *elder;* for Yashish (= an old man [1]) is Qashish in Aramaic; in 1 Chron. xxiv. 21, the LXX. so understand it, for they leave Yishiah untranslated, as if they considered it mere tautology for the eldest son to be expressed by two Hebrew words. In passing we may note the curious coincidence thus suggested that Saul and David should both have fathers known by the vague designation "the old man" Qish and Yishiah = Jesse. The lists referred to are as follows:

1 Chron. xxiii. 21.	1 Chron. xxiii. 17; xxiv. 21.
Machli (? Mushi);	Moses = Mosheh;
Eleazar;	Eleazar;
Qish.	Rechabiah;
	Yishiah = Qishiah.

Of course, if we acknowledge the accuracy of these genealogies, even if we accept the identification of Mushi with Moses, and the confusion between Machli and Mushi, there is nothing to prevent Qish being the name of both a brother and a grandson of the same Eleazar. But if we recognise in these early names only family *sections*, not individuals, then the order is not a matter of testimony, but the author's opinion—*i.e.*, in one case, tradition represents the Eleazar family section as older than the Qishite, in the other they are coeval.

220. More evidence of the ignorance, and attendant confusion, displayed in the compilation of the Levite genealogies, is obtained from the ensuing considerations. In chap. xxiv. the *intention* is to give the names of the officers in David's reign, but we cannot accept Yishiah above as a cotemporary of David; for in xxvi. 25, Shelomith is the representative of Rechabiah, whose son is Yesha'iah, the same letters as Yishiah

---

[1] Job xii. 12; xv. 10, &c.

with 'Ain inserted; but this Shelomith, here the son of Zikri, is said to be the representative of the family of Yizhar.[1] All this is very illustrative of the confusion likely to result from the attempts of the chronicler after the Exile to reconstruct from the family-trees and house-names of Levites in his own days, lists of officers in the reign of David, and more ambitious still to provide each with a genealogy right back into mythical periods.

221. QORACH.—The Qorachites appear to be an important branch of Levites, but we have seen that their genealogy is unreliable, being traced through Ephraimites to Yizhar in one case, to Amminadab of Judah in the other. Samuel and Heman the psalmist are both assigned to this family. In 1 Chronicle xxvi. they are called *porters*, which is in accordance with the youthful duties of Samuel. There can be no doubt that the historian[2] describes the utter destruction of the family of Qorach, for their presumptuous claim to the priesthood. A difficulty was naturally felt, as to whence the subsequent race of porters sprang (see above and Numbers xxvi. 58). So in referring to the episode in connection with the Reubenite rebels, Dathan and Abiram, a gloss was inserted:[3] "Notwithstanding the children of Qorach died *not*." Subsequent authors evade the difficulty by avoiding mention of the priestly ambition of Qorach, while recording the royal pretensions of the Reubenites.[4] The fact is that the whole history of the wanderings is only illustrated by episodes, that bear on the importance of Moses and the Levites, and is entirely unhistoric. This particular narrative

---

[1] xxiii. 18; xxiv. 22.   [2] Num. xvi. 32.
[3] Num. xxvi. 11.   [4] Deut. xi. 6; Ps. cvi. 17.

may have been introduced in the reign of David or Solomon, as a warning to the Qorachites, who doubtless thought themselves slighted in the menial work assigned to them of door-keeping. Of the psalms whose titles claim for them Qorachite authorship, Psalms xlii.–xlix. five have a slight reference to the Temple; Psalm lxxxiv. 10 has a distinct allusion to the Qorachite occupation, doorkeeping. Psalm lxxxviii. has a reference to their early rising to open the Temple gates with the key,[1] Psalms lxxxv. and lxxxvii. are of a general character.

222. Who were the Qorachites? In 1 Chronicles ii. 42, Qorach is the son of Chebron, *i.e.*, the Qorachites are a branch of the Chebronite Qenite family. Here too we have further evidence of the attempt, if it be not a fact, to trace the Qenites to Esau,[2] for Qorach is assigned to him, and we have observed (216) the remarkable fact that the Qenizzites (akin to the Qenites) and the Zuphites (Samuel) claim the same parentage. Not only also is Reuel, the tribe of the Qenites into which Moses is said to have married, assigned to Esau, but in the descendants of Reuel his son, a strong affinity to the names of the sons of Gershom, the Levite, is apparent:

Gen. xxxvi. 17.	1 Chron. vi. 26–28 (41–43).
Reuel.	Gershom.
Nahhath.	Yachath.
Zerach.	Shime'i.
Shammah.	Zimmah.
Mizzah.	Zerach.

In the Hebrew characters, Zimmah and Mizzah only differ in order of letters, while in comparative tables,

---

[1] 1 Chron. ix. 27.   [2] Gen. xxxvi.

Neglect of Ark proves Non-existence of Levites 217

such interchanges as Nachath and Yachath, Shammah and Shime'i are of the commonest occurrence? We are thus urged to the conclusion, that either the family-tree of Esau is a fabrication, pure and simple, or that apart from the Edomite race he was the ancestor of the Qenites also. This relation would account for the unwillingness of the Qenite Moses to force a passage through Edom, when the alternative was a long digression, wasting much time and attended with considerable loss of life. We should also note that the rare word *terioth*, E.V. castles, is found only of the villages of the Qohathites,[1] of the Hagarenes or Ishmaelites,[2] of the Midianites[3] and affected by later authors.[4] It would thus appear to be a survival of an ancient word, belonging to the Qenites in common with other southern races, and cherished by the later Levites.

223. Outside the priest-written narratives of the Pentateuch, we have no evidence of the existence of an hereditary high-priest, clad in gorgeous apparel, and ruling over a large army of Levites, divided into three chief sections, to each of which were assigned its several duties. On the contrary, we have seen that no mention of a high priest is made between the days of Joshua and David. Further, the history of the Ark is inconsistent with the establishment of a priesthood, whose special function it was to be in continual attendance upon it. When the Philistines restored the Ark to Israel, it was taken care of at Qirjath-Jeearim[5] by a non-Levite, Abinadab, and his sons Eleazar and Uzza,

---
[1] Chron. vi. 39 (54).   [2] Gen. xxv. 16.   [3] Num. xxxi. 10.
[4] Ez. xxv. 4, xlvi. 23; Cant. viii. 9; Ps. lxix. 26.
[5] 1 Sam. vii. 2,

for *twenty* years.¹ During this long period of time, the priests, so-called highpriests, Abimelech and his son Abiathar, abandoned the Ark to its fate. Their first station was Nob, where the main object of their regard was the Divining Ephod and the Table of Shewbread! This piece of furniture, which by the law of Moses was to be stationed near the Ark and to be replenished every Sabbath,² is left desolate after the massacre of the priests, for Abiatha escapes only with the ephod, to offer himself to David as a medium for anticipating the designs of his enemies. With what caution, then, must we read notes as 1 Chronicles vi. 34 (49) which would make Aaron and his sons, without intermission, always to have offered at the two altars of burnt-offering and incense, and to have made atonement which not only required the annual visit to the Ark, but demanded the presence of the Ark in the Tabernacle; the note concludes with the statement that this arrangement was of Mosaic origin, which is inconceivable when we have just seen that in the pious David's reign the Ark, Tabernacle, and Priest were all three in different places at the same time.

224. When the kingdom was assured to David by the murders of Ishbaal and Abner, the king bethought him of the Ark.³ No Levites go to escort it, no public ceremony was observed, an ox-cart is employed to convey it which results in catastrophe, if indeed the whole narrative is not a novelette to account for the name Perez-Uzzah.⁴ David, without consulting priest

---

¹ Ln. 2 Sam. vi. 3; 1 Chron. xiii. 7. for Uzzah and Achio, read Uzzah and his brother, LXX. "his brethren"; *cf.* 1 Sam. vii. 1, where the name of the brother is given as Eleazar.

² Lev. xxiv. 8.   ³ 2 Sam. vi.   ⁴ See below under Judah.

or prophet, in despair abandons the Ark to the care of a Philistine, Obed-edom; but after observation of three months regains his confidence, and this time decides to employ Levites and a full choral service with every pageant. This is not mentioned in Samuel, but in 1 Chron. xv. 2 an important announcement is made: "Then David said, None ought to carry the Ark of God, but the Levites." Clearly because of the previous story, in which is recorded the untimely fate of the non-Levite; there is no reference to "as Yahveh commanded Moses" or the like. The note in verse 15 is a gloss, for the intention of the story is clear; the Ark is to be borne by Levites, not because Moses had provided rings for that purpose, but to preclude the possibility of a repetition of Uzzah's fate. The Ark at that time could not have been considered the special seat of God himself, but a mere interesting national relic, otherwise it could not have been so long neglected, nor could it for even three months be entrusted to a foreigner, however worthy in himself, who was a Philistine, and possibly a Moabite by birth.[1] As evidence of the absence of restrictions as to the appointment of priests, the family of this Obed-edom became permanently attached to the sacred service.

225. The next noteworthy point is, that David is described as providing a tabernacle of his own invention for the reception of the Ark. Although he considers it necessary to ask Nathan's advice before building a superb temple for this purpose, it does not occur to him previously to obtain permission when superseding the old tabernacle, which we are told was still in existence at Gibeon, rich in historic

[1] Deut. xxiii. 3.

family viewed this story of the "only-begotten"[1] with reverent affection, and would have no scruple in calling a *section* of their race after this name, Judah.

229. Accepting for the sake of argument the Genesis story as *history*, we find that this important name for the leading tribe of Israel, said to have been coined by the exultant mother of Jacob's fourth son, was *already* employed by the Hittites since years before Esau had married *Yehudith*, the daughter of Beeri the Hittite.[2] This might then be urged as evidence of the common early use of this Phœnician name. I fear, however, that in this connection the name is suspicious and testifies rather to the habit of the author, to fabricate names for *wives*, which shall at the same time convey and conceal the fact that two different tribes inhabited the same region. Nearly all the names given to Esau's sons are those of Qenizzite tribes dwelling in Judah, finally claimed and absorbed by that Israelite tribe. That Yechud was an early Israelite name for a god may, moreover, be observed from its use in combination, as an alternative for other divine names:

Num. i. 10, Ammi*hud* = Ammishaddai = Ammiel.
1 Chron. viii. 3, Abihud = Abiyah = Abiel.
Num. xxxiv. 27, Achi*hud* = Achiyah = Achimelek.
1 Chron. vii. 18, Ishhud = Ishbaal.

We should note also that the Benjamite name Ehud is to be referred here, as we find, amongst his Gerite section, the names Abihud, Achihud. The absence on Phœnician inscriptions of names compounded with Yachud can, I imagine, be only satisfactorily explained by the supposition that some other expression has

[1] Gen. xxii. 2. [2] Gen. xxvi. 34.

supplanted the older one for this purpose. This would appear to reveal itself in the name *Bada*,[1] which means alone, only and alone, *cf.* Hebrew *lebhadh*,[2] and which is frequently found in composition: Bodashtoreth, Bodashman, Bodtanith, Bodmelek, Bodmelqarth, Bodzephon, Bodbaal, &c.

230. The story of the *Man* Judah is not historic; but it is interesting to note the following points: his wife is daughter of Shua,[3] *i.e.*, Bathshua', strangely identical with the wife of David [4] and his daughter-in-law Tamar, self-devoted to prostitution, recalls the story of the rape of David's daughter Tamar. There can be but little doubt that the names of Bathshua' and Tamar were transferred from the times of David to the relations of his mythical ancestor, Judah. The incestuous origin of the descendants of Judah, is partly suggested by various mixed nationalities found in this tribe, and partly an insult from the northern author, for Judah is viewed as a northerner by Kuenen, Reuss, Schrader; as a southerner by Dillman, Stude, Driver. The last in the "Literature of the Old Testament" (p. 116) actually employs Gen. xxxviii. as proof of the southern source of this document, because it "records traditions relating to the history of Judahite families which would be of subordinate interest for one who was not a member of the tribe." This argument would assign a Moabite or Ammonite authorship to the story in Gen. xix. 30–38, as it could be of no possible interest to an Israelite. But the venom in each case is the interest to the outsider. The submission of Judah before Joseph, and his protection of Benjamin, are clear

---

[1] C.I.S., x. 3. [2] Gen. xxxii. 24, &c.; and of God, Ps. lxxxiii. 19.
[3] Gen. xxxviii. 2. [4] 1 Chron. iii. 5.

indications that the story was not written till after the secession of the Ten Tribes.

231. Of the sons of Judah we observe that one family is called Zarchite or Ezrachite—*i.e.*, native, indigenous, as opposed to alien races found in Judah; but we have the most meagre accounts of it, unless, indeed, the important district of Carmel[1] is to be considered part of this section of the tribe, for in Joshua vii. 1, Achan is a Carmite, *i.e.*, a Carmelite, and of the Zarchite section. It is, however, to be noted that this Zarchite section is relegated to Simeon, the Ishmaelite tribe; and its sub-section, Carmi, to Reuben.[2]

232. Of the Perizzites, which so were connected with the Zarchites that, like Jacob and Esau their ancestors, are described as twins, we know still less. They were, however, a recognised section of Judah after the return from the Captivity.[3] Now the Perizzite aboriginal race of Canaan is associated with the Jebusites[4] who it is admitted were absorbed in Benjamin[5] and who it is distinctly stated[6] were conquered by Judah. I take it then that these Perizzites submitted to Judah in early times, and were by them admitted by the league, being viewed later as one of the earliest accretions of that tribe, and hence called his eldest surviving son. How far tradition succeeded in preserving the names of the aborigines of Canaan is a problem difficult of solution. We can recognise the mellowness of antiquity about such names as Emin and Zamzummim, or Amaleq and Anaq; but in Palestine itself there is an indefiniteness about names, which are so vague as to be capable of application to any people of any time; Amorites and

---

[1] Josh. xv. 55; 1 Sam. 25.   [2] Num. xxvi. 13, 6.   [3] Neh. xi. 4.
[4] Josh. xi. 3.   [5] Jud. i. 21.   [6] Jud. i. 4.

Canaanites, or Highlanders and Lowlanders, Perizzites and Hivites (= Havvoth); both mean villagers, the latter perhaps cities. The number of these nations is uncertain: in Deut. vii. 1 we find *seven* of them, and in Gen. xv. 19, 20 exactly *ten*, both very suspiciously sacred numbers; it being specially worthy of observation that in the latter case, to arrive at the number desired, Qadmonites or Aborigines, Rephaim or departed heroes, have to be requisitioned along with Qenites and Qenizzites elsewhere considered posterior to Abraham, but here assigned to Esau as his progeny. Similarly the LXX. and Samaritian Pentateuch correct the Massorete and Peschitto in Ex. xxiii. 23; xxxiii. 2; xxxiv. 11 by adding mention of the Girgashites to preserve the number seven. In Esther ix. 19 we find "the Judahites, the Perrizzites" as synonyms where the Aramaic Zain has replaced the Hebrew Ssadde, a frequent practice. If we suppose the converse to have taken place in the change from the Canaanite tribal name to that of the Judite section, the word has a sensible etymology "the villagers," a name much akin to *Chesron* the fabled son of Perez. Of the latter we probably have traces in Baal-Perazim;[1] and Har-Perazim;[2] very possibly too in Perez-Uzza.[3]

233. Chezron is one of those ancient plurals in *n*, like Sime'on, Reuben, &c., and signifies the Chazors. This is supported by Josh. xv. 25, "Chezron, which is Chozer," and the fact that several cities in Judah bore this name; Chazar-Addar,[4] Chazar-gaddah,[5] Chazor-chadattah = New-chazor;[6] besides, in the tribe of

---

[1] 2 Sam. v. 20.
[2] Is. xxviii. 21.
[3] 2 Sam. vi. 8 (224).
[4] Num. xxxiv. 4; Josh. xv. 3.
[5] Josh. xv. 27.
[6] Josh. xv. 25.

Simeon, Chazor-shual[1] and Chazor-susah,[2] and in the equally adjacent tribe of Benjamin, Chazor,[3] we have here sufficent grounds for stating that Chezron was a *district* of Judah; he is called the son of Perez, or a Perizzite, being a portion of the ancient race and having a synonymous appellation. The kingdom of Chazor, in the north, to which Sisera and Jabin belonged, and to which Num. xxxix. 9, 10; Ez. xlvii. 16, 17 refer; must not be confounded with the southern Chazor, though at one time they were doubtless akin, as were the Reubenites and the northern Rechoboth.

234. The royal line of descent from Chezron is exceedingly doubtful, Ram is both his son and grandson, son of Yerachmeel, *i.e.*, traditions varied in assigning the family of Ram to the Chezron and the Yerachmeelites. Nachshon is[4] called the descendant of Caleb the Qenizzite (or Celubhai) not of Ram, whose son Salmon is in 1 Chron. ii. 51 also assigned to Caleb, while his identity with the Salmon of the Book of Ruth is established by the definite statement that he was Father of Bethlehem.[5] As we have already seen that the genealogies of the high priests are, in the days prior to David, unreliable, so we shall find that the ancestry of that king himself is supposititious. Nothing is really known of his grandfather, the name Obed is suggestive of Moabitish origin, which is the material on which the plot of the story of Ruth is based. It has been shown above that the coincidence in the fathers of both Saul and ·David being known by the indefinite cognomen " the old man," Qish and Yishshi respectively is too marked for us to afford to disregard it in any

---

[1] Josh. xv. 28. [2] Josh. xix. 5. [3] Neh. xi. 33.
[4] 1 Chron. iv. [5] *Cf.* 1 Chron. iv. 5.

appreciation of the historical value to be accorded to their personality. In considering the line of David, we are, moreover, at once confronted with the problem of the Caleb family, which is so fully dealt with by Kuenen. The main points to be noted are, that the genealogies of the five Calebs are from internal evidence clearly shown to relate to one and the same man; that we thus discover evidence of the mixed character of the component parts of the tribe of Judah; and that in these genealogies betraying secrets, otherwise undiscoverable and plainly at variance with the generally received notion of the purity of the royal lineage, the intimations thus provided cannot be over-estimated; nor can we sufficiently praise the integrity of purpose displayed by the original scribes, who preserved these conflicting fragments of lost geographical knowledge, though they could not but have been aware of the manifest discrepancy thus exposed from the position they elsewhere so strenuously advocated.

235. In Genesis xlviii. 22, Jacob says to Joseph: "I have given thee one *Shechem* (shoulder) above thy brethren, which I took out of the hand of the Amorite with my sword and my bow." The pun is patent, but the historic truth underlying Jacob's remark shows a quite different author from him who reports the conquest of Shechem to have excited feelings of shame and dread on the part of the fabled aged patriarch, culminating in his solemn curse. The Blessing of Jacob is full of similar plays on the names of tribes, which conclusively demonstrate a late date for its publication. Some of these are recondite, such as the reference in Genesis xlix. 11 to *Carmi*, the vineyard district of Judah, and verse 21 (see under Naphthali); others were

explicit, as verse 22, *Porath* = Fruitful, a play on
Ephrath ; and so in verse 9 we must see in *U-kelabhi*,
"and as a lion," a reference to Caleb, as if he should
say: "And Caleb who shall stir him up. The association of the lion with the tribe of Judah is very ancient ;
but is strangely mixed up with the Calebite family, for
the hero Othniel = Lion of God, is called the younger
brother of Caleb = the Dog ; though it may very well
be questioned whether he lived at or after the time of
the Josephite conquests under Joshua.

236. The following are the five genealogies of
Caleb:

(1) 1 Chronicles ii. 18–20. He is called the son of
Chezron and identified with the Chelubai of
verse 9.

(2) 1 Chronicles ii. 42–49. By being called the
brother of Yerachmeel, he is identified with
the preceding (see verse 9).

(3) 1 Chronicles ii. 50–55 still identical, by the
allusion to his wife (verse 19), Ephratah,
though, we must read "the sons of Hur, the
son of Caleb, and firstborn of Ephratah," for
"the sons of Caleb, the son of Hur," which is
a manifest error (see verse 19). In this
marriage with Ephratah we can only understand a latent historical allusion to a previous
occupation of Ephraimite territory by Calebites, which throws grave suspicions on the
trustworthiness of the story, which makes
Caleb a fellow-spy of Joshua and his subordinate in the latter's fictitious universal conquest
of Canaan.

(4) 1 Chronicles iv. 11, 12. Chelub, the brother of

Shuach. The allusion to Ir Nachash = City of Nachshon, is a strong indication that this is none other but the same Chelubai of verse 9, though Nachshon is represented as the grand-nephew of that man, who is certainly Caleb (see No. 1). As regards Shuach, it appears improbable that this should be a metathesis for Chusah in verse 4 (Gesenius), who is there described as many generations younger than Carmi = Caleb. It recals rather the name of Shuach of the Qeturite family[1] and seems to convey the usual idea of blending of races, here Qeturite and Qenizzite.

(5) 1 Chronicles iv. 15 19. Caleb, the son of Yephubneh, whose sons are found in previous tables, as descendants of the Chezronite Caleb, viz., Ziph iv. 18 (cf. ii. 42); Chebher, iv. 18 (cf. ii. 42); Gedor iv. 18. (cf. ii. 51). These being the names not of men but of places, do not justify the hypothesis that there were two or more Calebs who chanced to have sons of the same name. The text of 1 Chron. iv. 11–20, especially 15–19, is in a corrupt condition. We read "the sons of Yehaleel were," "the sons of Ezra were," and "his wife Yehudiyah bare," without any explanation as to who Yehaleel and Ezra were, or whose wife Yehudiyah was. The latter is described as the "sister of Nacham"; but when we remember that in the ancient Semitic characters *m* and *sh* are easily confused, we feel little scruple in restoring Nacha*sh* here. Yehudith = Jewess,

---
[1] Gen. xxv. 2.

sister of Nachash, was the wife of Caleb the son of Yephunneh, as her descendants clearly show. Thus here again we have an instance of a supposed marriage describing the blending of two races, here Jewish and Qenizzite.

237. Contrariwise, the other genealogies of Caleb, the so-called son of Chezron, stand confessed of Qenizzite origin (ii. 54); the house of Joab is Qenizzite (cf. iv. 14), evidently a district (ii. 45); Me'on (cf. iv. 14), another district;[1] last but not least, Caleb the brother of Yerachmeel has a daughter Achsah (ii. 49, while Caleb the Qenizzite also has a daughter of the same name.[2] The evidence given above is cumulative, and seems to preclude the possibility of our believing in the existence, in these tables, of more than one Caleb. We are told in the plainest, most unmistakable language that Caleb the son of Yephunneh was a Qenizzite,[3] and equally distinctly that he was not a Judahite;[4] for both these passages affirm that Caleb the son of Yephunneh, on account of great services rendered to the Israelites, was allowed by Moses to have settlement in Judah *as if* he had been one of the tribe by birth. Joshua is magnanimous enough to give him Hebron, though as a matter of fact the same narrative makes the conquest of this city due to Caleb's own valour and generalship, and the tradition prevailed that the whole southern district of Judah, Ziph, Gedor, Carmel, Me'on, &c., belongs to this champion of the south, who was doubtless, in accordance with the facts elsewhere observable, simply a warlike tribe personified and deified. Here, however, he is viewed as a single

---

[1] 1 Sam. xxv. 3.
[2] Josh. xiv. 14.
[3] Jud. i. 13.
[4] Josh. xv. 13.

hero, assisted by his younger brother, who, though not by birth an Israelite, occupies the proud and semi-royal position of Israel's first Judge. In Seraiah = warrior of Yahveh,[1] brother of Othniel and ancestor of the Joabites, who dwelt in the valley of the craftsmen, we recognise but thinly disguised Caleb the son of Yephunneh, champion of Yahveh, brother of Othniel,[2] and ancestor of the house of Joab.[3]

238. Inquiry into the root of Yephunneh affords what may be called a demonstration of the conclusiveness of the foreign origin of this Caleb. In Genesis xxxvi. 41, 42 *Pin*on and Qenaz are in juxtaposition as Edomites; in Numbers xxxiii. 42, *Pun*on, a halting-place in the wanderings, lies between Edom and Moab. The Atroth-Sho*phan* of Numbers xxxii. 25 is probably akin; but the Ishpan of 1 Chronicles viii. 22 seems more allied to Shephuphan.[4] *Penin*nah, wife of Elqanah the Qenite,[5] is the only individual bearing a name with this root. Later offshoots of the Caleb family still had a fancy for this root, *Penu*el with a sister Hazelel-*poni* are descendants of Hur,[6] himself son of Caleb. We gather from the above facts that the root of Yephunneh was common in names amongst Qenites and Qenizzites. Caleb then was not an Ezrachite, *i.e.*, he was recognised as extraneous to Judah, though the alliance between them was of so remote an antiquity, that attempts were made by the chronicler to make it appear that he was called a Qenizzite, not because of his connection with that ancient race, but because he was son of a certain man named Qenaz,

---

[1] 1 Chron. iv. 13. [2] Jud. i. [3] 1 Chron. ii. 50-54.
[4] 1 Chron. viii. 5. [5] 1 Sam. i. 2 [6] 1 Chron. iv. 4.
[7] 1 Chron. ii. 19.

who without introduction, *i.e.*, without a father, is thrown amongst the Judahites with the hope that he would be mistaken for a descendant of Judah. This ruse has proved very successful to the present day.[1]

239. The Mosaic sanction for the acceptance of the influential Calebites into the Israelite league is of very doubtful historical value, beyond illustrating the fact that Moses, a Qenite, was glad to secure the assistance of the powerful Qenizzite race, already established in the south of Canaan. If on the contrary, instead of the vague royal pedigree based on late narratives of the character of the Book of Ruth, we accept on the strength of the above evidence the plain statement that, amongst other places, Bethlehem was peopled by Qenizzites, we shall be driven to the conclusion that the Calebite connection with Judah must be referred back to remoter times than would appear from the Hexateuch narrative; a date more in accordance with the position, which Caleb, the father of Hur, assumes in the genealogies.

240. Considerable light is thus thrown on many incidents in the Scriptural narrative. Samuel, a Qenite, when choosing the first king of Israel, knowing the jealousy existing between the north, where he had not so much influence, and the south, where his congeners abounded, made his selection from Benjamin, a comparatively small tribe, not likely from its size to usurp excessive authority, though sufficiently renowned for valour to protect the interests of the realm, besides occupying a natural central position. On his quarrelling with Saul, he resolved to run the risk of appearing to favour his own kindred, and choose a Qenizzite of

[1] *Vide* Keil on 1 Chron. iv. 13-15.

Bethlehem for the next king. Saul retaliated by massacring the Qenites at Nob, in Ephraim, whereupon David immediately espoused their cause, and Qenites were the backbone of his army of brigands in the wilderness of Judah. On his accession to the throne, he requited these Qenites, whose loyalty he had proved, by appointing Chebronites to positions of trust throughout the land. In anticipation of the erection of the temple, he seems to have organised the body of Qenites for its service, though it is very improbable that this was done on anything like the enormous scale, with which he is credited by the chronicler. Gradually withdrawn from their military posts, they came to occupy various ranks of the priesthood, up to that of highpriest, whose influence was second to the king's. Solomon pursued the same tactics, but, on the severance of the northern kingdom, Jeroboam's dislike to the employment of Levites = Qenites as priests was due, not to religious, but political scruples, for he feared their national interest in the Qenizzite house of the south. No other explanation satisfactorily accounts for Jeroboam's action, as prior to his time, even before the organisation of the priesthood, Levites were always welcomed at the northern shrines ; nor assigns a reason for the acerbity with which the southerners declare that he took of "the lowest of the people," *i.e.*, *not* aristocratic Qenites, to serve as priests.

241. SHELACH.—In Numbers xxvi. 20, we read "of Shelah, the family of the Shelanites," but Shilonites, 1 Chronicles ix. 5 ; Nehemiah xi. 5. Now the sons of Shelah as given in 1 Chronicles iv. 21, 'Er and La'adah, recall the names of the sons of Ephraim,

Shuthelach and 'Eran in Numbers xxvi. 35; but Shuthelach, La'adan and 'Ezer in 1 Chronicles vii. 20, 21, 25. Shuthelach, a puzzle to Gesenius, appears to be an irregular ancient form for Eshtelach, the usual Ethpa'al of sibilant verbs, and compare Eshtaol from Shaul, Eshtamoa' from Shema', also Shobal for Eshbal, and Shuphan for Ishpan. As, according to Gesenius, there is no root Thelach, we must in 1 Chronicles vii. 25, either correct Shelach or Shu-thelach. The identity of 'Eran and La'adan in the two family-trees is palpable, and there is little ground for hesitation in seeing in Shelach, or Shuthelach the same name as Shelah; if not we are confronted with a greater difficulty in believing that there were in both Judah and Ephraim, families of Shilonites with offshoots 'Eran and La'adan, but this will be further discussed below, under Ephraim. Briefly the sad fatality that befel the sons of Judah [1] and the building up of his family by an incestuous marriage, are the author's method of describing the fact that the Jacobean element in the tribe of Judah was almost lost while its strength and numbers are to be attributed to aliens, Perizzites and Qenizzites.

242. JOSEPH.—Various roots are given or hinted at. "God hath *taken* away (asaph = saphah) my reproach;"[2] which is immediately supplemented by another author with a second derivation, "May Yahveh *add* to my family" root Yasaph.[3] Joseph is also the *collector* (asaph, its more usual meaning) of corn, though two other verbs are employed[4] to prevent its

[1] Gen. xxxvi.
[2] Gen. xxx. 23.
[3] Gen. xxx. 24.
[4] Gen. xli. 48, 49.

being too readily perceived that the introduction of the story of his warehousing corn in Egypt is simply based on a derivation of his name. In a somewhat similar way the name Daniel is *only* derivable in the tale of Susannah, where he gives judgment; not from the canonical book, where he is a soothsayer and interpreter of dreams, solving no problem in judgment. Professor Sayce[1] refers all Hebrew names of heroes, up to the time of Solomon, to Assyrian etymologies. According to his view, Joseph = Ispu = divination.[2] It would be quite in accordance with the system pursued in the composition of Hebrew narrative, for a knowledge of this Assyrian root to have suggested the introduction of the reference to the divining cup, which is not essential to the narrative. If we accept Sayce's further conclusion that the tribe received its name from a deity, Joseph, we should discover that fully half the tribes, Judah—Joseph, Dan, Gad, Asher, Sime'on [3]—were called after ancient deities. In the Osarsiph of Manetho, whom he identifies with Moses, moderns recognise the name of Joseph, which is suggestive that the Josephite *race* was the one with which the Egyptians were acquainted, not the Jacobean nor Israelite. What if Osar-siph should have meant Helper of Joseph, Osar being not the Egyptian god Osiris, but a transliteration of the Hebrew 'asar, to help.

243. From subsequent history it would appear that the name Joseph simply implies that later some great accretion was added to the Jacobean federation; the names of two tribes, Ephraim and Manasseh, being often combined in one designation, Joseph, *i.e.*, addition,

[1] Hibbert Lectures.   [2] *Cf.* Gen. xliv. 5, 15.   [3] *Vide* Isma'el.

supplement, are taken as the names of the two sons of the man Joseph. It is only when we realise this later admission of Joseph, that we can fully understand the rivalry between the North and the South. Judah was a *long established power before* Joseph came on the scene. Joseph's claim to the birthright does not imply a claim to greater antiquity but rather to dominion, which, according to patriarchal ideas, was seldom given to the first-born. It is in this sense we must interpret 2 Samuel xix. 44 (43), reading with the LXX.[1]: "And I am, moreover, *firstborn* rather than thou," *i.e.*, held the birthright, instead of: "And also in *David* I [have] more than thou," which was not a fact, and, if it were, would be mere tautology after: " I have ten parts in the king." In the same sense we must understand the words of Jeremiah[2]: " I was a father to Israel, and Ephraim was my firstborn." This is more distinctly enunciated in 1 Chronicles v. 2: " Judah was a hero among his brethren, and was a prince over them, but Joseph's was the birthright," where just before, the occasion of this transfer had been given as the consequence of Reuben's incest. Consistently with this statement, we have the narrative in Genesis xlviii. 5, that after solemnly adopting Ephraim and Manasseh as sons instead of grandsons, the aged Jacob invoked the blessing of the firstborn on Ephraim the younger son of Joseph, precisely as he himself had been invested by Isaac with the birthright, though in his case procured with guile. Here again we have abundant support for the conviction that the details in Genesis were provided from the subsequent experience of later history. Jacob's blessing Ephraim and giving him the

---

[1] Professor Driver.   [2] xxxi. 9.

authority over his brethren is one of those numerous prophecies after the event with which the Hebrew writers loved to embellish their early history; they delighted in believing that their ancestors by some divine gift enjoyed the power of foreseeing the greatness of their descendants; but before we discuss the probability of such prophetical power, in the abstract it will be necessary first to have more conclusive evidence than we have as yet discovered, of the actual existence of a *man* Jacob, whose utterances have been miraculously preserved.

244. Ephraim (= Fruitful) would appear to have been the name of a district, not of a man. It is even probable that this district was in very early times known by this name, as we find a Hittite family known as the Ephrites, Ephron.[1] Its occupation by Judah prior to the Josephites is described as the marriage of Caleb with Ephratah, of which historical fact traces survive in names like Bethlehem-Ephratah, and the Ephrathite origin of Samuel's family, which lived at Ramah in Judah. Further, if we are correct above in identifying the Shelanites with the Shilonites (241), Judah must have occupied this district before Joseph and the narrative 1 Chron. vii. 21, which is a puzzle to most commentators as appearing to have occurred *during the time of the Egyptian bondage*, is really a disaster that befel the earlier Judite occupants of Ephraim, while the Josephites were still in Egypt. Corroborative of this hypothesis is the statement in 1 Chron. iv. 21, under guise of genealogy, that La'adah the Shelanite (Shilonite) founded or occupied Moresheth-Gath and Akzibh,[2] both of which are towns of Judah.[3] Observe

---
[1] Gen. xxiii. 10.   [2] *Cf.* Micah, i. 14.   [3] Josh. xv. 44.

also that in Gen. xxxviii. 5 Bathshua' is said to have given birth to Shelah at Akzibh, and we have testimony to the connection of Shelah,[1] with Akzibh, though the two traditions vary very considerably as to his relation with the place, in point of time. The mourning then of Ephraim over the fate of his son La'adan, who was slain by the men of Gath, is a reference to an encounter between the Judite Shelanite La'adan who afterwards successfully established themselves in this Philistine district; it must be considered as a poetical expression for the grief of the district Ephraim, at that time occupied by Judah.

245. In Genesis xlix. 10, it is plainly stated that Judah shall hold the supremacy for a time, till some one shall come to Shiloh, when the union of the tribes shall be with the later comer, *i.e.*, Joseph.

> "The sceptre shall not depart from Judah,
> Nor the divining-rod from between his feet;
> Until *one* come to Shiloh,
> And his shall be the union of the peoples."

This rendering is admitted by Professor Cheyne[2] to be "certainly the *most natural* meaning of the four Hebrew words, taken by themselves," as also did Ewald (ii. 283), but the latter read until *Judah* come to Shiloh. The Messianic interpretation of the passage "until Shiloh come," or "until he come whose right it is,"[3] is inconsistent with the context, for the meaning would then practically be "Judah shall *never* lose the supremacy," for Messiah of the tribe of Judah shall take it up when David of the same tribe lays it down. This is certainly

---

[1] Shuthelach, 1 Chron. vii. 20, 21; Thelach, 1 Chron. vii. 25.
[2] Isa. ii. 189.   [3] LXX. *cf.* Ez. xxi. 32.

not correct; for if it be not admitted that Judah lost the sceptre, when Joseph took away ten-twelfths of the peoples = tribes, no ingenuity can bridge over the 600 years between the destruction of Jerusalem by Nebuchadrezzar and the Advent of Christ. The sceptre swayed by the Asmonæans was of too tottery a character to be seriously viewed as a continuance of Davidic power. The LXX. translation of Genesis xlix. 10 was influenced by Ezra 21, and thus the application to Messiah arose; on the other hand Ezekiel cannot have intended to quote Genesis, for the conditions are diametrically opposite; in Genesis, Judah is to *retain* the *power*, till something or other happens, but in Ezekiel, the place is to *remain* in *ruins* till a lawful governor arises. When Joseph came to Shiloh, the Judites withdrew from the land of Ephraim, but the families from that district retained the name, hence Bethlehem-Ephratah, and Ephrath employed of Qirjath-Yearim [1] suggesting an Ephrathite district in Judah.[2] This coming to Shiloh was only the beginning of the end; quarrels and bickerings were maintained for a long time, before the final secession which shore Judah of its supremacy.

246. "And his shall be the *yiqqehath* of the peoples," this ἄπαξ λεγόμενον is doubtless selected as a play on the name Qohathites, whose dwelling had been so long at Shiloh. The access of Joseph to power is markedly associated with Shiloh,[3] for Achiyah the Shilonite it is who proposes to Jeroboam, the Ephraimite, that he should become king of the ten tribes. The real cause of the revolt is demonstrated by Renan, to have been

---

[1] Ps. cxxxii. 6.   [2] Ruth i. 2; 1 Sam. xvii. 12.
[3] 1 Kings xi. 26-40.

the exactions on the northern tribes made by Solomon, for the embellishment and fortification of Jerusalem. This jealousy between North and South reminds one of the Civil War in the States of America; and if we further accept the very probable theory of Renan, that the North revolted on account of forced labour amounting to slavery, the parallel is more complete, though somewhat inverted. In both cases, the Northerners were anti-slavery and successful; but in Israel the Northerners fought for secession, in America for union; again in America the Southerners were not of so long standing in their position as the Northerners, while the opposite was the case in Israel.

247. But Achiyah, the Shilonite had personal motives of revenge to gratify, albeit he availed himself of the popular feeling to foment the outburst. He was, with a high degree of probability, son or nephew of Abiathar, whose father was also an Achiyah. This Abiathar, for supporting Adonijah, David's eldest son in his claim to the throne, was by the anointed son of the favourite wife, banished from Jerusalem and excluded from his former high-priesthood. Solomon's ordering him to betake himself to his patrimonial estate at Anathoth appears to present some difficulty; of course Anathoth was a Levitical town, famous as the birthplace of Jeremiah, but no mention is made of it in the previous history of Abiathar's family, who dwelt far north of Anathoth. Ewald's conjecture that he was subsequently put to death, is supported by the ominous words, "Thou art worthy of death,"[1] a sentence deferred as in the case of Shimei, to whom it was said, "I will *not to-day* put thee to death." Achiyah, had thus great

---

[1] 1 Kings ii. 26.

personal cause for hatred of Solomon, both in the death of his father or uncle, and in the loss of the hereditary priesthood.

248. MANASSEH.—Joseph gives this name to his firstborn, saying,[1] "God hath made me to *forget* my affliction," &c., but like the derivation of Judah from *praise*, this is open to the objection, that it is manifestly too much of the nature of a pun, to be accepted as the *source* of a tribal name. Considering that this tribe occupied the region known earlier as Gilead, which is interpreted to mean, Heap of Witness, it is not impossible that some author would derive the name Manasseh from *Nes*, a *standard*, and also the pole or pillar, from which the standard floated.[2] Thus in Exodus xvii. there may be some allusion to the victory of this tribe under the leadership of Joshua, which is commemorated in the name "Yahveh-nissi," itself an alternative derivation for Massah, which is rendered Provocation or Temptation, and frequently confounded with Meribah, quite another place and occasion. It is, however, the taunt of the Ephraimites, which reveals the most satisfactory etymon of Manasseh, viz., the word *nus* to *flee*: "Fugitives of Ephraim are ye."[3] This expression is of the greatest historical interest in two ways; first as it stands, it denies the truth of the repeated statement, that half-Manasseh had first dwelt east of Jordan, for it asserts that it was well known that their withdrawal thither was to escape from the Ephraimite government; and second, which is far more important, because it has a bearing on the *fugitive* character of the *Exodus* from Egypt, for two of the prominent tribes that came forth from Egypt are thus

---

[1] Gen. xli. 50. [2] Num. xxi. 8, 9. [3] Jud. xii. 4.

known by names combining to emphasise the nature of their exit, the Levites are called Gershonites, *Expelled*, and the Josephites before they reached Palestine are called Manasseh, *Fugitives*.

249. The early history of Manasseh is as strangely interwoven with the fortunes of Judah, as we have seen above to have been the case in the history of Ephraim. In 1 Chronicles ii. 21 23, we are told that Caleb's father, Chezron, married the sister of Gilead, and was the grandfather of Jair, who had twenty-three towns, Havveth-Jair in the land of Gilead, and conquered Geshur, Aram and Qenath. A footnote is added that " all these were the sons of Machir, the father of Gilead," as if implying that the descendants of Chezron the Judite were reckoned to Machir the Manassite, as side-issue through his daughter; though if one were to appeal to the case of Sselophehad[1] for evidence of patrimony remaining inalienable after a daughter's marriage, we should find that this right was restricted to marriages *within* the tribe. There does not, however, appear any sufficient reason to divert us from the interpretation, hitherto uniformly maintained above, viz., that Judites formerly occupied Havvoth-Jair, Geshur, Aram, Qenath, certain districts which afterwards fell to the lot of Manasseh. The confused attempts at giving an authentic account of this region shows that its early history was but little known. In Numbers xxxii. 41, during Moses' lifetime a certain *man* named Jair, son of Manasseh took certain towns and called them after himself, Havvoth-Jair,[2] and another *man* named Nobah took Qenath, and called it Nobah ; all which has no more meaning historically than if we were to say

[1] Num. xxxvi.   [2] Deut. iii. 14.

Elsass son of Germany conquered the land beyond the Rhine and called it Elsass, Lorraine also his brother captured cities in the same neighbourhood and called them Lorraine. In Judges, an attempt is made to throw the story still later, Jair a Gileadite gives thirty cities to his thirty sons and calls them Havvoth-Jair. This antique name survives in that region in the days of Solomon.[1]

250. The connection between Judah and the Gileadite district is further shown by the statement that Caleb had a concubine, Maachah[2] by whom he became father of certain districts, Madmannah, Macbenar in Judah, and Gibea', probably in Benjamin. This must either mean that Caleb conquered the Maacathite district,[3] and brought some of the inhabitants captive to Judah: or, which is more probable, that the Qenizzites as well as the Chezronites (see preceding paragraph) formerly dwelt in this region east of Jordan. Machir, who is called father of the district Gilead, is also said to have married the adjoining district Maachah;[4] but she is called sister of the Benjamites, Huppim and Shuppim. Consistently with this in 1 Chronicles viii. 29, the wife of the Benjamite father of Gibe'on is called Maachah too, which harmonises also with the previous statement.[5] That the name Maachah may have been in common use for women in the adjacent Geshurite district, and thence imported into Israel by David's marriage with a princess of that name[6] has no bearing on the interpretation of the name of a *district*, introduced us the name of a *woman* in primæval history.

---

[1] 1 Kings iv. 13.
[3] Deut. iii. 14; 2 Kings xxv. 22.
[5] 1 Chron. ii. 48, above.

[2] 1 Chron. ii. 48
[4] 1 Chron. vii. 15.
[6] 1 Chron. iii. 2.

251. About Sselophehad, a branch of the Manassites, a novelette of considerable interest is written in Numbers xxxvi., to support the entail of property, through the female branch, if the male heirs had died out. Before the absolute acquisition of the land to be inherited, questions of this sort are *primâ facie* unsuitable, for Joshua xvii. is evidence that the allotment to Manasseh and the settlement of Sselophehad's property really took place, if at all, some fifty years later, under Moses' successor. If we could restore 1 Chronicles vii. 15-19, we should see pretty clearly the source of this; for three of these five sisters, Machalh, Moleketh (= Milkah) and Ani'am (= No'am = No'ah; see par. 64) are represented as mothers of families in Manasseh, Shemida', Abiezer, and Cheleq (Lecheq, by metathesis), which in Numbers xxvi. 29-32, appear as contemporaries of their father. Elsewhere marriage is only reported where the mixture of tribes and races is intended, the allusion here to blending of families in the *same* tribe afforded opportunity for ascribing to Moses a law relative to the rights of heiresses, which can only be attributed to him by the common prolepsis, disguised under the sacred name of prophecy. Sselophehad, as an ancient tribal name, cannot be viewed as a compound = Shadow of Fear (Fear = God[1]); for we have seen that such, as Reuben, Ishmael, were not used in primitive times. The final -*d* is probably the generic final (par. 67), which leaves a root Ssilpach, recalling Zilpah, fabled concubine of Jacob, and mother of Gad and Asher, tribes contiguous to Eastern and Western Manasseh. We have already seen in Bilhan the origin of the other concubine, Bilhah.

[1] Gen. xxxi. 42, 53.

252. BENJAMIN.—No intimation is given in Genesis xxxv. 20, of the meaning which is intended to be conveyed by making Jacob call his twelfth son, Benjamin; the most natural interpretation is Son of Days = Son of my old Age, which like Reu-ben, See a Son, was thought so manifest as not to require a note. The literal meaning, Son of my Right-hand, finds support in the repeated statement that the sons of the *right-hand* were, on the *lucus a non lucendo* principle, remarkable for being left-handed.[1] Bney-Yamin means Sons of the *South*, just as Bney-Qedem stands for Saracens, Eastern Tribes. The only applicability of the name lies in their position *south* of *Joseph* with whom they are associated.[2] If the narrative in Exodus and Numbers is correct, the name is inappropriate. If Benjamin arrived at the Holy Land at the same time with Judah and the rest, his central position would have precluded the origin of the name, while his subsequent absorption in Judah as one tribe would have suggested Sons of the North, as more apposite, considering their relative geographical sites.

253. The district occupied by Benjamin was, in remoter times, the home of the sons of 'Anaq, which word[3] is not a man's name, but a race-name in the plural form.[4] These people are doubtless identical with 'Anah, a race of Se'irites, connected with 'Esau by marriage.[5] 'Anaq-im is a double plural, like 'Amaleq-im, who also are referred to 'Esau himself, known as 'Eseq.[6] Several Benjamite family names are, moreover, apparent in the Se'irite list; Ashbel;[7]

---

[1] Jud. ii. 15; xx. 16; 1 Chron. xii. 2.   [2] Ps. lxxx. 2.
[3] *Paw* Josh. xv. 13.   [4] See above, under Isaac.
[5] Gen. xxxvi. 2, 25.   [6] ? Gen. xxxvi. 12.
[7] 1 Chron. viii. 6.

cf, Shobal, its elder form,[1] as Shuthelach for Eshtelach.[2] The identity of Shobal with Ashbel is corroborated by 1 Chronicles viii. 1, 6, where Ashbel removes to Manachath; with this compare the statement of 1 Chronicles ii. 52, that the Manuchathites are descendants of Shobal, and Genesis xxxvi. 23, where the same descent is announced; though in Chronicles the reference is to Caleb as the later occupier of the Se'irite territory of Genesis. Shepho is a son of Shobal,[3] and the Shuppites are a Benjamite family;[4] the *M*uppin of Genesis is evidence of a slip, only possible when the books were written in the archaic character,[5] where Nacha*m* occurs for Nacha*sh* the *Bilhan* are also common to Seirites and Benjamites.[6]

254. Again, Benjamin in root and meaning is akin to Teman, a family of Esau,[7] and Esau is represented as marrying a daughter of 'Anah [8] though there are several mistakes in this verse, 'Anah being called *daughter* instead of son of Zibe'on [9] who himself is termed *Hivite* by mistake for Horite.[10] We find further a tribe of *Esauites* called Ye'ush, the same name occurring in connection with the *Se'irite* Bilhan and amongst the *Benjamites*[11] also with variations of anagram, Yo'ash [12] and Yeshua'.[13] This leads us to the belief that the territory of Benjamin was first occupied by Se'irites, when it was known as part of the land of 'Anaq, a race akin to the *Rephaim*, who accordingly alluded to 1 Chro-

[1] Gen. xxxvi. 20.
[2] See under Ephraim.
[3] Gen. xxxvi. 23.
[4] 1 Chron. vii. 12; Num. xxvi. 39.
[5] Cf. 236, 5.
[6] Gen. xxxvi. 27; 1 Chron. vii. 10.
[7] Gen. xxxvi. 11.
[8] Gen. xxxvi. 11.
[9] Gen. xxxvi. 24.
[10] Gen. xxxvi. 20.
[11] 1 Chron. viii. 10.
[12] 1 Chron. vii. 8.
[13] 1 Chron. viii. 4.

nicles viii. 2 as sons of, *i.e.*, dwellers in the land of Benjamin. Later the Edomites dwelt there till dispossessed by Qenizzites under Caleb, who in their turn moved further southwards to make room for the Benjamites, on the arrival of the Josephites from Egypt.

255. The usual supposition that the word 'Anaq means giant and that they were called Sons of Neck; *i.e.*, Long-necked savours, of the absurd, as Longshanks would be more appropriate: it testifies, however, to the difficulty attending attempts to find a derivation for 'Anaq, and to the influence of the simple etymologies given by the Hebrew writers. The same root survives in the Benjamin 'Anathoth, and Shamgar, the son of 'Anath. Cheyne,[1] refers these to an Assyrian root, Anu, the name of a male god, and supposes Anath to be a Phœnician goddess.[2] An inscription at Cyprus,[3] opens with a dedication to this god or goddess who is called the *strength* of life; the later Greek translation takes considerable liberties with the original, rendering Baal-shalom by Praxidemos, and 'Anath by Athena. If 'Anath was a God of Strength, we can see the significance in a powerful tribe taking this deity as their patron saint, and calling themselves after him or her; this, too would be in keeping with the constant reference to the marvellous physique of this people, in whose sight the children of Israel felt as grasshoppers.

256. When then we read[4] that Benjamin was formerly known as the children of 'Anah, we see that ethnological history is, as usual, conveyed in the form of family idyl. Natural and touching is the

[1] Isa. x. 30.
[2] See Sayce, "Hibbert Lectures," 187-190.
[3] C.I.S. 95
[4] Gen. xxxv. 18.

statement that the dying mother, in her throes, called the child "Son of my sorrow," Ben-'oni, and that the father, partly from pride at the birth of a son to him at his advanced age, and partly from a desire not to be daily and hourly reminded of his lost favourite wife, changed this name of ill-omen into Beneyamin, Son of Days. No one can fail to admire or to be moved by these pathetic touches of the Hebrew novelist, but no good reason can be alleged for supposing this instance to be an exception to the general rule; episodes are always ready to hand to represent historical changes of much later date. Observe, too, the high degree of improbability attending the conception that the Dodecad of Jacob's family should begin and end with affliction recorded in the names of the eldest and youngest sons: 'he looked on my affliction,' and 'son of my affliction.'

257. In I Chron. vii. 6–11, there is a list of Benjamites which is out of harmony with all the rest, but is worthy of careful attention for the following reasons. Beker is called one of Benjamin's sons, who is mentioned elsewhere, only in 2 Sam. xx. 1, and that incidentally, Sheba the Bikrite, the Benjamite; this then is a case of preservation of some old tribal name, not thought worthy of record in the other lists which possibly aim at a purer lineage; amongst his sons are the villages ʿAnathoth and ʿAlameth. More remarkable still is the avowal, in verse 10, that Benjamin had the following sons: Benjamin and Ehud along with Yeʿush[1] and Canaʿan and Tarshish, all of which are manifestly names of races and occupations, the two last probably meaning merchants and

---

[1] An Esauite tribe (see above).

mercantile marine. How then are we to account for the name of Benjamin recurring as a family name among the sections assigned to the tribe Benjamin itself? The only satisfactory explanation is, that the territory afterwards known as Benjamin was occupied by the Bilhites and Esauite Ye'ush, before the arrival of Benjamin in company with Joseph from the land of Egypt.

258. DAN.—"Judgment" appears to be a natural derivation, but from what association? Is it from the series of retaliations wreaked by the Danite Sampson in the south; or from Judges xvii. and xviii., where the Danites stole from Micah, the image molten from money already stolen by him from his mother; or because Rachel succeeded in retaliating on her sister Leah, obtaining a son by a substitute.[1] Is it not rather to be acknowledged that these stories are attached to this tribe on account of the previously determined derivation? From the story of his sister Dinah, we see that the notion of Judgment(= retribution) prevailed. Probably there was a deity of this name, or it may have been contracted from Adon(=Lord), in which case it would be akin to Yechudh, the patron-saint of Judah.

259. Of the Danite family, we have no genealogy. Chronicles is silent concerning him, unless with Bertheau, Dan is to be understood in the ambiguous expression (vii. 12), "Hushim the son of *another*." Hushim is the name of Dan's son in Gen. xlvi., where he occupies the same position between Muppim, Huppim and Ard, sons of Benjamin, and the sons of Naphthali. There can be no doubt that the genealogies are here

[1] Gen. xxx. 6.

intended to be identical, in fact, vii. 12 has a suspicious appearance of being inserted, after totally dissimilar matter, bodily from Genesis, and the Hushim in Chronicles must be held to be the Hushim of Genesis. It is, however, with Keil, very doubtless whether Dan is here, as Bertheau suggests, intentionally called "another," seeing that there is no shrinking from mentioning his name (ii. 2; xii. 35; xxvii. 22). A lacuna is attested by the Peschitto, and very probably some scribe after comparing Num. xxvi. 38 with Gen. xlvi. 21, unable to understand why this name of the *Benjamites* was omitted, wrote in the margin *Achiram*, afterwards mutilated into Acher = Another, and introduced into the main text, which doubtless originally ran:

> "Shuppim also and Huppim,
> The sons of 'Ir (= 'Ard)
> And the sons of Achir[am.
> The sons of Dan] Chushim."

There is only one man, Sibbeca, spoken of as a Chushite or Chushathite.[1].

260. In 1 Chron. viii. 8, 11, it is very strange that Achiram, there called Shacharaim, is said to have married a wife, Chushim, which should be an indication of Benjamite possession of a district formerly held by Danites. But in Num. xxvi. 38, instead of Chushim, the name is Shucham, which if it be the true reading, simply implies that the Danites seized a district formerly the home of the Shuchites, a Qeturite tribe, with which Caleb was intimately connected (iv. 11) and to which Bildad in the Book of Job was fabled to belong.

261. From Judges xiii. 25, xviii. 2, 11, we learn that

[1] 2 Sam. xxi. 18; xxiii. 27.

the Danites originally dwelt in the neighbourhood of Eshtaol and Zorah, a region peopled by Calebites,[1] which formerly belonged to the Se'irite Menuchathites[2] and was later occupied by Calebite Menuchathites.[3] The interest culminates in the statement that Sampson the Danite mythical hero, who dwelt between Eshtaol and Zorah, was the son of a *man*, *i.e.*, a Manuchathite. This raises doubts whether we ought not to read Manuchath-Dan instead of Machaneh-Dan = Camp of Dan, in Judges xiii. 25 ; xviii. 12.

262. NAPHTHALI.—Here we have a flagrant instance of a perverted derivation. Gen. xxx. 8 is wrong: "I have prevailed after mighty *contests* with my sister"; for the root is *Nepheth* (= a wooded height), not *Pathal* (= to contest with). The employment of the word in Joshua xi. 2; xii. 23, Nepheth-Dor, and again "three of the Nepheth," apparently Dor, Taanak and Megiddo (xvii. 11) shows this word to have been freely used in the North; in the South we find a modified form of it, Nepth, in Psalm xlviii. 2. Naphthali, then, a hilly district, received its name from this natural fact, and not from the circumstances attending the birth of his pretended ancestor, which occurred some two or three centuries earlier. These wooded heights are referred to in Jacob's Blessing,[4] which is translated by Ewald: "Naphthali is a luxuriant terebinth, beautifying the heights."

263. GAD.—Though Isaiah lxv. 11 would make the word appear of late use, its antiquity is attested by the

[1] 1 Chron. ii. 53.
[2] Gen. xxxvi. 23.
[3] 1 Chron. ii. 52–54.
[4] Gen. xlix. 21.

name Baal-Gad.[1] In the Phœnician inscriptions it appears in composition, Gad-no'am,[2] its meaning is unquestionably "Luck." Leah said,[3] "(I am) in luck," there is no need to read "Luck cometh," the Massoretes thought an Aleph was missing, and read "A troop cometh," taking Gad as a synonym of Gedhudh. Both this tribe and Asher were called after Gods of Luck. Dan, Naphthali, Gad and Asher are viewed by ancient tradition as of less pure Jacobean descent than the other tribes; and are accordingly relegated to concubines not wives of Jacob.

264. In the Moabite stone inscription, line x. we read, "And the men of Gad dwelt in the land of 'Ataroth, *from eternity*." If the story of the Israelites coming forth from the land of Egypt, in twelve tribes, is correct, the above words have no meaning. If the Moabites were the ancient occupants of the land, and dispossessed by the twelve tribes, who awarded it to Gad, as related in Joshua, it is inconceivable that Mesha should not rather have exulted at regaining Moab's ancient possession; he certainly had no motive for seeking to gratify the vanity of the people he had just vanquished. According to the Hebrew account Moab had dwelt there fully four centuries before Gad came on the scene; but, if we see no reason for doubting Mesha's unbiassed statement, we shall conclude that Gad must have been dwelling in Gilead at the very time that the Biblical narrative places him in Egypt.

265. ISSACHAR. — The root Sakar = bribe or tribute, is too tempting to escape notice. Accordingly

---

[1] Josh. xi. 17.   [2] C. I. S., 378, 383.   [3] Gen. xxxix. 11.

the tribal name was conferred because the mother Leah bribed Rachel with her son Reuben's love-apples,[1] and in Gen. xlix. 15, reference to it is made in the allusion to the tribe's paying tribute to Tyre and Sidon There is, however, a very different opinion formed of this tribe in Deut. xxxiii. 19:

> "They summon nations to the mountains,
> Where they offer righteous sacrifices,"

which is more consonant with 1 Chron. xii. 32, where the men of Issachar are described as "having understanding of the times, and knowing what Israel ought to do." I cannot suggest the probable derivation, but it might be looked for in the direction of some priestly or literary attribute, consistent with the description given above.

266. ZEBULUN.—Here we have another ancient plural, Zebulites, *cf.* Sime'on, Reuben, Chezron, &c. The root *dwelling* is not to be sought in a euphemistic expression, "Now will my husband dwell with me,"[2] but rather with the habitation of the sun and moon,[3] and is a relic of old Baal worship; compare the name Jezebel, daughter of Ethbaal[4] and C. I. S. 158. Baal-izbal, which the privative force of *I*-in Jezebel = *un*married, very doubtful. The connection of Zebul with marriage seems to be entirely based on Gen. xxx. 20, a very slight foundation. "The dwelling of Baal" is more the idea, as appears from Gen. xlix. 13: "Zebulun shall dwell," &c.

[1] Gen. xxx. 18.
[2] Gen. xxx. 20.
[3] *Cf.* Hab. iii. 11.
[4] 1 Kings xvi. 21.

CHAPTER VIII

SYNTHESIS

267. Though mathematical precision cannot be expected in the discussion of historical problems, where the points at issue are often very delicate, and where the direction of a subtle truth may be indicated by the slightest oscillation of the compass, or the weight of arguments decided by the faintest turn of the scale; still we may be allowed the use of mathematical expressions, and as in the preceding chapters we have analysed the material at our disposal, it is only fitting that we should proceed to reconstruct the disarranged facts in synthetical order. But before doing this, and as a preliminary to secure greater nicety in expression of the argument, I cannot refrain from following the example of the Great Master of Geometrical Reasoning, and accordingly set forth Postulates, Axioms, and Definitions which, I trust, will justify the investigations in the preceding pages, and elucidate subsequent conclusions.

268. Postulates. Let it be granted— .
   (1) That without irrefragable proof of *cause* to the contrary the history of any one nation may be investigated after the manner customary to research into the history of all other nations but that one.

The cause alleged why exception is to be made in favour of Hebrew History, is threefold; first, that the subject is often the direct Revelation of God; second, that the writers were inspired; third, that the events were handed down by tradition from eye-witnesses. On Revelation, see paragraphs 148, 162-164; on Inspiration, paragraphs 149-151; on Tradition, paragraph 46. As from the arguments there adduced, we can only accept a very modified definition of these factors, we conclude that no cause exists why we should believe otherwise than that the History of the Israelites is only one of many national histories, and has no authoritative claim to special treatment.

(2) That cumulative evidence in favour of the probability or improbability of the occurrence of events may establish their possibility or impossibility.

Thus the improbabilities attached to the accounts of the Ark, the One Holy Place (136-143), the High Priest's genealogy (110), and the Power and Functions of the High Priest (144-147), establish the impossibility of the historical accuracy of the descriptions of the High Priest and his office, given in the Priestly Code, and purporting to be of Mosaic origin. Kuenen says:[1] "It is not only our right, but our duty to invoke the aid of historical probability, and to allow it a second vote in deciding the result."

(3) That when given derivations of names are puerile, search may be made for more reasonable and suitable etymologies.

On this it will suffice to refer to Gilead (81), Isaac (189), Reuben (200), Judah (228), Naphthali (262), &c.

[1] I. 139.

269. Axioms.
  (1) All History is more or less biassed (40).
  (2) The manifest presence of a religious bias vitiates history more than the presence of any other deflecting element.
  (3) Constant Prolepsis in history is evidence of late authorship.
  (4) The persistent and consistent silence of history as to any given national custom is proof that at the period described, such had not come into force.
  (5) Evidence of manufactured narrative is proof of ignorance of times described by later writers.
  (6) Stories based on improbable derivations of names are unworthy of historical credence.
  (7) Exaggeration in figures is evidence of unreliable sources or even conscious manufacture.
  (8) Two conflicting accounts cannot both be true.
  (9) Of two conflicting traditions, that has more credibility which is opposed to the general manifest aim and purpose of the history in which it is preserved.
  (10) Unsuccessful attempts in a history, to explain away difficulties or inconsistencies, are evidence of the serious nature of the latter, and their ancient recognition.
  (11) The history of a nation, written by its own authors, will *not* uniformly *vilify* its particular heroes.
  (12) The history of a nation, written by its rival, requires specially careful criticism, being *a priori* unreliable.

270. Definitions.

(1) Genealogy is a Family Tree, showing the main and side issues in descent from a given stock.

(2) Hebrew Genealogy is a list of Races, Tribes, and Towns, which are arranged geographically, with some regard to a traditional order of their historical existence.

(3) Marriage is the union of two human beings of opposite sex, to preserve the sacredness of family connection.

(4) Marriage in Hebrew Genealogy is the union of two races or districts by the conquest of the weaker, or, as in some cases, by the dispossession of the old by the new.

(5) Birth is the reproduction of the human race, properly the fruit of marriage.

(6) Birth in Hebrew Genealogy is the offshoot of one tribe, or the reception of strange tribes into a common league, or the erection of towns and villages.

(7) Incest is an improper marriage connection between people of too close a degree of natural consanguinity.

(8) Incest in Hebrew Genealogy is the mixing of tribes of pure Jacobean descent with Aborigines, or even with other tribes claiming common descent from Abram.

271. The following I claim to be somewhat the form assumed by the early history of Israel, a lost tradition, unexpectedly decipherable in the dry pages of confused genealogy, and so manifestly at variance with the very aim and object of the Hexateuch narrative, that by axiom 9, we cannot refuse to award to it the palm of truth. As we examine the *disjecta membra*, turned up by spadefuls in the exploration of this antiquated mound of apparent rubbish, we discover that they are not solitary relics of different individual legends, but that there is observable a continuity and manifest relation, by having regard to which we are able to collect and at length satisfactorily to fit together the scattered bones of the shattered skeleton.

272. About 3000 B.C. the Canaanites dwelt on the shore of Palestine, the Amorites on the hill-lands of Ephraim and Judah; the sons of Anaq in Benjamin; while scattered tribes in villages were known as Perizzites. East of the Jordan, were the Zamzummim and Emim; in the neighbourhood of the Dead Sea, the Rotenu or Lotan = Children of Lot. In a southerly direction lay the Se'irite or Horite race, Troglodytes or cave-dwellers, for which Sayce prefers white men, as opposed to their successors, the red men, approving the derivation of the name of Edom, from the distinctive ruddiness of the race, instead of the natural characteristic of the soil, red-sandstone.

273. Some centuries later, new names occur. Hyksos, or Isaacites, are found in Judah; Ammonites and Moabites supplant the Zamzummim and Emim; Edomites dispossess the Horites; Ishmaelites swarm in Philistia, and Midianites in Arabia. All these newcomers claim to be descended from one great Hebrew hero, Abram, who migrated from the far east; or a more modified relationship with him is asserted, as in the case of the Ammonites and Moabites.

274. Years roll on, and Qenizzites and Judites

Gradual appearances of Jacobean Tribes 259

appear in the north, both east (249) and west (244) of the Jordan; Reubenites occupy the land of Judah and Benjamin (201); a section of Jacobeans is found in Ishmaelite Philistia, adopting the name Simeon as a modification of Ishmael (203). Other smaller tribes of Jacobeans are scattered about, and, like the tribe of Dan, seek a secure home where the natural configuration of the country shall offer protection to the paucity of their numbers. A remarkable race, not yet definitely enrolled in the Jacobean League is seen freely sprinkled all over the country. Its name is Qenite, its national characteristic, religion, and its chiefs are known as Lewan (Levites). But few of the Hyksos are to be found, as they have settled in Egypt.

276. The Hyksos had strange experiences in Egypt. Their period of prosperity and supremacy is represented in the Genesis idyl, as the rule of the man Joseph. They were, however, dispossessed by the eighteenth dynasty, who proceeded to oppress them. After a futile attempt, with the aid of other Hyksos, to recover their lost position, they were driven across the last Egyptian province of Mafka, long miscalled the Sinaitic Peninsula,[1] and permitted to escape into the land of Midian and Edom. Two of their most important tribes were known by names, whose derivations betray testimony to the accuracy of Manetho's statement that they were forcibly *expelled*, viz., Gershon (217) and Manasseh (248). Their leader was Moses, the Qenite whose return from Midian in the Exodus story is probably to be identified with the response to the call for succour, narrated by Manetho as made upon the Hyksos of Jerusalem. As

[1] Sayce, "Verdict," p. 271.

Jerusalem was at that time a Jebusite city, Manetho can only be supposed to employ the name of that town for the whole district of which it was the capital in his own day, meaning thereby the Hebrew race in the neighbourhood of Palestine. The fugitives, after wandering about, up and down, on the east of Jordan, elect to cross that river near Jericho, *south* of the then Judite territory.

276. After the conquest of several strong cities, under the leadership of their hero, Joshua = Victory, an arrangement becomes necessary with the Jacobeans already resident in Palestine. Solemn meetings are for this purpose held at Shiloh, and finally confirmed at Shechem,[1] where the Jacobeans and Josephites in the most solemn manner swear allegiance to Yahveh, and *thenceforth* become known as one race, Israel, warriors of Yahveh. This, in idyllic form, is narrated in Genesis as the change of the man's name from Jacob to Israel, after the *birth* of Joseph. The Reubenites, who are unable to cope with the Aborigines in the districts of Chezron and Carmel, are glad to move into a district east of Jordan to the south of Gad, already pacified by the Josephites. The Judites agree to go south,[2] and leave the region known as Ephraim (the Fruitful) to the Josephites, who later[3] complain that their limits are too confined, and obtain permission to acquire property "in the land of the Perizzites and Rephaim," where a section of their tribe settles, calling itself Benjamin or Southerners. In Genesis, this is described as the birth of a son Benjamin, *after*

---
[1] Josh. xviii. 1; xxiv. 1.
[2] This, though somewhat misstated, is referred to in Josh. xiv.
[3] Josh. xvii. 15.

the change of Jacob's name to Israel; and the name first given to the latest born of Jacob's sons, is Ben-'oni, or Sons of 'Anaq = Rephaim; while in 1 Chronicles viii. 2, Rapha, a son of Benjamin, unmentioned in the Hexateuch, is clearly an allusion to Rephaite families still remaining in that locality. The history of Israel Proper, opens with the close of the Hexateuch.

277. Let us now invoke, the aid of archæology to appraise the value to be attached to the details of the above sketch. Considerable satisfaction has recently been expressed by conservative and orthodox writers, at the identification of Amraphel of Genesis xiv. with Khammurabi of Assyrian monuments.[1] We need not concern ourselves with the discussion of the date at which this episode was incorporated into the Hebrew story; but are content to accept the decision of critics who have made styles of Hebrew Literature their special study, that this composition. has nothing in common with the recognised styles of J., E., D., and P. The date of Khammurabi is fixed by Assyriologists as about B.C. 2350. Abram's migration cannot well be put much later, if he was already established in the neighbourhood of Palestine, when he routed the host of that Babylonian monarch.

278. Kuenen accepts 1325 B.C. as the approximate date of the Exodus.[2] The great festival held in honour of the conclusion of a Sothic Cycle would at once be a motive for clearing Egypt of strangers, and a source of confidence in the chance of victory, if any encounter should arise. *One thousand* years, then, at least, elapse

---

[1] See Addenda to Schrader and Sayce "Verdict," p. 165.
[2] See above, 178.

between the lives of Abram and Moses. Sayce throws the Exodus even still later, and yet only *five* lives are reported to have existed between these two heroes. The 'Verdict of the Monuments' appears, in no uncertain voice, to condemn the literal acceptation of the detailed human history given in Genesis. If, on the other hand, we admit that in the story of Genesis we have the history of tribes, an average of a couple of hundred years apiece will not come amiss. The difficulty of an impossible rate of propagation observable in the races claiming descent from Abram (106, 107) is removed.

279. Zoan was founded by the Hyksos, about B.C. 1806;[1] Qirjath-Arba', the home of the Ribqite Hyksos, seven years earlier. There would therefore be an interval of 500 years between Abram and Isaac, which is mildly indicated[2] by assigning the age of 100 to Abram at the birth of his son. Thus corroboration is afforded to the statement[3] that these great ages assigned to the patriarchs are not to be taken as proof of the belief of the original authors in their exceptional longevity, but as testimony to the difficulty, of which they were conscious,[4] in bridging over the abyss of time, which they saw yawning before them. It is also to be noted that Egyptian kings are described as reigning for periods, which would not be out of place in quite modern history; the old-fashioned argument, that mankind in its infancy attained greater ages than at present, finds no support. There is no doubt that the Hyksos present one of those problems, for the solution of which we can only patiently await the

---

[1] Sayce, "Ancient Empires," p. 33. [2] Gen. xxi. 5.
[3] Par. 97. [4] Axiom 7.

discoveries of archæologists; but from Josephus to the present day, there has been a keen sense of the necessity of recognising some intimate connection between them and the Hebrew race. The subsequent joining of Joseph in Egypt by his eleven brethren, appears only to represent a later advent of Hebrew races, when the Hyksos were firmly established in that kingdom.

280. The events attending the Exodus have been seen (177, 179), fanciful and unreal, while "Dr. Neubauer has pointed out that the Song (of Miriam) contains a curious piece of Edomitish colouring" (in the use of the word Alluphim), and Sayce gives strong arguments in favour of a site for Sinai[1] in the neighbourhood of Midian and Edom, already hinted at by Wellhausen.[2] The presence of Jethro in this vicinity corroborates the hypothesis that the Mosaic form of religion was derived from Qenites; the old idea of Egyptian influence is now exploded.[3] In investigating the history of the Passover, we have found reason to agree with Wellhausen and others, in the belief that there were originally two feasts connected with the opening of the solar year (128, 132), but these were of great antiquity, long prior to the time of Moses. Further, that the detail of the death of the firstborn in Egypt is due to a reminiscence of the sacrifice of firstborn at the Equinox, at which time the Israelites were driven out of Egypt. A confusion of this sort is not to be expected in history based on coeval tradition, but is quite explicable, if the result of later research. The sacrifice of Egyptian Firstborn further suggested a requital for some mischief previously perpetrated on the

[1] "Verdict," pp. 265-272.   [2] Israel 430, n 2.   [3] Sayce.

Hyksos, and this with the necessity for discovering some occasion for the exposure of Moses on the river Nile, an expedient in itself very commonly adopted, for the introduction of a hero of unknown antecedents, gave rise to the story of the massacre of Hebrew infants (177).

281. The Forty Years' Wandering (179) is eked out, with ritual and legislation of a much later date. The stories that illustrate this period are all to the honour and glory of Moses and the priestly tribe, and of Joshua, the subsequent leader of the Josephites. The only prominent allusions to other tribes are made occasions to record fact to their discredit, based on later jealousies, as the pretensions of the Reubenites to royalty, and of the Qorachites to highpriestly office. The specious accuracy with which specific figures are given of a census, held on two occasions, is well exposed by Kuenen, who shows that, in spite of lapse of time, the sum total remains unaltered, itself a suspicious circumstance; while it is truly remarkable to observe how, in so short a space of time, small tribes have waxed sufficiently to take a first-class rank, and large tribes have dwindled into insignificance. The greater part of Numbers is attributed to the Priestly Code, but the pre-existence of traditional stories belonging to this period is attested by Deuteronomy and the Prophets, though sufficient antiquity is not thereby ensured to prove authoritative.

282. That all the twelve tribes went down into Egypt, and thence issued again at the Exodus, and all arrived at the same time at Palestine, is a story confined to the Hexateuch. In the Prophets and Psalms, allusions to the Exodus are in a significant manner

reserved for the Josephite section, to whom alone they are considered appropriate. Psalm lxxxii. 3 : "Thou that leddest Joseph like a sheep, stir up thy strength .... before Ephraim, Benjamin and Manasseh." Psalm lxxxi. 6 : "A solemn covenant made he with Joseph, when he came forth from the land of Egypt." In Hosea xi. 1 the phrase "called my son out of Egypt" is immediately explained by verse 3, "I also taught Ephraim to walk," *cf.* also xii. 9.

283. Again, the expression "Jacob and Joseph" must be of great antiquity, as, in the light of historical events, we should have expected Judah and Joseph, in reference to these two kingdoms. We look in vain in the Hexateuch for a scintilla of light as to the reason why Judah should be known as Jacob, and Joseph as Israel; more consonant with the family idyl would have been a constant use of the terms, sons of Leah, and sons of Rachel, respectively. If the name, Israelites, had been common to the race from remote antiquity, its restriction to the Josephite section, in the expression Israel and Judah, even before the rupture between the two kingdoms,[1] cannot appear natural. Nor do the longlived, almost eternal jealousy and hostility between the two kingdoms, and the assertion that the birthright was Joseph's (243), accord with the tradition set forth in the Hexateuch, that they had shared prosperity and oppression in Egypt, miraculously escaped thence, and together borne the hardships of the Wilderness, after which the conquest of Canaan was their joint labour and glory. Surely one cannot conceive a more complete series of links in a chain to bind two tribes of one race indissolubly together ; one could not devise a more

---

[1] 2 Sam. xi. 11; 1 Kings iv. 20, 25.

thorough process of welding to unify the most antagonistic and refractory atoms. It is opposed to the lightest shade of probability, that twelve small tribes should have succeeded in keeping their families separate in the midst of the debasing slavery described, and should have desired to maintain individual interests in the face of powerful foes, and should have allowed petty jealousy to urge them into a suicidal severance of national policy, when danger passed the watchword, " Union is Strength."

284. On the other hand, if the Jacobeans did not go down into Egypt, all these difficulties vanish. Judah, as the prominent tribe in Canaan would naturally retain the name Jacob. The name Israel, devised at Shechem (276), by Joshua or Phinehas, for the league there formed would more easily be employed as a synonym for the Josephites, whose advent had provided the occasion for its introduction; while the fact that Shechem was chosen [1] for the dissolution of this bond, greatly corroborates the accuracy of the hypothesis that the league between Yahveh and Israel solemnised by Joshua, is the original occasion of the choice of a new national name for the scattered units. We now see that the absence of the name, Israel, on Egyptian monuments is only what was to be expected, as the Hebrews in Egypt had not yet adopted it. Thus the ' Verdict of the Monuments ' affords negative support to the theory here advanced.

285. Further, the discrepancy between the narratives of the Colonisation of Canaan, as reported in the Book of Judges, and of the Conquest of Canaan, as depicted in the Book of Joshua, is accounted for;

[1] 1 Kings xii. 1.

and the pre-Mosaic narratives of Ehud, Tola, Jair, and other judges, become natural if the Jacobean tribes remained in Palestine during the Hyksos and Hebrew epoch of Egyptian history. Ehud is described[1] as the grandson of Benjamin, when he should have been in Egypt and not Palestine. He is rather the name for some Judite section (229) dwelling in the region afterwards occupied by Benjamin. His father, Gera, probably signifies merely that the Judites felt themselves or were known by the Jebusites as "strangers and sojourners." If we accept the total destruction of Jericho by Joshua, without regard to details, as historical, we have in the occupation of that city by Moab[2] further indication of a pre-Mosaic date, which more than counterbalances the slight anachronism (327) of substituting Israel for Jacob. Renan[3] rightly asserts that Tola and Elon are sections *not judges* of the tribes Isaachar and Zebulun, respectively. As evidence of his antiquity, Tola is called great-grandson of Issachar,[4] but even this appears to be an attempt to modernise him,[5] as Tola is coeval with Puah; and we must not forget that, though these lists are composed of tribal names, their claim to any title of genealogy is their attempt to preserve some historic sequence.[6] Jair again was a district in Gilead, first occupied by Judites (249). This northern site for Judah is confirmed by his residence in Ephraim (244), which must have been pre-Mosaic. It is well known that in Judges i., where the same conquests are recorded as given in Joshua, Judah and Caleb occupy the place of Joseph and Joshua. The reason why

[1] Jud. iii. 15.   [2] Jud. iii. 13.   [3] i. 337.
[4] Jud. x. i.   [5] Num. xxvi, 23.   [6] Def. 2.

Judah went up *first*[1] is partly that it was necessary for Judah to move down from the north, *before* room could be made for Joseph, without friction or collision, and partly as an indication of his *priority* on the scene. The note that these events took place after the death of Joshua is more an author's connecting link with a preceding chapter, than a correct indication of historic sequence, being, moreover, flatly contradicted by verses 9-15. The Calebite conquest of Chezron and Carmel falls naturally in the days of Joshua, when the removal of Reuben from the same district to the East of the Jordan also took place; though the man Caleb, with his experiences as a truthful spy, is a pure fabrication, and the acquiescence of Moses in Reuben's desire to occupy the land south (?) of Gad, an absolute fiction. Ewald had some inkling of the facts underlying the above theory, for he speaks[2] of Judah's turning *back* to the south, which acknowledges a previous more northerly site, formerly in his possession.

286. To the pre-Mosaic history of the Jacobeans must also be referred the capture of Shechem by Simeon, in conjunction with Qenites (203), and the incident of the loss of Judah's earlier sections, who failed to dispossess the newly-arrived Philistines from Gath;[3] though, later, the occupation of Moresheth-Gath and Akzibh was successfully accomplished.[4] The latter episode is reported as occurring to the tribe of Ephraim, for the expedition set forth from that region, when occupied by Judah (244). In Genesis xxxviii. these facts are narrated as incidents in the family of the man

---

[1] Jud. i. 1.
[2] ii. 307.
[3] 1 Chron. vii. 21.
[4] 1 Chron. iv. 21.

Sihon and Og doubtful contemporaries

Judah, and two of his sons, Er and Onan, die prematurely for disregarding the Law of Moses, a proleptic crime, while Shelah lives to grow up, but apart from his father, who subsequently begets the Perizzite and Chezronite races. As in Shelah, we have no difficulty in recognising the success of the Shelanites in the vicinity of Philistia, so we need not scruple to identify the fatal raid on Gath with the early demise of Judah's elder-born sons.

287. Ancient poetry, probably a part of the lost Book of Vasher, testifies[1] to a conquest of Moab by Sihon, King of the Amorites. Whether or not the conquest of these Amorite possessors of Moab by Moses is a fact, must appear doubtful, when we remember that Balaq (itself a doubtful name, as Belqa is the name of the district to this day), king of Moab summoned Balaam, king of Edom, to his assistance against the Josephites; which combination is further complicated by the slaughter of the Midianites, among whose slain is found the corpse of Balaam. If Sihon was king of Heshbon, Ar, &c., where was the king of Moab's seat of power? Again, if the latter was in a state of subjection, why did he not seek the assistance of the Hebrews, in accordance with every historical precedent? Another legendary, foreign here, is Og, king of Bashan, whose conquest is also assigned to Moses. In view of the confusion and inconsistencies observed above, and of the errors demonstrated in the history of the conquest of Canaan by Joshua, we can only accept these stories as *vaguely* recalling some heroic struggle between Hebrews and other races, but of *uncertain* date. Perhaps some day

---

[1] Num. xxi. 28.

the very sarcophagus of Og[1] may be exhumed, and an inscription like that of Aschmanuzar may enable us to fix his date.

288. It may be as well here to collect a few references to various critics, as showing that many of the details of the above synthetic theory, have already been exercising the minds of men.[2] "The author of the Book of Origins, who, with the eagle glance of his legislative wisdom, discerns as the weak point of the national settlement the scattered and isolated condition of the tribes beyond the Jordan; and therefore *makes* Moses hesitate in giving his assent to their settling there" (298). "Respecting the division of the cities between Gad and Reuben, a discrepancy exists between these two earliest authorities, which we find it difficult to reconcile" (300). "It will be presently seen that this eastern direction was that in which the tribes in later times spread most widely." Ewald thus admits that the history of the Hexateuch, as regards the trans-Jordanic tribes, is unreliable.[3] "If this tribe (Judah), like Joseph, remained at first in *Central* Canaan . . . . Judah directed his marches first against Galilee . . . . but he turns towards the south." Ewald thus corroborates the northerly and central positions occupied by Judah, before he withdrew to the south.

289. Wellhausen (430), "To a not very numerous people, such an undertaking presented no great difficulty" (431). "For a civilised community of from two to three millions, such a settlement would, of course, have been impossible." The Josephites alone coming forth from Egypt instead of the twelve tribes, relieves this felt difficulty (442). "It might be

---

[1] Deut. iii. 11.   [2] Ewald ii. 303.   [3] ii. 284.

supposed that Judah had not taken the longer route to the eastward of the Dead Sea at all" (30). "Sacred localities are so well known to the narrator, and are punctually and accurately recorded, notwithstanding the 400 years of the Egyptian sojourn, which otherwise would have made their identification a matter of some little difficulty" (pp. 188, 189). "Israel (Joseph) was the cradle of prophecy; Samuel, Elijah, Elisha, exercised their activity there; what contemporary figure from Judah is there to place alongside of them? Assuredly the author of the Book of Kings would not have forgotten them, had any such there been; he is a Judæan with all his heart, yet is compelled, purely by the nature of the case, to interest himself chiefly about the northern kingdom" (p. 333). "Herder's theory of the development of history out of genealogy will not apply here." Unfortunately I have not had the opportunity of consulting this work.

290. Kuenen (i. 113): "Our present investigation does not concern the question whether there existed men of those names, but whether the progenitors of Israel and of the neighbouring nations who are represented in Genesis, are historical personages. It is this question which we answer in the negative" (115). "It is not impossible that a single tribe had preceded them thither" (121); "a few slight touches furnish us with proof that the Israelites were supported by the nomadic tribes of Arabia, that is to say, by the Hyksos." Yes, but did these claim descent from Abram? (p. 122); "the drowning of the newborn sons can scarcely be accepted as history" (133); "as yet there is no such thing as an *Israelitish* nation, the unity of the people is as yet unborn, and only comes into being by degrees,

under Samuel and the first kings. How is this possible, we ask, if the twelve tribes have been united and have acted as one man, first, for forty years under Moses, and then for some time under Joshua (134)?" "Events, which in reality were distributed over a very long period, deeds which were achieved by more than one generation, and mostly by particular tribes, were compressed by tradition into a very short space of time, and were ascribed to all Israel . . . . if in the course of time the boundaries of the domains of the separate tribes were frequently modified according to tradition, Joshua fixed them as they existed centuries afterwards" (138). "Entirely dismiss the idea that all Israelites were sons of Israel [1] (143). "Therefore, in order to form a correct idea of the history of this period (Judges) we must free ourselves as much as possible from the views of the author."

291. Renan (i. 109): "Beni-Israel, an asylum among Hebrew races as Rome amongst the tribes of Latium" (112). "After the establishment of Israel in Canaan, we shall be struck with the superiority of the Josephites over the rest of the Beni-Israel" (141); "it is not impossible that the origin of the name, Joseph (= addition, conjunction, annexation), should be sought in this circumstance, that the first emigrants and their families had become, as it were, strangers to their brethren, and required a sort of rejunction to become once more part of the family of Israel" (155). "One is led to believe that some of the Beni-Israel, at least, the Josephites, had a share in the deeds, and participated in the favours of the Hyksos" (161). "But it is also possible that all these stories of the Exodus where a fable has

---

[1] *Cf.* Romans ix. 6: "For they are not all Israel which are of Israel."

penetrated to such an extent, may be still more mythical than one generally supposes, and that it is only necessary to preserve the simple fact of the Exodus of Israel from Egypt." These specimens will suffice to show that, in my hypothesis, I have merely followed in the footsteps of these four, the greatest of critics in the field of Hebrew History. I have, however, I trust, not made a servile use of their labours; I have not scrupled to deviate to the right or the left, and may claim, whether successfully or not, to have broken new ground, especially in the matter of derivations, and the paramount importance to be attributed to this factor, as determining the value and date of the historical compositions.

292. It will doubtless be asked, "Why should the *old* tradition, traces of which are occasionally perceptible in poetical and prophetical writings, and even in history and genealogy, have been deliberately ignored or purposely obscured by native authors?" The reply to this objection is exceedingly simple. The History of Israel was written in the North. The two earliest editions, J and E, Yahvist and Elohist histories, are attributed to Josephite authors; the latter unanimously, while on the former opinions are divided (230). The standpoint of the authors is uniformly hostile to Jacob, Judah and Reuben.[1] It is not till after the birth of Joseph, that, in the Genesis story, Jacob becomes a reformed, or in modern parlance, a converted, man. His new character is assumed with his new name, Israel; previous to that event, his story is not a model, but a beacon.

293. As regards Judah, the mixed elements

[1] "Axioms," 11, 12.

of his race are the subject for scorn, the Perizzites and Chezronites are the offspring of his incestuous connection with his daughter-in-law, Tamar; his occupation of the Carmelite and Chezronite districts, on their evacuation by the Rechoboth (Reuben) is depicted as the marriage of his descendant Salmon with the harlot Rachab, who, further to pile up the agony, is represented as a denizen of the doomed city, Jericho; in the untimely death of his two sons, alluded to above, occasion is found for the manifestation of Divine wrath; when it is desired to find an historical association for the name 'Akar, sufficiently evident in the repulse from before 'Ai, the cause of the defeat is brought home to "'Akar, the son of Carmi, the son of Zabdi, the son of Zerach, the son of Judah,"[1] where the given genealogy teems with difficulties. Victories may be taken away from the credit of Judah and claimed by Joseph;[2] but disaster is impossible to Joseph, and must therefore be attributed to Judah.

294. As regards Reuben, we have seen that his presence in the land of the Bilhites, afterwards occupied by Benjamin, is described as incestuous connection between the man Reuben and his father's concubine, a sort of fostermother to Benjamin; and above his intimate connection with the tribe of Judah, has provided opportunity, not neglected, for the reprobation of his name, though in a slight disguise, by means of the story of Rachab, the harlot. In the forty years' wanderings, outside the jealousies of the Levite sections, Reubenites alone are held up to public contumely as rebels; and a sudden convulsion of the earth is requisitioned to leave an indelible impress of Divine

[1] Josh. vii. 18. [2] Josh. x. 36-39.

Judah's Acquiescence in Misrepresentation 275

wrath and rejection, in the history of a tribe, which, by its hoary age, could best dispute with Joseph the claim to the birthright. Jealousy and hostile bias mark the author's attitude towards the four eldest sons of Jacob, for Levi and Simeon are obsecrated in their fabled father's fictitious blessing. That there is an intentional motive, not innocent unconsciousness, in the compilation of these stories, is manifest, not only from the undisputed evidence of malicious purpose in a very similar story told of the birth of Moab and Ammon, but from the careful avoidance of the employment of the same method in the case of Benjamin; when it is necessary to describe the fact that Benjamin occupied the previous home of the sons of 'Anaq, recourse is not had to the expedient of introducing the crime of incest, but a pathetic tale, accounting for the change of race by a change of name in the same person, is inserted.

295. But it may be futher asked, "Why should Judah acquiesce in this misrepresentation of his early history?" In the course of desultory reading, I came across the following passage in Jessop's "Studies by a Recluse" (p. 261), which appears to provide an excellent parallel in more modern history. Speaking of a work by M. Fustel de Coulanges, "Recherches sur quelques problèmes d'histoire," he says, "It has dawned upon the new generation of intelligent Frenchmen, that all this talk about a German immigration—a colonisation—a settlement of a whole people with their wives and children upon French soil in the fifth century, whereby all the institutions of the invaded lands were moulded according to the pattern of things beyond the Rhine, is a mere German figment, a specimen of mere German brag and bluster." Read

Joseph for German, and Judah for French, and we have an almost identical condition of affairs with the one I have been endeavouring to describe. If the French as a race, have been content for nearly 1500 years to accept the German story of their own early history, why should it be deemed incredible that Judah failed to repudiate the perverted story of their ancestors.

896. There remains, however, the main factor, in the history which reconciled Judah to its acceptance, and that is its religious character. The real history of Israel began with the solemn league and covenant at Shechem; and there and then, Judah and the other tribes swore allegiance to Yahveh, and accepted the modified form of ancient Hebrew religion, proclaimed by Moses' follower and probable descendant Phinehas. The redistribution of the country, effected by mutual arrangement between Joshua and the powerful Calebites, would tend by change of scene to loosen the traditional memories of Judah. By means of heroic songs, and instruction from the Qenite Lewan, who were chiefly from the north, while the warrior Qenites were in the south; all the tribes would readily believe that their ancestors experienced the bondage of Egypt, and date back their national existence to the era of Joseph, the Exodus. As gradually the traditions of the early national history were embellished with stories of miraculous divine interposition, and as the observance of Sabbath, Passover, and all national feasts was by degrees thrown back to that event, it would indeed be surprising, if any man of Judah or Reuben had had the temerity or the desire, to cut himself off from the accepted form of Universal Israelite history.

CHAPTER IX

HEBREW AND CHINESE HISTORY AND RELIGION : A PARALLEL

297. Of the gay young Israelite cavalier, we are told (2 Sam. xviii. 18) that "Absalom in his lifetime had reared up, for himself, a pillar ; for he said, I have no son to keep my name in remembrance." As we gaze on the Pyramids of Egypt, or the Winged Bulls of Assyria ; on the pillars at Karnak and Palmyra, or the temples hewn in solid rock in Mexico, and Hindustan, we hear voices from the most distant antiquity, in whispers growing fainter and still more faint, declare, "These are the pillars we reared in our lifetime, to keep our names in remembrance against the time when our national existence should have become extinct." Two highly civilised races whose history can be traced back back for four millenniums, can boast no such everlasting monuments of Art and Architecture; but as a solace for lack of notoriety in this particular direction, they are conspicuous for the preservation of their individual life and characteristics, language and relation. As far as the east is from the west, these two races are sundered geographically by the full width of the vast

CHAPTER IX

HEBREW AND CHINESE HISTORY AND
RELIGION: A PARALLEL

297. Of the gay young Israelite cavalier, we are told (2 Sam. xviii. 18) that "Absalom in his lifetime had reared up, for himself, a pillar; for he said, I have no son to keep my name in remembrance." As we gaze on the Pyramids of Egypt, or the Winged Bulls of Assyria; on the pillars at Karnak and Palmyra, or the temples hewn in solid rock in Mexico, and Hindustan, we hear voices from the most distant antiquity, in whispers growing fainter and still more faint, declare, "These are the pillars we reared in our lifetime, to keep our names in remembrance against the time when our national existence should have become extinct." Two highly civilised races whose history can be traced back back for four millenniums, can boast no such everlasting monuments of Art and Architecture; but as a solace for lack of notoriety in this particular direction, they are conspicuous for the preservation of their individual life and characteristics, language and relation. As far as the east is from the west, these two races are sundered geographically by the full width of the vast

istic of conceit attributed freely to Chinese and Jews arises in precisely the same way; they are satisfied with the wisdom of their forefathers, Europeans refuse to welcome them on an equal platform; there is nothing for them, therefore, but to be content with their own aims and reflections; they receive the arrows of insolence on the shield of calm indifference. If, occasionally, self-assertion replaces self-conceit, what marvel? Individual men and nations are alike subservient to the primary Laws of Nature. Force may be transmitted but cannot die; the angle of refraction equals the angle of incidence, &c. The more you endeavour to repress a man or a race, the more, if there is any elastic vitality left in him, will he rebound, and the height of his bounce will be in direct ratio to the energy employed in keeping him down. But there is no conceit, no bumptiousness amongst the favoured of Society! Undoubtedly, but it causes amusement, not offence, and, when not very pronounced, will escape the notice of any but outsiders. In the same way, the foibles of Western nations are mutually treated with forbearance, the pompous pride of the Britisher, the swagger of the Frenchman, afford each other occasion for playful satire, while both combine to denounce the self-complacency of the Jew and the Chinaman. We want the Roman satirist with his apt rebuke, " Quid rides ? Mutato nomine de te fabula narratur."

301. Another point of comparison between these two races is their tenacity of historic life. No conquest, no massacre, no oppressive severity has succeeded in crushing or sweeping them out of existence. In Europe the Goths and the Huns were practically absorbed in the countries of their ravaging conquests; barbarism

exulting in its might being obliged finally to succumb before the influence of existing civilisation. Similarly in China, Mongols and Manchus have successively conquered and governed China; the most famous instances being the Yuan dynasty, which was contemporary with the period from John to Edward III.; and the present Ts'ing dynasty which assumed the dominion about the time of our Civil War, and is still in power. The religion and language of the Chinese are not interfered with; the substitution of the *queue* for the coiffure on the top of the head is the only outward visible sign of the displacement of the native paramount influence. The Chinese race dwells where it did; and if the natives of 2000 B.C. were to revisit the earth now, though they could not recognise the dress or understand the dialect of the present day, they would find no change in the daily religious observances and points of etiquette, which receive the same regard as ever and in unaltered form. The anomalous effect of conquest on China Proper has been extension into the Chinese Empire; China has not been added to Mongolia, but Thibet, Mongolia and Manchuria have become annexed to the Chinese Empire. As regards ritual, the Jews, on the other hand, deliberately discarded a large amount of the practices and aids to religion deemed essential by their forefathers, but which their later sages denounced as idolatrous; so that Hebrew services, as seen now, do not carry us back to the same remote period as Chinese rites. A contrast, too, is manifest as regards their national preservation; the Jews for nearly two thousand years have been strangers to their native land, but their internal, social, and religious life is unaltered.

The striking anomaly in their case is that dismemberment and dispersion, which in a few generations would suffice to obliterate the identity of any other race, have had no appreciable effect towards producing the extinction of the Hebrew nation. As this is undoubtedly due to their ritual observances, may we not suggest that if the Mosaic Ritual had been formulated as common tradition asserts nearly 1400 B.C. it would be unaccountable that the Ten Tribes, possessed of the same distinguishing daily practices and hedged in by the same peculiar rites and ceremonies, should have been so completely lost; while, further, the fact of the utter disappearance of these, provides additional motive for the institution of a strict and distinctive ritual after the return from captivity, for the Jews said in their hearts, " Why should we die, and our name perish ? "

302. As we have been prying into the secrets of one of these races, the only two survivors of immeasurable antiquity, it appears appropriate to turn aside and consider briefly the history, literature, and customs of the other, as we not unnaturally conclude that some light, by means of a study of their points of comparison and contrast, may be thrown on our ignorance of the early history of the one, by actual observation of the customs and rites of the other, unaltered for thousands of years. The labours of archæologists, in their successful researches into the forgotten past, cannnot be overestimated, nor can a due recognition ever be made of their Herculean labours both in excavating buried monuments, and deciphering inscriptions in languages so long dead, that the very key to unlock their treasures had to be manufactured in the 19th century A.D., from what may

be called impressions of the wards of the lock, bearing a stamp of nearly five thousand years previous. There is surely, however, no need of an apology, for the suggestion that living monuments may be equally instructive in interpreting the history of the past, and as regards daily life and simplicity of primitive ideas, even more authoritative. Greater illuminating power will not be denied to the living flame, never extinguished for thousands of years, than to modern lamps kindled at a flash struck out from flints, buried in darkness for the same length of time.

303. Before proceeding with the work of comparison and contrast, I cannot refrain from drawing attention to the remarkable series of parallels, observable in Chinese and Hebrew history. For the division of the fabulous period into ten sections, they are doubtless, like the Hebrews, indebted to a Hindu source. Of later and less fabulous times they have rulers[1] whose names recall a similar process of selection, noticed in Genesis (par. 63), Nest-havers (cf. Qain), fire-producers, and service completed of Chenok; we also find Fuh-hi and Shen-nung, inventors of musical and agricultural arts, reminding one of the sons of Lamek. The first three great heroes of Chinese are Yao Shun and Yü; the first-named was almost a cotemporary of Abram, his date being 2356 B.C.; his reign lasted 101 years. As Jacob, the third Hebrew hero, was the ancestor of a separate race, so Yü in Chinese history founded the first important dynasty. It may here be remarked, that a universal flood is unknown to Chinese history, the great Yü has nothing in common with Noah. He was the prototype of engineers, not of shipbuilders,

---

[1] Mayers, p. 365.

he coped successfully with forest swamps and river inundations, but knew nothing of a deluge piling water three or five miles above sea-level. B.C. 1122, the first Emperor of the Chow dynasty, Wu, defeated and slew a dissolute monarch, Chow,[1] who had persecuted and imprisoned Wu's father Wan, who had carefully prepared the way and trained his son for his subsequent career. This bears a rough likeness to the events that occurred in Palestine, about a century or so later, when Saul drove David into exile, who afterwards returned and obtained the sovereignty, which, after continued troublous times, he bequeathed, with solemn injunctions, to his son Solomon, whose magnificence marked an era in Israelite history. The parallel is more exact when we note that the annals give Wan a priestly and prophetic character, worthy of David, and that the important Odes are referred to the times of Wan and Wu, precisely as Hebrews love to assign Psalms and Proverbs to David and Solomon. If thus the golden epoch of Chinese history is almost cotemporary with that of the Hebrew, no less so are their periods of greatest national degradation. B.C. 213, the first great universal emperor, gave orders to destroy all the Chinese Scriptures, and to slay or bury alive all scholars who persisted in fidelity to the ancient sages. Well might then have been heard throughout the length and breadth of China, the sad, keen, "The dead bodies of thy servants have they given to be meat to the fowls of the air, the flesh of thy saints to the beasts of the land," which, forty years later, resounded through the extent of Palestine, as Antiochus Epiphanes tortured and slew the faithful

---

[1] The characters for these two words Chow are totally different.

Jews who adhered to the religion and sacred books of their ancestors.

304. "It was to the Accadians," we are told, "that the beginnings of Chaldean culture and civilisation were due. They were the teachers and masters of the Semites, not only in the matter of writing and literature, but in other elements of culture as well."[1] But if the Semites, who extended westward, were thus primarily indebted to the Accadians, no less is the obligation of the Chinese, whose written language preserves to the present day, the characteristics of Accadian writing, thus described by Sayce:[2] "On the one hand, every character had more than one value, when used phonetically to denote a syllable; on the other hand every character could be employed ideographically to represent an object or idea. And, just as simple ideas could thus be represented by single characters, so compound ideas could be represented by a combination of characters." The question of the relation between Accadian and Chinese, was discussed philologically by Professor Terrien de la Couperie, but whatever degree of acceptance may have been accorded to his theory, it appears as impossible to attribute the coincidence in invention of two systems of writing possessing the same remarkable features, and both originating in Central Asia, as it would be to deny that all modern European alphabets may be traced back through the Greek to the Phœnician, and according to Sayce,[3] to a more remote parentage, the Minæan.

304. Prof. Gabelentz has shown that the Chinese

---

[1] Sayce, "Hibbert," p. 5. [2] *Ibid*, p. 3.
[3] "Verdict," pp. 43, 44.

must originally have been a pastoral people, wandering about with their herds and flocks, like the Hebrews led by Abram and Jacob. According to Professor Legge[1] there is no evidence of this in literature of the country except the use of the term, "Pastors of men" applied to princes by Mencius, and in the annals to the ancient Shun; but Gabelentz discovers in the important part played by the character for *sheep* in the expression of ideas like *beauty, uprightness, equity, &c.*, traces of lost history, fossilised in language; for he rightly argues that unless flocks and herds were at one time the principal source of wealth, and main object of thought and attention to a people such an association of ideas would be inexplicable. Thus, then, from the area influenced by Accadian literature and civilisation, there wended eastward and westward, two caravans of flocks and herds, the property of emigrants setting forth in search of unknown lands; and as each settled down in the ultimate home of his adoption, agricultural interests superseded pastoral.

306. The isolation of the Chinese was more complete than that of the Hebrew race. The former dwelt, not in a retired nook, it is true, but still in so distant a region as to be practically unknown. Their conservatism originally was less a matter of choice than of necessity. They had nothing to learn from the barbarians surrounding them; of civilised visitors they had none. It was only natural that their customs and religion should become stereotyped. The Hebrew race, on the other hand, settled right in the high road between Egypt and two other mighty empires, the Hittite and Assyrian. Whatever isolation they had

[1] Classics III., part i. p. 191.

was purely artificial, they insensibly acquired ideas, religious and social, from the nations with whom they were perpetually thrown in contact.

307. If then we desire to behold the nearest approximation to primæval religious conception, we shall not turn to the anthropomorphic tales of Greek or Hebrew authors, which are comparatively modern imaginations, nor to the older legends of cruelty and obscenity which disfigure Phœnician, Egyptian, Assyrian and Hindu pantheons; but we shall esteem it our wisdom to gaze on the colourless, but truer, or rather colourless, and therefore truer, because more ancient, religious ideas of the ancient Chinese, as preserved in their Classics, where is to be seen religion in even a simpler garb than is portrayed in the lives of the Hebrew patriarchs; much of which also survives to the present day.

308. The Canon of Chinese sacred literature was the lifelong study of Confucius[1] strangely coincident with the final edition of the Priestly Code amongst the Hebrews. The six Classics may be roughly compared with the Hebrew Scriptures, as follows: the books on Music and Ritual, with Leviticus and Deuteronomy; the Annals, with Numbers, Joshua, and Judges; the Spring and Autumn Annals, with Samuel and Kings; while the later Tse Chuen corresponds surprisingly with Chronicles, and perhaps the unintelligible Book of Changes may be allowed to find a counterpart in Genesis. "The Annals is the oldest of the Chinese Classics, more than a thousand years before Wan. The Book of Changes holds only a third place in point of age among the monuments of

[1] B.C. 478–551.

Chinese literature."[1] Of the three books of Ritual the same authority says,[2] "The first two are books of the Chau dynasty B.C. 1122-225; the third may contain passages of an earlier date than either of the others, but, as a collection, in its present form it does not go higher than the Han dynasty, and was not completed till our second century." Here then we have a marvellous correspondence with the claims of Hebrew books to great antiquity, and the same cautious admission of truth as regards a *part* of them. The writings of Confucius and his disciples and Mencius form a sort of Apocrypha, but receive a more reverent regard, being indeed more commonly known than the six Classics, with the exception of the Odes. Other remarkable coincidences obtrude themselves; the labours of the Great Synagogue find a parallel in "the large assembly of great scholars convened by the Emperor Hsuan B.C. 51, to discuss the text of the recovered Classics,"[3] and in "the seventy disciples, those of Confucius' followers who had been most in his society and profited most from his instruction,"[4] we are reminded of the same legendary number of Moses' elders. The fabled origin of the Septuagint translation with all its miraculous accessories appears natural and commonplace alongside the stories of the miraculous tales of preservation of the Classic Texts (303) during the persecution under the universal emperor; as a specimen of these we may quote the following as partaking least of the marvellous, though still the improbable, "after the burning of the books, according to Gan-kwo, Fuh-sang of Tse-nan, being more than

---

[1] Legge, "Sacred Books," xxvi. p. 7.　　[2] xxvi. p. 2.
[3] Legge, "Sacred Books," xxvi. p. 6.　　[4] *Ibid.*

ninety years of age (when the emperor Wan was seeking for copies) had lost his originals of the text, and was delivering by word of mouth, more than twenty books to his disciples."[1]

309. The method of criticism employed in investigating Hebrew literature is precisely the same as that used in the discussion of Greek or Latin; but as the nature of these is so essentially different, special interest is evoked by observation of identical conditions, with the same exaggerations, futile explanations, prophecies after the event and inconsistencies, manifest in the ancient Chinese Classics. To illustrate this comparison I shall below quote largely from Legge's "Classics and Sacred Books of the East." Discussing the question of the assignment of the editorship of the Annals to Confucius, Professor Legge says: "The earliest authority for these statements is that of Gan-kwo about B.C. 90. Confucius died B.C. 478, and thus nearly 400 years pass by before we find the compilation of the Shoo King ascribed to him.... It is possible, it is not improbable, that Confucius did compile a hundred ancient documents, which he wished to be regarded as the Shoo *par éminence*. His doing so would have been in harmony with the character which he gave of himself as 'a transmitter, and not a maker, believing in and loving the ancients,' and with his labours on the classic of poetry and on the Ch'un Ts'ew."[2] He also quotes on the special question of the authorship of the preface to the same work, the opinion of Tsae Chin the disciple of the great commentator Choo He,

---

[1] Legge, "Classics," iii., part i. p. 16.   [2] *Ibid.* pp. 4, 5.

(par. 23), who says : "When we examine the text of the preface, as it is still preserved, though it is based on the contents of the several books, the knowledge which it shows is shallow, and the views which it gives are narrow. It sheds light on nothing, and there are things in it at variance with the text of the Classic. On the books that are lost, it is specially servile and brief, affording us not the slightest help. That it is not the work of Confucius, is plain exceedingly."[1]

310. The Chinese doctrine of inspiration, as applied to Confucius, Dr. Legge disposes of in the following summary manner, which should be equally applied to the doctrine of Inspiration as affecting the historic truth of the Hebrew Annals. "Time is at once a producer and a destroyer. Many records of Yü and Tang and their successors had perished before the Canon of the Shoo was compiled, but sufficient must have remained for the materials for a larger collection than was made. . . . . Where had Confucius got his own knowledge of the ancient times? Some critics tell us that *he was born with it;* an affirmation which no foreigner will admit. He *must* have obtained it by his diligent research, and his reasoning satisfactory at least to himself, on what facts he was able to ascertain. His words show us that while in his time there were still existing documents of a high antiquity, they were not very numerous nor complete."[2]

311. "We come now to inquire how far the documents of the Shoo can be relied upon as genuine narratives of the events which they profess to relate. And it may be said at once in reference to the greater

[1] Legge, "Classics," iii. part i. p. 9.   [2] *Ibid.* p. 13.

number of them, that there is no reasonable ground on which to call them in question. *Allowance* must be made for the colouring with which the founders of one dynasty set forth the misdeeds of that which they were superseding. The failures of a favourite hero may be glossed over, and actual defeat represented as a glorious triumph."[1] A few pages further on he proceeds to criticise the subject-matter in a manner required by common sense, as much in the Hebrew as in the Chinese Scriptures. "The accounts of Yae and Shun, and especially of the connection between them, are so *evidently legendary* that it seems *strange* how any one can accept them as materials for history. When Yao has been on the throne for seventy years, finding the cares of government too great for him, he proposes to resign in favour of his principal minister, the Four Mountains. That worthy declares his virtue unequal to the office. This brings Shun upon the stage."[2] The following inconsistencies and incongruities are pointed out on the same page, as occurring in the various accounts of this period. Shun, an unmarried man among the lower people, appears as a farmer, a fisherman, and a potter; his mother is converted into his step-mother, and his arrogant brother becomes his half-brother. Yao has nine sons, who are sent with his two daughters and a host of officers to serve Shun and test his ability. They reigned together for about a quarter of a century, till the death of Yaou, thirty-three years later, Shun being now between ninety and a hundred years old, summons Yü to share the government, which they do for fifteen years. It is

---

[1] Legge, "Classics," iii. part i. p. 48.   [2] *Ibid.* p. 53.

thus evident that the early history of the times coeval with Abram and the rest were not days of historiographers and court annals; in either case it is difficult to credit the survival of the minute details of family life, with which the story of those times is illustrated.

312. On the life of the Great Yü, Dr. Legge's words might be inserted bodily into the works of Wellhausen and Kuenen, without any fear of detection on the score of their being inapposite. We are at once forcibly reminded of the exaggerations apparent in the narrative of the Exodus and the Wanderings. I should here state that all the *italics* in the quotations are *mine*, not Dr. Legge's. "The accounts are not those of a great people, but of a *tribe*, which had little difficulty in migrating from one spot to another. The dimensions of the empire in the days of Yü have been greatly exaggerated. We can *no more admit* that he ruled over the nine provinces ascribed to him, *than* that he executed the stupendous labours of which he has the glory. Biot says: 'It is evident that these *symmetrical* divisions have nothing of reality. . . . . After Yü, the labours of draining the country and clearing the forests continued during some ages, and the *result of all* was attributed by Chinese tradition to the *first chief*.'"[1] "When Yü had reduced the empire to order, the inhabitants amounted to 13,553,923; and the oldest writer in whom I have met with it is Hwang-poo Meih, who died A.D. 282. The statement, occurring thus for the first time about 2500 years after the date to which it refers, is of *no historical value*. The writer is evidently writing at random. The estimate

[1] Legge, "Classics," iii. part i. p. 72.

of the population is no more to be received than any of all the other notices which he gives."¹ "The results which I have endeavoured to bring out in this chapter are: first that Yü is a historical personage, and was the founder of the Chinese Empire, but that nearly all that the Shoo contains of his labours is *fantastical exaggeration;* and second, that Yaou and Shun were also real men, chiefs of the earliest immigrants into the country; but that we must *divest* them of the *grand* proportions, which they have, as seen through the mists of legend and of *philosophical romance.*"²

313. Writing on papyrus-leaves has been found in Egyptian sarcophagi; and on tablets in Assyrian and lately in Egyptian excavations, such tablets being made of baked clay; but more than sixteen hundred years ago some bamboo tablets were by chance discovered in a tomb, where they had lain hid for six hundred years. The great interest attached to this discovery was not that they corroborated existing texts, but that they revealed serious discrepancies from the texts as published after the burning of the books, and the interment of these bamboo tablets was prior to that event. Considerable excitement was caused by this discovery on the interpretation of the small seal character, in which they were engraved. Some pronounced them a forgery, but others, including Too Yu (a witness entirely competent and disinterested), maintained their genuineness. They appear to bear the same relation to the Shoo, as the Ts'un Ch'ew does to the Tso Chuen. "The bamboo annals give but the skeleton of the history of ancient China; the Shoo gives the flesh and

---

¹ Legge, "Classics," iii. part ii. p. 77.   ² *Ibid.* p. 80.

drapery of the body at different times. The one tells of events simply, in the fewest possible words; the other describes the scenes and all the attendant circumstances of those events.[1] We conclude that not only were the cycle characters, for years, introduced into the annals, after their emergence from the tomb, but that the lengths of the reigns were also altered, so that the value of the chronicle as a guide in chronology is altogether taken away. There are points of agreement between the two, as could not but be the case, the authors of them both, whatever they might add of their own, drawing on the same general stock of traditions. But the details of the Annals present the men and their doings in reasonable proportions. We see them the chiefs of a growing tribe, and not the emperors of a vast and fully organised dominion.[2] Even if it could be substantiated, which it cannot be, that the Annals were fabricated in the Tsin dynasty; the fact would remain that their fabricator had taken a more reasonable view of the history of his country, than any other of its writers has done." Hebrew literature can boast no such interesting discovery of lost texts recovered from oblivion, and revealing quite a different and "more reasonable" text; but the want of this is supplied by the Versions, which in many cases serve precisely this valuable purpose, especially in the historical books where the text exposed by their translation often differs widely from the Massorete, and frequently is to be preferred, for the illumination it casts on dark, unintelligible, and contradictory passages.

314. It is very interesting, and at the same time instructive to note that the very time when scribes or

[1] Legge, "Classics," iii. part ii. p. 178.   [2] p. 182.

historiographers were keeping diaries of national events in the reigns of Israelite monarchs, the same system was being observed in the Far East, where the minutest occurrence was duly recorded without comment also by court historiographers, of whom there was a staff in each separate state. These are best preserved to us in the dry pages of the Ch'un Ts'ew, while the Tso Chuen shows us the manner in which writers of continuous connected history would take the material thus provided, and work it up into shape, colouring it according to their own predispositions and predilections, and often introducing fatuous notes rather than recognise the presence of a simple error in the original text. The following extracts from Dr. Legge's preface to the work in question, will set forth these characteristics so plainly that no word of comment will be necessary. "The paragraphs are always brief. Each one is assigned to commemorate a fact; but whether that fact be a display of virtue calculated to command our admiration, or a deed of atrocity fitted to awaken our disgust, it can hardly be said that there is anything in the language to convey to us the shadow of an idea of the author's feeling about it. The notices, for we cannot call them narratives, are absolutely unimpassioned. A base murder and a shining act of heroism are chronicled, just as the eclipses of the sun are chronicled. So and so took place; that is all. No details are given; no judgment is expressed.[1] I have in a hundred places pointed out the absurdities in which such a method 'of explaining away inaccuracies and mistakes' land us. The same peculiarity of the style, such as the omission of the clan name, becomes in one passage the sign of

[1] Legge, "Classics," v. part i. 3.

censure, and in another the sign of praise.[1] An example may be of interest; the *Duke* of Cheng is by mistake called *earl;* this is explained as a studied slight on the part of the historian, who meant thereby to indicate his disapprobation of the duke's conduct towards his younger brother; if history were persistently written in such a manner, it is manifest that no reliance could ever be placed on the simplest statement. That there were records of events kept in the offices of historiography must be freely admitted; but the entries in the various Ch'un Ts'ew were not made from them, not made from them fairly and honestly, as when one tries to give in a few words the substance of a narrative which is before him. . . Maou K'e-ling says they were merely slips of subjects and not summaries or synopses, containing barely the mention of the subjects to which each of them referred."[2] The following is a specimen of the scrappy notes of which the Ch'un Ts'ew is composed.

1. It was his first year, the spring, the king's first month.
2. In the third month, the duke and E-foo of Choo made a covenant in Meeh.
3. In summer, in the fifth month, the *earl* of Cheng overcame Twan in Yen.
4. In Autumn, in the seventh month, the king by Heaven's grace sent the sub-administrator Heuen with a present of two carriages and their horses for the funerals of Duke Hwuy and his wife Chung Tsze.
5. In the ninth month, the duke and an officer of Sung made a covenant in Suh.

---

[1] Legge, "Classics," v. part I. p. 5.   [2] *Ibid.* p. 10.

6. In winter, in the twelfth month, the Earl of Chae came to Loo.

7. Kung-tsze Yih-tsze died.

315. The Tso Chuen takes the above as a text, and explains and expatiates—*e.g.*, line 3 becomes half-a-dozen pages; you learn who are the duke[1] of Cheng's parents, and how like Isaac and Rebecca the father favoured the elder and the mother the younger of two brothers, which resulted in a lifelong quarrel between them, and the rebellion of the younger, resulting in his defeat and death. Some occurrence took place at the birth of the elder, about which commentators differ; myself, I am inclined to believe it is a mere invention to account for the agnomen Ng-shang—which literally means Sleeping-Birth, whence they conclude that either the mother or child was insensible at the time. I have said that generally we have in the work of Tso, the details of the events of which we have but a shadow, or the barest intimation in the text of the Ch'un Ts'ew; but we have more than this. Of multitudes of events, that during the 242 years of the Ch'un Ts'ew period took place in Loo and other States, to which the text makes no allusion, we have from Tso a full account. Where he got his information he does not tell us. Too Yu is probably correct, when he says that Tso, who died at least fifty years after Confucius, was himself one of the historiographers of Loo.[2] The events and the characters of the time pass, as in reality and life, before us. In *no* ancient history of *any* country have we such a vivid picture of any lengthened period of its annals, as we have from Tso. To myself it appears plain that Tso's work was compiled on a twofold plan.

[1] Earl.   [2] Legge, p. 27.

First he had reference to the text of the Ch'un Ts'ew, and wished to give the details of the events which were indicated in it. Occasionally also he sets himself to explain the words of that text. He lays down canons to regulate the meaning and application of certain characters.[1] Wang Cheh says, But though his book was made as an appendix to the Classic, yet apart from and outside that, it forms a book by itself, the author of which was led away by his *fondness* for *strange stories*, and carried his collecting them beyond what was proper.[2] Much of the above would be appropriate as a criticism on the Book of Chronicles, but for similar detail of style we must turn to the earlier books of the Bible.

316. "There is a host of passages, which contain predictions of the future, or allusions to such predictions, grounded on divination, meteorological and astronomical considerations, and something in the manner of deportment of the parties concerned; predictions which turn out to be true. *We may be sure that none of these was made at the time assigned to it in the Chuen.* Some of them which had their fulfilment, before the end of the Ch'un Ts'ew period, may have been current in Tso's days and incorporated by him with his narrative. Others, like the ending of the Chow dynasty after an existence of so many hundred years, the fulfilment of which was at a later date, were no doubt *fabricated subsequently to that fulfilment and interpolated* during the time of first Han."[3] Have we not here another trait in common with the Hebrew Scriptures, which is generally regarded as their speciality and to which special treatment is therefore by some accorded?

[1] Legge, p. 28.   [2] *Ibid.* p. 30.   [3] *Ibid.* p. 35.

317. "Kung-yang," says the Ch'un Ts'ew, "conceals the truth on behalf of the high in rank out of regard to kinship, and on behalf of men of worth. On V. i. 1, Tso says that it was the rule for the historiographer to conceal any wickedness which affected the character of the State. But this concealing covers all the ground occupied by our three English words, ignoring, concealing, and misrepresenting." It is true that the Hebrew writers do not scruple to report anecdotes to the discredit of their heroes, but it would appear that they are not entirely free of this charge of misrepresenting for historical purposes, especially as regards their portraiture of the kings of Israel, and of such of the kings of Judah as failed to adopt the modern forms of religion and reject the old. "In X. i. 11, it is said, in winter, the eleventh month on Ke-yew, Keun, viscount of Ts'oo *died*. The viscount or king as he styled himself, was suddenly taken ill, of which Wei, the son of a former king, was informed, when he was on his way in discharge of a mission to the State of Ching. He returned immmedately, and, entering the palace as if to inquire for the king's health, *he strangled him*, and proceeded to put to death his two sons. Here certainly was a murder, which ought to have been recorded as such."[1] This tale involuntarily recalls the murder of Ben-hadad by Hazael under identical circumstances, and it occurs to one to ask how far Dr. Legge's criticism of the Ch'un Ts'ew views on murder, do not apply to such cases as Jehu's murder of Jehoram and his brethren, and the wanton slaughter of Ahaziah of Judah and his retinue. "The deaths of princes and great officers recorded in the Ch'un Ts'ew took place in

[1] Legge, p. 40.

various ways, but they all appear under the same form, died."[1] This sentence might have been penned after the perusal of several chapters in the Books of Kings.

318. As the Jews delight to ascribe to Moses a large part of their literature that he could not have seen, so the Chinese have a similar failing with regard to Confucius. Writing on the Yi King, Dr. Legge says, "I regretted that Confucius had stooped to write the parts of the appendices now under remark. It is a relief not to be obliged to receive them as his. Even the better treatises have no other claim to that character besides the voice of *tradition, first heard nearly 400 years after his death.*"[2] Like the Jews, the Chinese carefully count the number of letters or characters in their scriptures, and "Confucius tells us (Analects XV. xxv.) that even in his early days a historiographer would leave a blank in his text, that is, would do so, rather than enter anything incorrectly, of which he was not sure."[3] Fanciful as the following statement undoubtedly is, it still possesses interest, as showing that the later notions of inborn knowledge or inspiration had not always prevailed. There is as great a difference between the two explanations of a difficulty, as between the ancient song of the Elders digging a well and the narrative of the miraculous striking of the rock by Moses. "Confucius, having received the command of Heaven to make his Ch'un Ts'ew, sent fourteen men in all to seek for the historical records of Chow, and they got the precious books of 120 States, from which he proceeded to make his chronicle. This is, however, one

[1] Legge, p. 13.   [2] "Sacred Books," xvi. 31.
[3] "Classics," v. 50.

of the wild statements which we find in many of the writers of the Han and Tsin dynasties."[1]

319. Another noteworthy point of touch between these two races is the importance attached by both to the value of parallelism in composition, both prose and poetry. Occasional parallels will be discovered in the best works of all nations and ages; but as a carefully studied system, which is invariably followed in all writings with any claim to classical style, parallelism appears to be a distinct feature of Hebrew and Chinese composition. It will occasionally be observed in the finest prose writings of the West and even in rhetoric, that a regard to rhythm and musical cadence has led the author or speaker to a choice of words such that, if counted, the number of syllables in two members of an impressive period will be found to be the same; but this frequently appears to be spontaneous, and is not sustained for any length of time, as its manifest artificiality would be betrayed, and to be artificial is a cardinal sin against the ancient canon, *Ars est celare artem*. In poetry, the balance of syllables is a natural adjunct of metre; it is therefore surprising that so much objection should have been raised to the elaboration of a system by Merx and Bickel[2] for establishing a principle for reducing Hebrew Poetry to a system of carefully counted syllables, following some scheme, however irregular it may appear to modern notions, or even when compared with the euphonious, well-balanced verse of Greece and Rome. Chinese poetry appears to com-

[1] Legge, p. 9.
[2] See also the Introduction to my critically revised translation of the Book of Job.

bine the rhyme of the West with the somewhat erratic difference in number of syllables in adjacent couplets. But in Chinese and Hebrew *Higher Prose* the same regard to assonance produced, by an exact number of syllables in parallel clauses, not only affords at once a criterion of merit, but in several instances enables the critic to detect the insertion or omission of a word, the presence or absence of which mars the general scheme otherwise observable. Have we not in these two distinctive features of Chinese and Hebrew literature further indication of a common indebtedness to the same source, in primitive times, probably Accadian.[1]

320. Dr. Legge's remarks upon the religious ideas and practices of the Chinese, as recorded in their Classics, again appear equally appropriate to what we know of ancient Hebrew notions on the same topics. "There was *no* sacerdotal or *priestly class* among them; there were *no revelations* from Heaven to be studied and expounded. The *chieftain* was the *priest* for the tribe, the emperor for the empire, the prince of a State for his people, the *father* for his *family*. .... Shun always commenced his proceedings by presenting a *burnt-offering* to Heaven, and sacrificing in order to *hills* and *rivers*. I do not refer to these passages as veritable records of what Shun *actually* did; but they are valuable as being the *ideas* of the *compilers* of the Shoo, of what he *should* have done in the supposed circumstances. ..... The name by which God was designated the Ruler, and the Supreme Ruler, denotes emphatically his *personality*, *supremacy*, and *unity*. We find it constantly inter-

[1] See above, 304.

changed with the term Heaven, by which the ideas of supremacy and unity are equally conveyed, while that of personality is only vaguely indicated and by an association of the mind. By God, kings were supposed to reign, and princes were required to decree justice. All were under law to him and bound to obey his will. Even on the inferior people he has conferred a moral sense, compliance with which would show their nature invariably right. All powers that be are from Him, He raises one to the throne and puts down another! Obedience is sure to receive His blessing, disobedience to be visited with His curse. The business of kings is to rule in righteousness and benevolence, so that people may be happy and good. When they are doing wrong God admonishes them by judgments, storms, famines and other calamities; if they persist in evil, sentence goes forth against them, the dominion is taken from them and given to others more worthy of it."[1] Who, reading the above, might not well believe that he was perusing a sketch of Hebrew religious thought, which could without trouble be identified by occasional reference to quotations in the Bible.

321. It is clear from the above that Dr. Legge does not share the opinion recently expressed in the *China Review*, that the Chinese have *no* idea of a *personal* God. It appears, however, as well to cite a few passages from Chinese authors outside the Classics, to illustrate the views held by enlightened men, and by them derived from their ancient sages. Su She, who flourished about A.D. 1050, in his "Narrative of the Lucky-Rain Pavilion," writes: "Now God has

[1] "Classics," iii. part I. 193.

not forgotten his people, for after some drought first He favoured them with rain." Liu Ki, A.D. 1350, in a monograph on Excess of Anxiety, writes: "For those matters only are human, for which human foresight avails; but that *which lies outside the power of his wisdom* is unattainable, and *belongs to the realm of God*," and again, "The ancient sages.... merely relied on their extreme sincerity and great virtue, to identify themselves with the divine plans, to induce God to regard their virtue, *like a fond mother* who protects *her new-born child* and *cannot desert it*. Then although their descendants might be sufficiently dense and worthless to ensure the destruction of their State, still *God in the end would not permit their utter extermination*." Surely this is all that anybody could desire in the way of a personal conception of God. In Li Wa's "Lamentation on an Ancient Battlefield," we read: "In this time of bitter cold, *Heaven aided* the hardy Mongols, who availing themselves of the deadly weather, slew and massacred our troops." If this is pure Nature Religion, vague and unsatisfactory, what are we to say of the hailstones at the battle of Beth-Horon, and of passages where God is described as riding on clouds; while one Psalm is devoted to the grandeur of Thunder which is repeatedly called the Voice of God? If these are poetry, why deny the same explanation to the Chinese composition? But what if they are all alike remnants of Nature Worship, into which more exalted ideas have been introduced by later development of thought?

322. The Chinese and Hebrews bravely acknowledged an ignorance of immortality, though both had a vague belief in a continuation of existence, especially

manifested in their dread of the influence of ghosts and spirits. "There is no promise of rest or comfort beyond the grave. The virtuous man may live and die in suffering and disgrace; let him be cheered, his posterity will reap the reward of his merits, some one sprung from his loins will become wealthy and attain to distinction."[1] Any one who doubts that this corresponds exactly with the faith of the Israelites up to the third or even the second century B.C. should read an Essay by the late Professor Mozley; but I will state the case briefly in an Appendix.

323. "Although the Chinese can scarcely be said to have had the knowledge of a future state, and were not curious to inquire into it, they were anxious to know about the wisdom and issue of their plans for the present life. For this they had recourse to divination. The Duke of Chow certainly practised it, and we have a regular staff of diviners among the officers of the Chow dynasty.[2] Divination was practised in China from a very early time, I will not say 5200 years ago, in the days of Fu Hsi, for I cannot repress doubts of his historical personality; but as soon as we tread the borders of something like credible history we find it existing. Twenty-third century B.C. divination by means of the tortoise-shell is mentioned; and somewhat later we find that method continuing, and also divination by the lineal figures manipulated by means of the stalks of a plant.[3] The Decider was held to be Heaven, the error was in thinking that the will of Heaven could be known through any manipulation of the tortoise-shell or the stalks."[4] The

---

[1] "Classics," iii. part i. 196.   [2] *Ibid.*
[3] "Sacred Books," xvi. p. 40.   [4] *Ibid.* xxvii. p. 233.

Israelites were equally addicted to having resort to the casting of lots, which was supposed, with equal futility, to reveal the will of God in any perplexity. How this was managed remains at present a mystery, but that it was connected with the Ephod worn by certain hereditary diviners is manifest from the stories in the Books of Samuel and the Kings; whether or not Urim and Thummim partook of the nature of *odd* and *even* like the unequal stalks in Chinese divination cannot be asserted.

324. The legend of Pwan-ku, and his moulding the heavens, and chiselling out the earth is not classical; while the doctrine of emanations from male and female essences, reminding one so strongly of the Valentinian Gnostics, is first met with in the Appendix III. of the Yi King, which is subsequent to Confucius.[1] I cannot refrain from alluding to a hidden allusion to creation in the very ancient trigrams which are open to two interpretations, the one abscribed to Fu Hsi B.C. 3322 and the other to Wan B.C. 1143. The former explained these mysterious signs, by objects in Nature, but King Wan "altered the existing order and position of the trigrams, with regard to the *cardinal points*, simply for the occasion that he might set forth vividly his ideas about the springing, growth and maturity in the vegetable kingdom, from the labours of spring, to the cessation from toil in winter. The marvel is that he *brings God upon the scene,* and makes Him, in the various processes of Nature, the *All-in-all.*[2] The author of Appendix V. speaks of the work of God in Nature in all the year as a progress through the trigrams, and as

---

[1] "Sacred Books," xvi. p. 40.   [2] *Ibid*. p. 51.

being effected by His Spirit."[1] Liang Yin A.D. 13—
says, "The Spirit here simply means God, God is the
substantiality of the Spirit; the Spirit is God in operation; He who is *Lord over and rules all things is God*,
the subtle *presence and operation of God* is by *His
Spirit*."[2] The following translation of the interpretation
of the trigrams is taken from the same work, Yi King,
Appendix V. chapters 5, 8:

1. God comes forth in *Kan*, to His producing work
   E Thunder
2. He brings his processes into full and equal action
   in *Sun* SE Wind
3. They are manifested to one another in *Li* S
   Sun
4. The greatest service is done for him in *Khwan*
   SW Earth
5. He rejoices in *Tui* W Sea
6. He struggles in *Khien* NW Sky
7. He is comforted and *enters into rest* in *Khan* N
   Rain
8. He completes the work of the year in *Kan* NE
   Hills

We note at once the statement that God enters into
rest as His *seventh* action or station, which is the more
remarkable, as there is no special preference shown
to His number, as a common practice, in Chinese
literature. To account for its presence here, we can
only refer once again to Accadian influence—*i.e.*,
survival of ideas imbibed along with the principles of

---

[1] "Sacred Books," xvi. p. 50.
[2] *Ibid.* 53. The Chinese words for *chaos*, Woun tun (Cheng Yü Kao) are said by Dr. Faber to be of foreign origin, and suggest *tohu* and *bohu* in inverted order, which are also foreign to Hebrew.

writing, which are common to Chinese and Accadian. Again, by Wan's interpretation, Nos. 3 and 7, God manifests himself in the South, and enters into His rest in the North; this is in accordance with observation of the sun's course, for that luminary is manifest in the South, and hidden in the North. On this account I cannot but think that in Job xxiii. 9 there must be a confusion, resulting in an inversion of the idea:

"Northwards, where he *works*, I cannot seize him;
Southwards, where he *hides*, and I cannot see him"

The assembly of the gods in the mountain of the north, Isaiah xiv. 13, is to be viewed as the place of their secret deliberation, not of their public manifestation in work. See Professor Cheyne on this passage, who says: "The north being used loosely for the northeast"; in this connection it is strange to note that N.E. of Wan corresponded to *hills* of Fu Hsi. Thus the whole passage from the Chinese Classic, with its authoritative native interpretation, seems to transport us to the same region of thought known to the Babylonians and the later Hebrew writers. Once more we have evidence of religious ideas surviving from remote antiquity, bequeathed to the Chinese from their ancestors, who were acquainted with the Accadians.

325. The doctrine of *Filial Piety* is a conspicuous bond of identity in Hebrew and Chinese religious conceptions, and is the natural consequence of the want of belief in immortality. If there is no "sure and certain hope" of the permanence of the individual, all that tends to the preservation of the family and race becomes an imperative necessity and pre-eminent duty. Hence the propagation of the race is an obligation laid upon every man, and *concubinage* was on this account approved by Hebrew and Chinese philosophers alike, dating back to their hoary ancestors Abram and Yaou.[1] It is true that this permission is liable to abuse, but to state that concubinage is legalised vice, is deliberately to shut one's eyes to its origin, which is philosophical, logical, and, from a certain point of view, even religious. With the same object, special provision is made for the exceptional cases of childless couples; the Chinese elder brother *adopting* his eldest nephew, that the main line may not become extinct, and the Hebrew in like case, by the Levirate law, taking the childless widow of his deceased brother, to "raise up seed unto his brother."[2] *Earler marriages* are, for the same reason, a common practice in both races, from a morbid fear that an untimely death should cut off some branch, and the immortality of the family be endangered. *Registration of Births* was an ancient custom among the Chinese. A record to effect, In such a year, In such a month, On such a day, So and so was born, was made and deposited. The officer also informed the secretaries of the hamlets who made out two copies of it."[3] To the present day, every man who obtains a degree by examination publishes a book, setting forth his family tree for several generations. The interest in *genealogies* common to both peoples is also attributable to their belief in the immortality of the nation, to which genealogical tables prove a necessary adjunct, and afford a reliable safeguard. It is manifest then, that, in a religious system where the propagation of the

[1] "Classics," iii. part i. p. 199.   [2] Matt. xxii. 24.
[3] Li Ki, "Sacred Books," xxvi. p. 474.

race is a fundamental article, the father and mother must hold a *quasi*-sacred position, for on them depends the realisation of the hopes of many generations of buried dead; they are the link between the past and the future; as long as they live, they are the incarnation of the whole family history; it excites, then, no surprise, that their sons are expected to be exact in their reverence, and punctilious in their obedience to them. "Honour thy father and thy mother, that thy days may be long in the land that Yahveh thy God giveth thee" was the Hebrew injunction. "If a man be perfect in the observation of one hundred rules of conduct, and fail in Filial Piety, all his other virtues are nothing worth," so says the Chinese philosopher. The incorrigible refractory son may, in China, be condemned to death by the elders of the village, just as is recorded in the Hebrew Code.[1]

326. *Ancestral Worship*, or the commemoration of the forefathers, with a view to keeping their memory eternally green, is generally treated as an idiosyncrasy and idolatrous practice, peculiar to the Chinese nation. Intimately associated as it is with the doctrine of filial piety, it would be surprising if no trace of ancestral worship remained in ancient Hebrew history and literature; and we have seen that idea was not unknown to them (138–140). The worship of *trees* and *stones* or rather of the spirits which they enshrine, or natural powers which they typify, is still continued by the Chinese with the same simple faith, and plain ritual, that was observed by the patriarchs Yaou and Shun, Abram and Jacob; though it is true that, after the reign of Hezeqiah, the Israelites soon discarded it

---

[1] Deut. xviii. 18-21.

as a remnant of idolatry and barbarism. The *new moon* held a special fascination for both Hebrew and Chinese; while the *full moon*, specially observed at the spring and autumn equinox (128—133) by the Israelites, is also generally the occasion for religious services among the Chinese, especially in the first and eighth moons. On latter occasion, particular mooncakes are prepared, reminding one of the cakes made to worship the Queen of Heaven,[1] an old custom with their forefathers,[2] derived from Assyria, according to Kiel. The custom of putting orange-red labels, incribed with the characters invoking luck and blessing, on the *doorposts* and *lintel* of the entrance to Chinese houses at the *New Year* is probably a reminiscence of an older custom of smearing sacrificial blood in the same places at the same time.[3] "At the *Equinox* they make uniform the measures of length and capacity. They correct the peck and the bushel, the steelyard weights and the bushel-scraper."[4] This ordinance seems very appropriate at a time when Nature herself appears to be equalising measures of time and space; and the solemnity of the occasion more than suggests a similar custom on the part of the Israelites, which accounts for the spasmodic reference to perfect and just weights and balances in the midst of more important laws.[5] "The son of Heaven at this time offers a *lamb* to the ruler of cold, on the fourth and fourteenth cycle days."[6] We are thus vividly reminded of the manner and time of observing the Hebrew Passover which was also associated with the Near Year feast.

[1] Jer. vii. 18.
[2] Jer. xliv. 17.
[3] Ex. xii. 22.
[4] Li Ki, "Sacred Books," xxvi. p. 260.
[5] Deut. xxv. 13–16.
[6] Li Ki, *loc. cit.*

a human being into body, soul, and spirit. "Kwei denotes the animal soul or nature, and Shan, the intellectual soul, the union of which constitutes the living man.¹ All the living must die, and dying return to the ground; this is what is called Kwei; the bones and flesh moulder below, and hidden away become the earth of the fields; but the spirit issues forth and is displayed on high, in a condition of glorious brightness."² On the *evil*, the orthodox doctrine propounded by Mencius, is that every man is born perfect; but by example and practice he falls more or less from the implanted standard of good, and is guilty of sin or maintains virtue; the fall of man and his rise, are thus events perpetually recurring in the individual lives of millions; this is known in the West as Pelagian heresy. "Known ye not that your body is the temple of the Holy Ghost? ye are not your own," thus Paul³ preaches purity and *self-respect*, nor have these the Chinese philosphers failed to inculcate morality from the sanctity of the body: "Zang-zze said the body is that which has been transmitted to us by our parents, dare any one allow himself to be irreverent in the employment of their legacy?"⁴ The association of *affliction* with *guilt*, which forms the main subject for discussion in the poem of Job, is not unknown to the Chinese: "When Zse-hsia was mourning for his son, he lost his eyesight. Zang-zze went to condole with him, and said, 'I have heard that when a friend loses his eyesight, we should wail for him.'

---

¹ Yi King, "Sacred Books," xvi. p. 43.   ² *Ibid.* xxvii. 220.
³ 1 Cor. vi. 19.   ⁴ "Sacred Books," xxvii. 236.

Thereupon he wailed, and Zse-hsia also wailed, and said, 'O Heaven, and I have no guilt.'"[1] On the necessity of purity of *motive* in religious services, the Chinese writers are at one with the Hebrew prophets. "The rites should not be performed by the man, who is not right in heart and sincere. Confucius said one may repeat the three hundred Odes and not be fit to offer the sacrifice.[2] To speak and to carry into execution what you have spoken is ceremony ; to act and to give and receive pleasure from what you do, is music."[3] Parallels to the following quotations will suggest themselves at once in our Bible : "The Master said, The superior man exalts others and abases himself ; he gives the first place to others and takes the last himself.[4] He reaps without having ploughed that he may reap ; he gathers the produce of the third year's field without having cultivated them the first year.[5] When he asks about men suffering from cold, he clothes them ; or men suffering from want he feeds them."[6] Last, but not least, the well-known so-called silver motto, "Do not to others what you would not like done to yourself."[7]

328. In Hebrew history, ever and anon, at some crisis, there appears suddenly on the scene, some holy man, who utters remonstrance or warning, as the mouth-piece of God, prefacing his remarks with the formula, "Thus saith Yahveh." The place of these seers and prophets is taken in Chinese history by philosopher and sages, who without any assumption of inspiration, show the same intrepidity in denouncing vice in high

---

[1] "Sacred Books," xxvi. 135.   [2] *Ib.* xxvi. 414.   [3] *Ib.* xxvii. 249.
[4] *Ib.* xxvii. 287.   [5] *Ib.* xxvii. 296.   [6] *Ib.* xxvii. 348.
[7] Ana. xv. 23.

places and the disregard of ancient laws and customs; and even on occasion, like Elisha, have no scruple in interfering with military tactics. Many more examples and instances might be cited; but enough has been said to show, that the Confucian religion, which is only so called because Confucius codified it, is in its elements more akin to the Hebrew than Egyptian, Phœnician and Assyrian religions are, that these bear the same relation to Hebrew religion, that Buddhism does to Confucianism, for they provide the sensuous ritual constituents which our *a priori* conceptions assure us should be wanting in a primitive religion.

CHAPTER X

CONCLUSION

329. It is now time to gather up the scattered, though, I trust, not tangled, threads of the argument, and to endeavour to present it as a whole. I may as well at once confess that it is not so long since that some such title as "Fly Leaves from a Note-book in the Far East" or "Random Reflections on Hebrew Problems" suggested itself to me as appropriate. It was not till I had compiled the table of contents, that I was cheered by the discovery that I had maintained a certain scheme and unity of purpose better than I had feared. I had, as it were, been rambling over a large field, plucking flowers here and there, chiefly attracted by their size and colour, and I was gratified to find that the general effect of the nosegay was after all fairly harmonious.

330. My original purpose was to study the genealogies, especially with a view to ascertaining what historical facts underlay the family relationships represented in the tables. This was suggested to me by Kuenen's[1] inquiry into the connection between the Qenizzite race and the tribe of Judah. For this purpose, I wrote out, in Hebrew, all the genealogical trees I

[1] "Religion of Israel," vol. i. chap. ii. note 4.

the fatality that befel the Egyptians. And when we find that the history of the High Priest, the Ark, and the Tabernacle, &c., is at variance with the Hexateuch narrative, we have less hesitation in admitting that the origin of all these has been attributed to Moses, not because ancient tradition assigned them to him, but because tradition recognised the Exodus as the era of national beginnings; and the authors found themselves possessed of none but the most meagre materials, from which to construct their sub-patriarchal history.

332. A careful perusal of this remote period revealed that a very large supply of the events recorded is due to suggestions made from rough and ready derivations of the ancient names of men and places. I collected several of these, and demonstrated that from the very first chapter of Genesis onwards, this principle reveals itself as a motive for the authors' composition. Occasionally such stories may also bear the stamp of antiquity, but as a rule they are simple narratives, which at the most have no significance beyond conveying allegorical reference to historical events, which did not occur till 500 or even 1000 years later.

333. The motives that actuated Hebrew authors were the next object of inquiry, and some attempt at an explanation of the methods adopted by them, was made. This led to the recognition of critical ability manifested by them; and considerable evidence of painstaking research was adduced. It therefore occurred to me, whether it was not too generally assumed that criticism was a comparatively modern science, and whether it might not be advantageous briefly to sketch the development of this science, which is no more modern than grammar, mathematics, or astronomy.

334. Chapter i. therefore professes to contain a brief exposition of the expansion of critical labours, amongst Hebrew and Christian schools of thought. In these, religion and history are so indissolubly combined, that they act and react upon each other, in a manner tending to the utmost mystification, not to call it confusion. The standpoint of religious preconception perverts and distorts the account of historic events; and when it became necessary to find ancient authority for doctrines and dogmas of a later development, more or less logical, these were based on a literal acceptation of incidents, whose claim to be treated as history was already dependent on the genuineness of religious ideas of previous ages. Thus it is that the dogmas of Predestination and Election appear to be deduced from innocent narratives about Abraham, Pharaoh and Esau; whereas these stories were written by men who already held that view of God's relation to the affairs of mankind, in which He is conceived of as making an arbitrary choice without regard to individual merit. It is on this account that I venture to think that the religious activity of certain ages should be as much attributed to the exercise of the critical faculty, as those textual and historical researches to which the term is more usually restricted. I take this opportunity of repairing a strange omission in this chapter i., viz., the absence of reference to the great Hebrew critics and grammarians of the Middle Ages, Gaon, Jarchi, Ibn Ezra, Maimonides, Kimchi, and Tanchum, on whom see Keil's Introduction.

335. I divided criticism into two sections, Conservative and Liberal, as I considered that these sufficiently express the difference of thought, besides having the advantage of being applicable to all ages. Liberal criticism may be further divided into subjective and objective criticism. All that pertains to the study of archæology and of ancient texts suggested by versions, falls under the head of objective criticism. The subjective critic is he who by study of the author and his period endeavours to throw himself back into the circumstances and conditions of the past; who most successfully divests himself of all ideas and traditions that came into existence after the time with which he may be occupied; who, noticing the faintest difference in style and expression, classifies and assigns dates to works bearing similar tokens; who is keenly alive to internal evidence of anachronism and incongruity. I submit that this incomplete definition of the *subjective* critic appears sufficiently identical with one's impression of what is intended by the term *higher* critic, to justify the supersession of the latter, which by its tacit assumption of a criticism, which must necessarily be on a *lower* plane, causes needless offence, and is unduly suggestive of arrogant pretensions to superiority, of which there is no trace in the writings of the authors on whom this title is conferred.

336. In chapter ii., under the heading, "Hebrew Story and History," I showed that there was even more of story and less of history, in the times prior to David, than Ewald or apparently Renan would admit. Wellhausen ignores this period, with a silence indicative of intentional neglect and scornful rejection; while Kuenen speaks of the bare outlines as alone worthy of historic acceptance. I believe that the theory of stories, based on derivation there advanced, especially as illustrated with a modern parody, is a

novelty; in so far as it recognises this as a distinctive and systematic feature of Hebrew history.

337. Chapter iii. shows that stories based on derivation abound from Adam to Joshua. The discussion of the patriarchal names was deferred to chapter vii., as other important factors in their history had first to be considered. The effect of these stories can only be to make readers believe that the authors had at their disposal very full and complete information of the history of mankind from the foundation of the world; their purpose, however, was to show the guidance of Divine Providence in the choice and formation of the Hebrew race, and then, reaching still further back, the same motive was applied with greater boldness to the history of the world. As I state later on (par. 89), there probably existed originally long lists of names, which were learned by heart in the schools of the prophets, for there is considerable evidence in their arrangement of a definite aim at providing mnemonic aids, such as the distribution of the names in triplets, reminding one of the Chinese tri-literal classic. These skeletons their teachers clothed with interesting narratives; but it appears now next to impossible to be confident of the date of their composition, though we have (par. 116) a rough idea of the date of their publication in book form. It is well to bear in mind that many of those which occur earliest in the Bible are of latest date.

338. In chapter iv. we investigate Hebrew genealogies, pursuing Kuenen's line of investigation. From the manner in which the distinction between tribal and individual names is uniformly ignored, both being treated as interchangeable, even when of a definite plural form, we infer that they are for the most part of a very late date. This conclusion is further corroborated by the refusal of the genealogies to harmonise with the chronological system; by the manifestly vain attempts to connect David with the patriarch Judah, and the High Priests with Aaron; and by the boldness with which lists of officers are tranferred from the days of Hezekiah and Nehemiah to the reign of David. The importance of the fact that the fiftieth generation from Adam inclusive was in existence at the destruction of Jerusalem by Nebuchadnezzar is not to be over-estimated as evidence of the *terminus a quo*, the date, *before* which these tables could *not* have assumed their final form.

339. In chapter v., by consideration of the various and conflicting accounts of such important institutions, as the Sabbath, Circumcision, and Passover, we discover that the writers, who deal with these subjects, are themselves unconscious of the time, to which these should be referred. It is singularly instructive to note how each and all are reported first of comparatively late date, and then thrown back, and again still further back. Thus, the *Sabbath* would appear, from its eternal non-observance, to be a novelty in the days of Jeremiah, and even of Deutero-Isaiah, who are the first to declaim against its neglect; the Deuteronomist, a contemporary of Jeremiah, antedates it to the Exodus; and a later writer, having regard to the fact of its observance in Babylon, wisely deduces that it is not a peculiar invention of the Hebrews, and accordingly relegates it to the Creation. Similarly, *Circumcision* is described as first inaugurated as a national custom at Gilgal, by Joshua; some pious writer

thought this a reflection on Moses, with whom and his wife Zipporah, he therefore connects it; some one, endued with a more logical mind, or a deeper spirit of research, observed that other nations, claiming descent from Abraham, practised this rite, so we read that Abram was instructed by God to circumcise himself and his son Ishmael. In the same way, after the discovery of the Book of the Law, Josiah is the first to hold a universal *Passover;* this appearing far too modern, the feast is referred back to Joshua, where a pun on the name Gilgal suggested that place as a suitable site for the purpose; and finally the belief that this feast was peculiar to the Hebrew race, suggested Moses as its original founder. Here their research stayed, though one would have thought that the complex character of the feast, and the similar general observance of New Year and Spring Equinox by other nations, would have justified its relegation to Noah, along with the equally universal precepts ascribed to him by the Rabbis. It is to be noted that some of the latter, though not venturing to criticise too severely the Canonical Writings, felt this want, and experienced doubts as to whether this feast did not exist in the days of Abram, but contented themselves with asserting that the substitution of the ram for his firstborn was a *type* of the national feast.[1]

340. This backward method of writing history is a singular feature of Hebrew authorship, which appears to demand fuller attention. Thus we have Joseph's life manufactured after the model of Samuel's (176), incidents in David's reign are utilised with actual names preserved in the story of his great ancestor Judah (230);

---
[1] See par. 132.

Abram's life is filled up with episodes borrowed from Isaac's—indeed, it appears very doubtful whether all his experiences in the south of Canaan, in Egypt, and in the land afterwards know as Philistia, are not due to this practice, for ancient tradition associated him with Tyre (187) and Damascus. All the ancient kings of the latter place are not men, but tribes, including Abraham and Israel; Hadoram and Ozal, tribes in this vicinity,[1] are the origin of the so-called kings of Damascus, Azelus, and Adores, whom Ewald[2] endeavours to identify with Hazael and Eliezer. The note here referred to is of great interest, as it collects references to ancient traditions preserved by the early Fathers, which dilate on Abram's connection with the history of Damascus. The sanctity of Bethel, one of the Northern shrines, is first secured by asserting that after the change of Jacob's name to Israel he set up a pillar at Bethel[3]; further, to convince the *southerners* of its claim to veneration, it became necessary to show that Jacob had performed the same ceremony at the same place *before* his name was changed, the earlier story[4] is therefore inserted; and to provide greater antiquity still, and more neutral associations, Abram is represented as the first to consecrate the place.[5] Joshua[6] relates the solemn Treaty of Union at Shechem, where Yahveh, the God of the Josephites,[7] becomes the national god of united Israel;[8] the Deuteronomist prefixes chap. xxiii., which relates a conference with the elders, previous to the appeal to

---

[1] Gen. x. 27. [2] i. 312, n. 1. [3] Gen. xxxv. 15.
[4] Gen. xxviii. 18. [5] Gen. xii. 8. [6] chap. xxiv.
[7] "As for me and my house, we will serve Yahveh," xxiv. 15.
[8] "Nay, but we will serve Yahveh," xxiv. 21.

dation of the world were then revealed,[1] and others had to await a future revelation[2]; in other words, discoveries led to further development of doctrines, when the time is ripe, for there is deeper philosophy than is apparent on the surface, in the simple words: "It is not for you to know the times and seasons which the Father hath put in his own power."[3] That Revelation, as an extraneous influence, is synonymous with Inspiration, is admitted by Paul: "God hath revealed them to us by his Spirit;[4] further, that Inspiration, though in its highest sense apparently confined to "holy men of old, who spake as they were moved by the Holy Ghost,"[5] is, from another point of view, the common heritage of mankind, seeing that in God "we live and move and have our being."[6] Inspiration is a fertilising river, of infinite length and unknown breadth; a serious wrong is done to it, by the endeavour to dam it up and divert its course into narrow channels, that its energy may be confined to working one religious system for the selfish benefit of a small fraction of the human race.

342. If in making a railway cutting, the navvies were to come on a Saxon coin, and, on going deeper, discovered a Roman urn, and later on a stone implement; would you be justified in assigning them all to the same period, because they happened to be found in the same area? Again, if by any chance these articles had been discovered in an inverse order, would you not, by knowledge derived from many parallel cases, elsewhere, be unconscious of any need of apology for the assertion that some cause for this

---

[1] Rom. xvi. 22. [2] 1 Peter i. 5. [3] Acts i. 7.
[4] 1 Cor. ii. 10. [5] 2 Peter i. 21. [6] Acts xvii. 28

departure from the ordinary rule must exist, and should be sought for; even if you hazarded a theory of upheaval by earthquake? Research into Hebrew history is attended with similar phenomena; as we have seen in chapters v. and vi., ideas belonging to different epochs are found all within one compass: ideas of God, of customs, of the office of the High Priest, of the Ark and the Tabernacle; later, middle, and early periods are all combined to produce an ideal of primitive times. Penetrating the recesses of intricate genealogies, we find the same conditions; and it is the study of these which forms the subject of the seventh chapter. The suggestions of etymologies will probably meet with varying degrees of approval; if they are fortunate enough to escape general condemnation. The analysis of the history of Jacob's eldest and youngest sons, suggested by the hints of tradition conveyed in stories based on several different derivations, and the demonstration of the confusion of Judite and Ephrathite history, are the most interesting and satisfactory to myself. But I must restrain myself, or I shall be accused of writing an author's criticism of his own work; and I have, with one exception, executed the task, which I set myself, of explaining the system on which the book developed itself.

343. I had intended making an appendix of the chapter on the parallel observable between Chinese and Hebrew history and religion; but on maturer reflection, it appeared to demand a place in the main body of this book. This could well be made the subject of a monograph, and, in the hands of an experienced Sinologue, be developed into a bulky volume. It is strange, that without the bias of theological or anti-theological prejudice, critics assign a date for the commencement of reliable Chinese history, 780 B.C.,[1] which marvellously synchronises with the limits of true Hebrew history, as assigned by Kuenen and other "higher" critics. The lesson we learn from this is, that nations may have any amount of literature, of the most "sere and yellow leaf," but it is not till the race of editors arises that true history begins. Previously collections of facts, in the briefest, driest, and often most unintelligible form, may be piled up, as was the case with the Chun Ts'ew and the Bamboo Annals. The attempt to save the contents of these from oblivion, seems to have aroused the historic spirit. We cannot suppose that the writers of the Tso Chuen and Shoo King had in every case access to the fuller historiographical documents, of which the Chun Ts'ew and the Bamboo Annals provide the *précis* notes. They had probably oral tradition, local odes and folklore to aid them in the work of filling in and colouring.

344. This is most important in its bearing on the compilation of Hebrew history, for even though Qirjath Sepher, or Bookton, was furnished with a library before the advent of the Hebrews; and, though in early times, Issachar and the North were celebrated for the skill of their scribes; even though tablets in Babylonian cuneiform writing were stored all over Palestine, as is suggested by analogy from the Tel-el-Amarna tablets; the main points at issue are untouched. What was the nature of the news inscribed on these booktiles? What was their form? Surely

[1] Mayer's "Manual," p. 369.

of Oriental science. We learn how every decade marks a distinct advance in scientific knowledge. I deny, however, that recent discoveries overturn and nullify the labours of previous critics. Newly discovered facts may upset or disorganise existing theories, but they will never shake the foundations of abstract truth, on which Higher Criticism is founded.

346. It was the custom at Queen's College, Oxford, twenty years ago, for undergraduates at the end of Term, to appear before the "Dons" in Common Room, when the lecturers would comment upon the signs of improvement, or otherwise, perceptible in the examination papers written at "Collections." I well remember Mr. Sayce's addressing the late Provost, Dr. Jackson, in March 1874, to the following effect: "Mr. Wright, Sir, has done a very creditable paper, showing that he has made a careful study of the book of Isaiah; but "— and this with a friendly smile of encouragement—"but I think that a little more experience and further study will satisfy him that he has *not fairly represented* the *arguments in favour* of the *dual authorship* of Isaiah. Thenceforth, I determined to inquire into critical questions without an *a priori* bias that they must be wrong because they disagreed with tradition; I am therefore indebted for my present liberal views to the author of "The Verdict of the Monuments."

347. I must confess that this incident recurred to me, more than once as I read some of the indictments formulated against the advocates of "Higher Criticism." "A single error in detail, a single inconsistency, a single exaggeration, a single anachronism was considered sufficient to overthrow the credit of a whole narrative." This charge could only apply with force against some of the old-

fashioned difficulties about Sargon, and other historical problems, the solution of which by either conservative or liberal critic could only be temporary, till more light could be thrown from other sources, and such were then despaired of. As a rule, narratives are vitiated by the presence of more than one of these separate defects; and when, out of the multitude of stories in the Hexateuch, there is not one to which you can point with any feeling of security, as bearing the impress of simple truth unaffected by extraneous influence, allowance has to be made for the general atmosphere, so that the presence of a single defect may, in rare instances, suffice for the rejection of a particular narrative.

348. "The pages of the Old Testament were accordingly ransacked for arguments against itself. No point, however minute, which could tell against it was overlooked, no interpretation was neglected which could assist in the work of destruction"(p. 21). Surely rhetoric has taken the place of argument here. The picture of a "Higher" critic, seated pencil in hand scoring his Bible whenever an argument hostile to orthodoxy presented itself, is more vivid than real. Colonel Ingersoll might possibly prepare material for a lecture in this manner, but to suppose Kuenen and Wellhausen pursuing such a course is ludicrous when the method is compared with the result: the haphazard ransacking with the cool, almost cold, unimpassioned, most logical argument. Archæology does not disdain the aid of the microscope in deciphering characters, the omission or insertion of "a jot and a tittle" has the most serious consequences; why should critics be blamed for not overlooking minute points?

"The work of destruction" is a phrase to catch the jury, for "Higher" critics aim at construction, not destruction; they seek to expose lost reality, not to conceal existing truth.[1]

349. The use of the character *Shel*, a sort of possessive relative, on a northern coin of the eighth century, is supposed (pp. 6, 449) to prove that the Song of Songs may, after all, be the *bonâ fide* production of King Solomon, two hundred years previously. This assertion assumes or suggests that the argument for the late authorship of this book depends solely on this comparatively trivial point; whereas a reference to Driver's Introduction (pp. 421, 422) will provide a list of a dozen Aramaisms which are not found in the northern writers of the same period. If *shel* were in common use in the northern tribes, in the eighth century, *why* have Hosea and other northern prophets *carefully avoided its use*? It is possible—in fact, natural—that a contraction, made of necessity to meet the difficulties of circumscribed space in coins or cursive literature, may have been known long before it was introduced into the spoken language or classical literature.

350. It is true that one hundred or even fifty years ago, it was considered established that writing was an invention too modern for such phrases as "Moses wrote it in the Book" to be accepted as describing a real incident. Undue stress was undoubtedly laid upon this argument; but as it was generally applied to Greek classics, there was no cause of complaint, that an *a priori* objection to the Mosaic authorship originated the assertion. For the last quarter of a century this argument has been neglected, if not discarded.

[1] See above, par. 15-18.

Wellhausen and Kuenen not only do not build upon the inability of Moses to write, but, as far as my memory serves, make no allusion to this kind of argument. I cannot but think that it must mislead the general public, as to the method and force of the "Higher" critical reasoning, to read: "If we are to throw discredit on the history, we must have recourse to *other* arguments than those which rest upon the *supposed ignorance* of the *art of writing* in the early age of Palestine" (p. 60).

351. In the "Conclusion" Professor Sayce evinces a spirit of equity, which is not so conspicuous in the earlier chapters. "On the other hand, the same evidence, which obliges us to reject the conclusions of the newer critics in one place, *equally* obliges us to *reject* those of the *older school* of commentators in another" (p. 561). It was not to be supposed that a book published by the Society for the Promotion of Christian Knowledge would state very clearly the "Verdict of the Monuments," when adverse to the generally accepted outlines of Hebrew history, as recorded in the Bible. The reader must mark for himself the amount of discredit thrown on Biblical narrative by the testimony of the monuments, which is of much greater weight and volume than the negative charges of incomplete and insufficient knowledge with which its independent critics are here charged.

352. Subjective critics have never stated that Hebrew authors have simply given the reins to their imagination, and freely invented interesting tales without any foundation on which to rear the fabric. On the contrary, they have sought for, and

welcomed from others, the facts which provided the sources of such narratives. The discovery of particulars about the Dardani and Teucri and the earlier date of their history as attested by the Tel-el-Amarna tablets, is of the utmost importance to history generally. But the discovery of no number of names such as Achilles, Ajax, Hector, Cassandra, &c., could in any way establish the absolute truth of Homeric stories, as to the details of family history and conversations of heroes of the Trojan war. Still less could such discoveries discredit and destroy the theory of the composite authorship of the Iliad and Odyssey, which is based on purely literary and internal considerations. In the same time the monuments may continue to reveal any number of Biblical names, as yet undiscovered, such as Phicol, Hirah, Rachel, and Leah, without in any way establishing the correctness of the family incidents connected with them in Genesis, still less have they absolutely any weight whatever in depreciating the conclusions of the critics who have carefully catalogued the linguistic peculiarities of various authors of the Hexateuch, recognising even the faintest shade of variety.

363. The author of "The Verdict of the Monuments" writes : "Opinions may differ widely as to the authorship of certain passages and the dates to which the several documents are to be assigned, but about the general fact of the *composite character* of the Pentateuch, competent critics of *all schools are now agreed*" (p. 31). This hardly accords with the sweeping condemnation, "The archæology of Genesis seems to show that the literary analysis of the book must be revised, and that the confidence with which one portion of a verse is assigned to one author, and another portion of

it to another, is a confidence begotten of the study of modern critical literature, and not of the literature of the past. Such microscropic analysis is the result of short sight" (p. 561). On what principles then, may we ask, is the composite character of the Pentateuch to be established at all ? The reply would probably be that archæology graciously permits us to recognise dual authorship in the stories of Creation and the Flood, because evidence of the same phenomenon is observable in Babylonian accounts; or that the progressive character of the so-called Mosaic Code is established by the evolution of doctrines manifest in the various editions of the Egyptian "Book of the Dead." It is surely highly improbable that critical system should be shown consistently applicable to the first six books of the Bible, that vocabularies can be drawn up of words employed by certain authors whose date and standpoint are discernible from internal evidence, that all critics should agree about the main features of the case, and yet, after all, the principles of it are to be disowned because Hammurabi has been found to have suggested to some Hebrew author the introduction of Amraphel into the life of Abram. In fact, the defeat of the Babylonian warrior by the Hebrew ancestor is precisely the sort of story we should expect to be introduced as a *solatium* when the Israelites themselves had been conquered by Babylon. This was the date assigned to this episode by critics, before the Monuments had unearthed Hammurabi, and no testimony to the personal identity of Abraham, or to the antiquity of the story of his defeat of the former is borne by the proof that there once existed a king who was utilised in this manner.

354. As far as I can gather, it is not claimed that

The Nature of the Monuments Discovered

as yet any continuous work of Egyptian or Assyrian history of ancient date has been exhumed. Panegyrics of heroic kings, or pæans on their victories, with tabulated lists of the vanquished, or books of mystic ritual, form the bulk of the discoveries. Egypt provides the sensational literature; the novel of the Twin Brethren, which suggested the story of Joseph and Potiphar's wife, and the Journal of an Egyptian Marco Polo are evidences of that "touch of nature which makes the whole world kin." The Sacred Epics of Babylonian literature are more in harmony with Hindu than Hebrew literature, judging from specimens given in Professor Sayce's Hibbert Lectures. The question then arises, By what right are these "Higher" critics required to mould their researches into Hebrew literature, which, in its present form, is a vertebrate unity, after the manner indicated by the dislocated discoveries on the banks of the Nile or the Euphrates.

355. It is a matter of regret than an Appendix on the Tel-el-Amarna correspondence was not added to the "Verdict of the Monuments," showing the total number of kings and governors who addressed Khu-n-Aten, and the names of their cities and provinces. Brief references to it are scattered over 500 pages, and it is quite possible that one forms a wrong impression of its nature. This correspondence appears to be entirely *sui generis;* addressed to an Egyptian Pharaoh, it is written upon clay tablets in Babylonian cuneiform characters. The language is mostly Babylonian, transliteration of foreign, Canaanite, words is very rare. The motive of addressing Pharaoh in this language appears to be that on account of his mother being a Mesopotamian he was pro-Asiatic (pp. 47-49). The contents of the correspondence from the point of view of generally accepted ideas, sacred and profane, are singularly proleptic. "The Tel-el-Amarua tablets have enabled us to carry back a contact between Greece and Canaan to a still earlier period" (494), *i.e.*, from Hezeqiah, 700 B.C. to Khu-n-Aten, 1740 B.C. "In one of them mention is made of a Yivana or Ionian, who went on a mission in the country about Tyre," 300 years before the siege of Troy. "The districts south and north of the Ephraimite hills are already known as Jacob and Joseph" (p. 337). "On the other hand, Jacob is found in Cappadocia" (p. 338), "Judah north-west of Aleppo" (p. 305), "Simeon and Levi near Tyre" (340). These last, if substantiated, support my theory that the Jacobeans were chiefly settled in the north ; while the reference to both Jacob and Joseph in Palestine at the very time one, or both, is supposed to be languishing in Egypt, appears fatal to any Hebrew visit to Egypt whatever. I must honestly confess that my first impression on reading the account of the Tel-el-Amarna correspondence was that it was a hoax or forgery of some one, who, wishing to curry favour with an Assyrian or Median conqueror—Cambyses, for example—showed him that more than 1000 years previously an Asiatic king of Egypt had been addressed in Babylonian by his tributaries, irrespective of nationality and native tongue.

356. Ramses III., nearly 200 years after Khu-n-Aten, conquers Palestine, but does not mention Jacobel and Josephel.[1] How is this discrepancy accounted for ? As his victories took place at the time that Moses was making himself a name by the conquest of

[1] Kuenen, i. p. 141.

The "Verdict" discredits Hebrew Chronology 337

Og and Sihon, we are also surprised that he left such a formidable growing power unmolested, especially as, if the Biblical narrative is trustworthy, he should have been eager to recover the prestige lost by his father on the banks of the Gulf of Aqaba. The "Verdict of the Monuments" seems to mystify, if not discredit, the Hexateuch narratives. If, however, the Jacobeans were not a powerful race in the north, they would escape notice; and if the Josephites were wandering in the east, without any miraculous victories, after being driven out of Egypt, they would be treated by the Egyptians with natural contempt; and the silence of Ramses is accountable.

357. Egyptian chronology is still uncertain. In "Ancient Empires of the East" (p. 47), the date 1320 B.C. is approved for the Exodus; but in the "Verdict of the Monuments," about ten years later (p. 242), it is thrown a century later, as Ramses II., who preceded the Pharaoh of the Exodus, does not die till 1281 B.C. This last leaves only a couple of centuries for the wanderings, the conquest of Canaan and settlement before Saul arises 1037 B.C.[1] It also severs Abram from Moses by another 100 years; 1100 years from Khammurabi to Amenophis is irreconcilable with the seven generations. The "Verdict of the Monuments" is again adverse to the Hexateuch narrative.

358. Even if the Tel-el-Amarna tablets are genuine, which I suppose it would argue madness to deny, how does the existence of Ebedtob, king and priest of Jerusalem 1470 B.C. (or 1370), establish the truth of story about Melchizedeq in 2350 B.C., and substantiate the payment of tithes to him by Abram? The notorious

[1] Schrader ii. 320.

famine, that was still remembered in Egypt 500 B.C., does not prove that Joseph interpreted dreams; nor does a Semitic, Dudu, second to Pharaoh, nor the Babylonian etymology of *Arbrek* remove the impression forced upon us by various considerations that, like all the Hexateuch narratives, and even to a higher degree, the story of Joseph is a romance. Details were doubtless borrowed from all available Egyptian sources, including the novel of the Twin Brethren, to give an appropriate local colouring to a story, the main plot of which was taken from the life of Samuel (p. 176). The Tel-el-Amarna correspondence on the one hand shows that there would be no difficulty in the way of an author's finding "copy" of the sort required, and the Books of Job and Ruth on the other vindicate the claim of Hebrew authors to high rank as novelists and dramatic writers.

359. The "Verdict of the Monuments," then, so far from subverting the critical opinion that there is no reliable history of Israel before the reign of David, supports the conclusion that the writers of the Lives of the Patriarchs and the Judges were in such complete ignorance of the times that they were describing as to represent a period of 1100 years as 480, and to incorporate subsequent Egyptian anecdotes to give the necessary local tints. The main point of the "Higher" critics is untouched. These stories were written ages afterwards, and this assertion is made, not because of the inability of men in those primitive times to write, but because the authors knew only the barest facts about them, and with a lack of historic perspective introduce the conditions of their own days into those remote periods.

360. If the history is unreliable, it seems a work of supererogation to do more than assert that the miracles and prophecies which embellish it *must ipso facto* be more so. Miracles abound where ignorance is most evident, as in the lives of Moses, Joshua, and the Judges. The mental condition, that could accept stories of heathen origin like the Creation and the Flood, Abram and Isaac, Jephthah and his daughter, of Iphigeneia = Iphi's daughter and Samson[1] would not be slow to utilise the pious love of the marvellous in the manufacture of miracles, which should redound to the glory of the Hebrew race, by showing the special favour it enjoyed at the hands of the Most High, Who perpetually transcended the laws of nature in its behalf.

361. The Songs of Moses and Jacob are excellent specimens of prophecy after the event, which betray themselves so completely, that in their case the assertion cannot be ascribed to the fractious designs of critics. The prophecies to Abram, Isaac and Jacob of the greatness of their posterity, fall with the disillusion of their general history; nor do they stand, any more than the above-mentioned songs, by its establishment. The prophecies in Genesis[2] are mutually exclusive, as 400 years and the fourth generation refuse to be reconciled. The old explanation that the 400 years counted from Abram's visit to Egypt down to the Exodus inclusive, is shown by the Monuments untenable, as 1000 or 1100 years represent that interval. The first Messianic prophecy[3] is by a strict translation shown to be a simple statement of the natural warlike tactics pursued by the man and the snake.

---

[1] Ewald, ii. 395.   [2] xv. 13, 15.   [3] Gen. iii. 15.

Another[1] relates the national history of Judah, while the ease with which it has been perverted into the prophecy of Messiah, warns us not lightly to disregard the testimony of the bulk of Hebrew interpreters, who maintain that Isaiah liii. is also a simple narrative of the fortunes of the people. The belief in the power of prophecy led to the research for passages of ancient Scripture which could any way be strained in to prognosticating subsequent events or not seldom led to the manufacture of events which should fulfil prophecies whose fulfilment was not yet accomplished. It is thus that the otherwise manifestly unreliable early chapters of the Gospels of Matthew and Luke make Jesus born at Bethlehem, instead of Nazareth; while the latter is guilty of an anachronism, and shows his ignorance of the method in which a Roman census was held, to account for the presence of the infant's parents at Bethlehem.

362. The fulfilment of prophecy has been so much dwelt upon as a proof of its divine inspiration; and a belief in the history attached to such prophecies has been held to be so remarkably established by the fact of their fulfilment, that we may be excused for a brief practical consideration of the phenomenon. The existence of antedated prophecies actually written after the events they foretold is a powerful caution against a too ready acceptance of their inspiration. On the other hand those prophecies which appear to have been wonderfully realised, are just those which merely required keen observance of the signs of the times, and a study of the fate of adjoining nations, and reference to past history. I refer specially to the prophecies of

[1] Gen. xlix. 10.

Unfulfilled Prophecy Ignored

the desolation of Edom and Moab, Judah and Israel, the carrying into captivity and the dispersion of the nation; for the manner in which the empires of the East established their conquests by total destruction of capital cities and wholesale transplantation of populations, was well known before their full force was turned on Western Asia. There remains, however, quite another question, not sufficiently considered—viz., unfulfilled prophecy. To meet this difficulty, several stories have been invented, but there is a large number not so carefully guarded. Micah v. 6 foretells an Israelite invasion and conquest of Assyria; Isaiah xix. 24 predicts a triple religious alliance of Egypt, Assyria, and Israel; Hosea xi. 9–11· asserts the recovery of the lost tribes. Some interpreters of prophecy may console themselves with the possible contingency of the fulfilment of the last prediction in the remote future; but as Egypt and Assyria no longer exist, the first two cases appear hopeless. As to prophecies of shorter anticipation, the study of those of Jeremiah is instructive; he appears to have pronounced terrible curses on his enemies rather lavishly; on Hananiah (xxviii. 16); on Ahab, Zedekiah, and Shemaiah (xxix. 21, 32); but the fulfilment of the first is alone recorded. These blood-curdling anathemas are truly Oriental, but it is a relief to reflect that their realisation is so rare, as to indicate fortuitous coincidence, rather than divine approval and confirmation. The most conclusive instance of inspired belief in the course of future events, which eighteen and a half centuries of subsequent facts have shown utterly foundationless and misdirected, is Paul's fixed confidence that he should not die, but be translated with the righteous at the end of the world ;[1] Peter[2] and James[3] shared also the conviction that the end of the world was to be momentarily expected in their days.

363. Miracles and prophecies are the most improbable of the many improbable elements observable in the Hexateuch narratives ; they have absolutely no independent weight in assigning its date ; but rather contrariwise, the presence of miracles shows that the author lived so long after, as to feel less, if any, scruple at the improbabilities he was relating; and the allusions in the prophecies, by their reference to several historical incidents, long subsequent to the days of the Patriarchs and the Judges, confirm the critical assertion of the author's late date.

364. *Quousque tandem. . .?* Pray then how long are we to continue training children in an implicit belief in the historical truth of the first seven books of the Bible ? How long are the very foundations of religion and morality to be shaken in the young man's heart, by the discovery that these stories are not history, that this fiction is not fact? No line of demarcation is drawn. From cover to cover of the Bible all is equally revelation and inspiration. Such generalisation is most dangerous. The observation of manifest infirmities in some parts causes the pillars of the solid fabric of religion and even of morality to totter. The degree of the revulsion in manhood is proportionate to the keenness of imagination enjoyed, and the absolutely simple belief indulged by the child. Shall we then encourage children to cherish as flowers, what we are assured they will in their maturity reject as weeds ? Or what is worse, shall we stifle the

---

[1] 1 Thes. iv. 17; 1 Cor. xv. 51 ; Phil. iv. 5. [2] 1 Peter iv. 7.
[3] Jas. v. 8.

natural inquiries of children, and silence those logical objections, which arise naturally and unbidden in their little minds? Are our dull perceptions and blunted imaginations to be canonised as virtuous faith, and their innocent prattle to be stigmatised as vile heresy? It was once my duty, as part of their course of education, to teach two little boys, of ten and twelve years of age, Scripture lessons. I continually found myself in a dilemma. Had they been my own sons, I should have said to them, "This is an allegory, such is its moral lesson; it was written for the infancy of the Israelite race, and must not be accepted literally as a history designed for a people whose education was fully developed. One day we were taking the story of Abram and Isaac, when one of the boys exclaimed, "This cannot be true, God never ordered a father to murder his son." I was obliged to refer them to their own father for his opinion, I could not conscientiously affirm that it was in any sense true. I insert this anecdote as an illustration of the unbiassed effect produced upon juvenile minds, by the assigning to God of incongruous attributes, or of a dalliance with sin. Another boy of seven, as I have heard, was playing with his toys, when his aunt entered the room, weeping, to announce to him that his father had just died in the room overhead. The little boy hardly desisted from his play to remark, "Then, by this time he has seen Abram, Isaac, and all the patriarchs." Strange acme of bliss to associate with the departure into the new and unknown world of spirits; but how instructive as evidence of the firm grip of reality, secured by infants on these Biblical narratives: I ask what was the effect on that boy's faith in topics of greater moment, when his patriarchs no longer shone in his grasp, but as baubles, or dissipated into thin air as bubbles?

365. I would venture to make the following rough assertion as to the beliefs of the clergy of the Church of England and ministers of various denominations. Ninety-nine per cent. would reject the stories of the speaking ass of Balaam, and the ventilated dolphin of Jonah, as undiluted fables. Seventy-five per cent. would admit that the Garden of Eden, Noah's Flood, and the Tower of Babel were legends. On the other hand, the percentage of those who realise the unhistoricity of the lives of the Patriarchs and of Moses and Joshua, might probably be represented by decimal places. This is not to be taken as proof of their having investigated the subject, and concluded that the history of those times is established on an irrefragable basis; but rather as an indication that they fail to recognise it as a matter of vital importance; in the present state of warfare, to reduce the length of lines of defence; in the storm now raging, to cut away the wreckage that impedes the way of the ship, and threatens its total loss.

366. Far better were it with the Catholic Church, to discountenance the unrestricted acquaintance with the Bible, which is prone to lead to misconception. Or, if this is opposed to the liberal spirit of the times, let us share Reuchlin's dissatisfaction with the incompleteness of the work of Reformation; and admit once, and for all, that there is as great a gulf between the historical value of the Hexateuch and of the books of Samuel and Kings, as between the intrinsic merits of Daniel and Isaiah, of Jonah and Hosea, of Esther

and Nehemiah, of the Song of Songs and the Psalms, of Ecclesiastes and Job. We may, if we please, include them all under one category as inspired writings; but, as in comparing different works of the Old Testament, we recognise lower grades of genius contrasted with higher, and in some books actually more heathen and less spiritual standpoints; so, while not grudging the highest palm for literary work and religious sentiment to the Hexateuch, we cannot fail to see that these authors are writing of times of which they are completely ignorant, in comparison with the studies of life compiled from the notes of later historiographers. If we impress upon ourselves and our children that these are only fond dreams and pious conceptions of early times, whose reality is lost in the dimness and obscurity of remote antiquity; that the main points of the moral lessons remain untouched, though we frankly acknowledge their pictorial dress to be fiction; we shall find religion to be the gainer and not the loser; we shall remove one of those stumbling-blocks, one of those scandals which we are solemnly warned by Christ to beware of laying in the footpath of the little ones.

367. I have been writing neither as a theologian nor as a critic, but as one of the mass of thinkers whose hearts are stirred within them by the problems raised by the results of modern discovery, not modern invention. Mine is not the seat of the judge who pronounces sentence in accordance with the law after reviewing the arguments of both sides. My attitude is rather that of the barrister, who, in the desire to state his case clearly, finds its necessary to anticipate the objections likely to be raised by the other side,

and to strengthen his own position by showing the fallacies adduced by the opponent. I have endeavoured to avoid the use of expressions which might wound the susceptibilities of those whose simple piety accepts the Bible without inquiry, but as such are not likely to read a book of this character, I need hardly apologise to the stronger brethren for any inadvertence that may have crept in, despite my better purpose. I am confident that the host of earnest inquirers and seekers after lost and buried truth is waxing in bulk; and if any such are stimulated to further independent research, or find from the perusal of this book, with its many imperfections, any ray of light thrown on the trackless waste of primitive history, I shall be content.

APPENDIX

THE DOCTRINE OF IMMORTALITY IN THE OLD TESTAMENT

368. When Confucius was asked by one of his disciples what his views were on a future life, he replied with another question: "Have you solved the mysteries of this· present life?" As the disciple could not lay claim to such complete knowledge, the sage continued: "If the mysteries of our daily life are unfathomable, how much more beyond our ken must be hypotheses concerning a future existence!" The reply of Confucius contained, in embryo, an anticipation by 2000 years of the argument employed in Bishop Butler's Analogy of Religion.

369. It has been the custom on the score of this episode, to accuse Confucius of indifferentism towards this soul-absorbing topic, and to maintain that modern Confucianists are practically sceptics denying a future existence. It is true that strict Confucianists have no share in the Buddhist belief in a material Hell; but there are many grounds for supposing that there is an indefinable rational conviction concerning a future state, entertained commonly by the people, though not crystallised into the form of dogma. Such grounds are: belief in apparitions of the departed, the recognition by separate terms of the tripartite composition of man—body, soul, and spirit; the aversion to loss of limb in this life, as affecting happiness hereafter; the strict attention paid to the interment of the dead, including the choice of the most favourable situations and aspects for tombs; and above all ancestral worship. Ancestral Worship is viewed by many as a mere appanage of filial piety, as if its sole object were to sanctify the relation between father and son; whereas its remoter, one might say, its truer purpose is by frequent commemoration of ancestors to urge their descendants to emulate their virtue and deeds of renown, and to avoid bringing disgrace on their unsullied memories. It is hardly conceivable that such a custom could have been maintained for centuries, and yet for the worshipper all the while to be convinced in his mind that his interest and devotion were being expended on ancestors, who had long since ceased to be.

370. Very similar will be found to be the results of an inquiry into the existence of the doctrine of Immortality in the Old Testament. The few well-known passages commonly adduced in testimony will be found, on investigation, incapable of bearing this interpretation; the only indisputable passage being of so late a date as the second century B.C., in the Book of Daniel. Are we then, because of the silence of the literature on the subject, justified in concluding that the Israelites had no conception of the doctrine? Assuredly not, for we shall find that they too had narratives and customs, which not only imply the doctrine of immortality, but are direct evidence of their belief in it. We may not then assert that the doctrine of a life continued beyond the grave was unknown to the Israelites, because their

prophets and philosophers not only abstain from giving a formal utterance concerning it, but actually abandon themselves to melancholy and despair, when they approach the subject.

371. It has been said, and with much truth, that their souls were so filled with the threats and promises of divine rewards and punishments in this life, that no occasion remained to stimulate interest in the future world. Further, that their belief in the immortality of the Chosen People, the race not the individual, a belief nurtured by frequent divine promises, and manifested by the keen desire of all their parents for children, that this belief restricted their vision to an earthly horizon, and prevented their penetrating the mists that shroud the world beyond the grave. It remains, however, a question, whether these considerations may not be viewed as the very motive, the *divine* motive, if we may venture so to employ the word, in holding the doctrine in abeyance for so many centuries.

372. In order to make a complete search for expressions in the Old Testament concerning immortality, we will employ the following method. We shall begin with observing Hebrew ideas about death and the grave; we shall listen to their utterances in the immediate presence of death, on the bed of sickness, at the approach of old age and in the hour of bereavement; we shall sit at the feet of their philosophers as they discourse on the sublime topic of the moral government of the world; and then having observed the restricted view of immortality commonly entertained by them, the immortality of personal fame and family name, turn to consider the more hidden references to the doctrine in their historical narratives and social customs.

373. DEATH AND THE GRAVE.—Sleep is known as "Death's twin-brother" to all nations. The lapse into unconsciousness and the appearance of suspended vitality are respectively the subjective and objective causes, which from the earliest times have made the comparison between sleep and death self-suggestive. Thus, in the Book of Job, we read:

> iii. 13. For now should I be lying and at rest,
> Asleep then were there peace for me.
> 17. There cease the wicked to trouble,
> And there the toil-worn rest.
> Psa. xiii. 4. Regard and hear me, Yahveh, my God,
> Lighten mine eyes, lest I sleep (the sleep of) death.

Job xiv. 12[1] proceeds further and describes this sleep as *eternal*. Seas may ebb, but they will flow again; rivers be dried up, but they will be replenished by mountain torrents; while, on the other hand,

> Man lies down and rises no more,
> Till the heavens be no more, they shall not awake,
> Nor be roused out of their sleep,

i.e., they shall *never* awake; for from Ps. lxxii. 5, 7, 17, we find that the duration of the heavens is a poetical expression equivalent to "for ever." In Jer. li. 39, 57, "an eternal sleep that knows no waking" is associated with drunken stupor, and employed as a curse.

374. Death being viewed as a sleep, it is natural to find the grave described as a bed. Hence the frequent phrase, "lay down with his fathers," employed of Moses;[2] of David,[3] and elsewhere. The expression being "gathered to his people" or "to his fathers" is much

---
[1] *Cf.* vii. 9.   [2] Deut. xxxi. 16.
[3] 2 Sam. vii. 12; 1 Kings i. 21, ii. 10.

stronger and more suggestive, especially as in Gen. xxv. 8, xxxv. 29, xlix. 39, care seems to be taken to avoid confusing this act or condition with death and burial; for we read, " He *died* and was gathered to his fathers, and his sons *buried* him." Still we shall hardly be justified in taking this to mean, "His soul joined the assembly of the souls of his departed ancestors," as, after so explicit a statement, the position of the Prophets and of the schools of wisdom, would be inexplicably retrograde. It can only be taken as equivalent to the phrase above, "lying with his fathers," and conveys the idea of following his fathers to death, in obedience to the universal law, elsewhere otherwise expressed, "I go the way of all the earth," by Joshua,[1] and by David.[2] We may connect with this conception of death as *sleep* the representation of the grave as a place of *silence*.[3]

375. BLACKNESS OF NIGHT.—In common with many other nationalities, the Hebrews spoke of life as the time in which men "see the light," or "rejoice in the light."[4] By a natural sequence of thought, death is a condition in which men are no longer capable of beholding the light, and the grave is viewed as a place of darkness,[5] nowhere so graphically delineated as in Job:

> x. 21. I go hence, no more to return,
> To the land of darkness and gloom.
> 22. To the land which is pitchy dark,
> Of gloom without any order,
> Whose dawn is as pitchy darkness.

---

[1] xxiii. 14.   [2] 1 Kings ii. 2.
[3] Psa. xxxi. 18, 19; xciv. 17; cxv. 17; 1 Sam. ii. 9 (?), &c.
[4] See par. 80, Psa. lvi. 14: Job xxxiii. 28–30; Eccl. vii. 11.
[5] Psa. lxxxviii. 7, 13; Eccle. xi. 18.

The physical darkness attendant upon death, and the chilly gloom enveloping the grave and the vault sufficiently account for the origin of such ideas, but the expression of them by religious poets is inconsistent with their belief in immortality.

376. NO HEBREW LETHE.—It may be here observed that there is no idea in the Old Testament analogous to the Greek conception of a bath in Lethe, a preparation of the soul for the new experience by wiping out utterly the former associations. "The land of forgetfulness"[1] should rather be rendered "the land of forgottenness," an objective, not subjective, use of *neshiyah*,[2] "I am forgotten as a dead man, out of mind."[3] There is no need for a Lethean bath, simply because the dead do not exist, or have any conscious mental operations. The unconsciousness of the dead is absolute; it is not that they have entirely forgotten the things of earth, and awakened to perception of a new experience: "The dead know not anything."[4] The indifference to matters, formerly of a prime importance, expressed by Job:

> xiv. 21. His sons came to honour, and he knows not,
> Or are disgraced without his regarding.

is not due to forgetfulness, but to the cessation of existence. "There is no work, nor device, nor knowledge, nor wisdom in Sheol."[5]

377. GOD'S POWER DOES NOT EXTEND TO HADES.—A question of the deepest moment

---

[1] Psa. lxxxiii. 13.
[2] *Cf.* Psa. xxxi. 13.
[3] Eccle. viii. 10; ix. 5; Isa. xxvi. 14.
[4] Eccle. ix. 5.
[5] Eccle. ix. 10; Psa. cxlvi. 4.

now arises. Did the ancient Israelites believe that the grave was under the rule of Yahveh, their God? Would it be consistent for them to hold that the grave was a place of darkness and chaos,[1] and still maintain that the God who created light and brought chaos to a state of order, would allow such conditions to remain in the nether world, if it were a region under his control. In accordance with the henotheist belief of many ancient nations, the Israelites long held that Yahveh was their national God in the same sense as Chemosh was God of Moab, and that his power and presence were limited to Palestine.[2] Foreigners, who wish to worship Yahveh, must come to Jerusalem,[3] and Naaman, whose course of action was approved by Elisha, considered it necessary to carry away into Syria some of the very soil of Palestine[4] to form an acceptable altar for the worship of Yahveh in a foreign land.

378. The following passages would appear to suggest that this idea of the limitation of Yahveh's rule to the confines of Palestine, had been pressed to its logical conclusion, that his rule was restricted to the living of the Chosen People, and did not extend to the dead, who had perished from off the face of the *earth, i.e., country*.

Psa. lxxxviii. 4. My soul is sated with afflictions,
    And my life draweth nigh unto Sheol.
  5. I have been reckoned as one of them that go
      down to the grave;
    I have become like a hero who has grown feeble,
  6. *Free* to wander amongst the dead like the slain;
    The liers in the grave, whom *thou dost no more
    remember*,
    For they are *cut off from thy rule*.

---

[1] Job x. 22.   [2] Jud. xi. 24.
[3] Micah iv. 2; Zech. viii. 22.   [4] 2 Kings v. 17, 19.

Considerable light is thrown on the interpretation of this difficult verse, by reference to 2 Chronicles xxvi. 21, where of Uzziah it is said, that "he dwelt in the house of *freedom* for lepers, for he was *cut off* from the house of Yahveh." The restricted freedom is the same in both cases, liberty to wander anywhere but in the precise direction for which the soul yearns; while both are deprived of religious privileges. Similarly, a man, who had been suffering from some severe illness,[1] speaks of himself as doomed to death, in the words:

> xxxi. 23. I said in my alarm,
> I am *cut off* from the presence of thine eyes.

A dying saint entreats for continuation in the land of Yahveh.

> Psa. vi. 5. For in death there is no mention of thy name,[2]
> In the grave there is none to praise thee.

379. These quotations clearly indicate an idea of separation from Yahveh effected by death, as also do several other passages to the same effect, *e.g.*,

> Psa. cxv. 17. The dead do not praise Yah,
> Nor all those that go down in silence.

Job, too, entertains the same belief, for, after complaining of the continual inspection to which he was subjected by God in this life (vii. 17, 18), he expresses a wish,

> vii. 21. That now I might lie in the grave,
> Thou mightest seek me, but I should not be.

---

[1] Psa. xxxi. 10, 12.   [2] *Cf.* Ex. iii. 15.

Psalm cxxxix might appear antagonistic to the above notion, that, by dying, a man could escape from the rule of Yahveh.

> 7. Whither shall I go from thy spirit?
> And whither shall I flee from thy presence?
> 8. If I climb up to heaven, thou art there,
> And if I make my bed in Sheol, lo! there too art thou.

Heaven and Sheol are here intended to be only expressive of extremes of height and depth,[1] for if we take "the bed in Sheol" literally, what idea are we to suppose associated in the poet's mind with "climbing up to Heaven"? Both clauses must be taken metaphorically. In Psalm xlviii. 15, we have a distinct statement that God's protection and providence do not extend beyond death. "He shall be our guide up to the portals of death": *'al maveth*, cf. *'al pathach*, Job xxxi. 9. Bishop Alexander, in his Bampton Lectures on the Psalms gives as a translation, "*beyond* death," but I cannot find a passage to support this interpretation of the preposition *'al*. The LXX. evidently read *'ad mathai* = how long? which they render, *to eternity*. Ewald approves their conclusion, but recognises a difficulty in supposing that they read *'Olamoth*, which is removed above. He does not, however, admit allusion to immortality in Psalm xvi. 10; xvii. 15; xlix. 14; cxliii. 8.

380. Thus we find that the Israelites looked on the state after death as one of sleep and unconsciousness; that the grave was repellent to them; and that the dwellers in the tomb no longer worship God, and are no more under his government. If anywhere we should expect

---

Cf Amos ix. 2; Job xi. 8.

to find traces of the expression of a hope in Immortality, it would be on the approach of death in old age, at the end of the span allotted to man ; on the bed of sickness, when that span is threatened to be cut short prematurely ; or in the hour of bereavement, when we stand on the shore, and through the gloom, gaze after the bark launched on the waves of eternity.

381. OLD AGE.—In the final charges of Joshua and David, their piety finds utterance in gratitude for mercies vouchsafed in their own past lives, and in pronouncing promises and warnings for the guidance of their successors. There is not a word of Immortality, nor of its influence on the present life. Their silence is inconsistent with the supposition that they were cheered with any hope of a future existence for themselves, or of a reunion with those whom they were leaving behind. Neither does the panoramic view of Canaan granted to Moses before his death accord with a belief in the untrammelled flight of the conscious soul after emancipation from the body. In Psalm lxxi., an aged servant of God begs (verse 18) for continuance of life, urging, as a plea, that he may yet tell younger generations his experience of the power of God, and cries still more piteously for a renewed lease of life :

> 20. Thou who hast shown me many afflictions and ills,
> Wilt once more revive me ;
> Wilt once more rescue from the grave.

In Psalm xc., a psalmist, who has apparently exceeded the average limit of fourscore years (10), after praying (16) for a revelation of the mysteries of God's past dealings with him, utters a final plaintive prayer that the work of his life may be secured to his memory and not perish with him. Just as the former psalmist clings tenaciously to this life, in spite of age and afflictions, so the latter has no hope of the rewards of heaven for his faithful service in this world.

382. SICKNESS.—The Prayer of Hezekiah[1] is of great value, as revealing the secret reflections in the sacred privacy of a man's heart on the verge of the grave, in the imminent presence of death. He laments death as the end (11) of all intercourse with Yahveh, and of hope in the covenant mercies of God known as his *truth*.[2] The covenant of God with each man terminates with him personally at his death, though continued to his children (19).

> 18. For Sheol does not praise thee, nor death psalm to thee;
> They that descend to the grave do not hope for thy truth.
> 19. The living, the living shall praise thee, as I do this day;
> The father shall inform his children of thy *truth*.

God's truth is everlasting, being handed on, from generation to generation; as the "sure mercies of David,"[3] and the promises to Abram, Isaac, and Jacob were fulfilled through their descendant. The individual dies away from the promise, the promise does not fail him.

383. We have already had occasion to make quotations from the Book of Job; and though his utterances could well be cited here as the expressions of one described as suffering from an incurable disease, it will

---

[1] Is. 38.   [2] 18 *Cf.* Ps. xxx. 9; lxxxviii. 11-13.
[3] 2 Sam. vii. 12-16.

be better to reserve the consideration of them, as they represent rather the reflections of a philosophic school. Several Psalms—*e.g.*, xxx., xli., lxxvii., cxvi.—would appear to relate the experiences and reveal the heart-felt desires of the sick; but in all, the one cry is for recovery, whether the object is to continue the worship of God, or the more selfish one of wreaking vengeance on their enemies.

384. It is necessary to utter here a word of caution about the meaning imparted to the phrases "restoring to life," and "raising up"; which too strongly suggest the doctrine of immortality, to accord with the context. Raising up the sick from his couch of pain, and reviving him when at the very point of death is what the various writers intend to convey. "Yahveh killeth and maketh alive"[1] can in accordance with the *usus loquendi* mean simply, "God makes sickness, or wounds, fatal, and God it is who recovers the dying, even at the last gasp;" for compare the following Psalms:

> xxx. 3. I cried unto thee, Yahveh, my God; and thou didst heal me,
> Thou, O Yahveh, didst bring up my soul from Sheol.
> Thou didst *revive* me, even when amongst those who go down to the pit.
> xli. 11. But thou, Yahveh, take pity on me,
> *Raise me up* that I may repay them.

Manifestly the prayer of a sick man, *vide* verse 4.

385. Hence we discover that in Hosea vi. 2, the image employed is *not* one of *resurrection*. The children of Israel are represented as lying wounded and smitten, on a bed of sickness, from which it is promised that God will recover them:

[1] Deut. xxxii. 39.; 1 Sam. ii. 6; 2 Kings v. 7.

> 1. Come and let us return to Yahveh,
>   For he hath torn and he will heal us;
>   He smites and he will bind us up.
> 2. After two days, he will *recover* us;
>   On the third day, he will *raise* us *up*;
>   And we shall live before him.[1]

This interpretation is manifestly corroborated, by reference to Job:

> v. 17. Lo! Happy whom God doth chasten;
>   Then despise not the Almighty's correction.
> 18 (?) When he wounds, himself doth bind,
>   When he smites, his own hands heal.
> 19. Six times, he shall rescue from trouble,
>   The seventh, no evil shall touch thee.

It is surely by no accident, that in both passages we find, in the same context, the promise assured by the appended number.[2] If six times and the seventh, in Job convey the thought, that there is no limit to the number of troubles from which God is able to deliver; surely the two days, and the third, in Hosea promise that, however long the restitution tarry, it will surely come. Moreover, we must not overlook the fact that *yomayin* is not a literal period of *two* days, but an indefinite period.[3]

386. BEREAVEMENT.—In the calm that followed his futile, agonised entreaties for his child's restoration, David uttered the memorable words, "I shall go to him, but he shall not return to me." It is difficult to remove oneself from the subsequent standpoint of Christian hope, and to realise what the words really meant to David, but in view of the researches

---

[1] Cf. Psa. lxxxv. 7.   Micah v. 4; Prov. xxx. 18, 21, 29.
[2] Ex. xxi. 21 · Num. xxii. 9.

above, and the general feelings entertained by saints and prophets subsequent to him, it can hardly, without strain admit of any other interpretation than the following:

2 Sam. xii. 23. Can I restore him to life again?
I shall go to the grave, where he is;
But he will not return to life, where I am.[1]

Thus in old age, sickness, and bereavement, we find that the Israelites could not venture to express a hope in a life beyond the grave.

387. IMMORTALITY AND THE MORAL GOVERNMENT OF THE WORLD.

Nothing indeed is more remarkable than the absence of all reference to a future state, where the triumphant wicked shall be punished, and the despised and oppressed righteous rewarded. Men are encouraged to obey God's laws by the promise of length of life,[2] and of prosperity in their own days, and for their children after them.[3] Even when a more philosophical research into the problem of the moral government of the world is attempted, as in the Book of Job, Psa. xxxvii. 73, &c., the theory is maintained that rewards and punishments are confined to this life; even though it is frankly admitted that facts are often contrary to the theory. In Job, the only conclusion arrived at is, that as many mysteries in the natural government of the world as evinced by natural history, remain inexplicable; so man should not be surprised at the discovery of difficulties and anomalies in connection with its moral

---

[1] *Cf.* Job vii. 9, 10.   [2] Deut. iv. 40; v. 16.
[3] Deut. iv. 40; vi. 3, 18; xii. 25, 28; xxii. 7.

government. No light gleams from the future, no prospect of restitution and compensation is derived from the hope of immortality.

388. The Book of Job, written certainly *not earlier* than the Exile, may be accepted as an unimpeachable witness for the state of Jewish religious thought. Though evidently composed with a certain freedom in combating the then orthodox idea [1] that the righteous are rewarded and the wicked punished in this life, it has nothing in common with the more sceptical tone of the author of Ecclesiastes. M. Halevy says, "In Job, a redoubtable mark of interrogation is inserted before the problem of human destiny, a problem which the author abandons without a definite solution." As the author of the Book of Job makes his characters profess the deepest reverence for ancient tradition,[2] the absence of reference to immortality is strong evidence that the doctrine was not then formulated.

389. Is it possible for utter despair to find finer expression than in

xvii. 13. Am I to hope for Sheol as my home,
That I should spread my couch in darkness?
14. Should I call corruption, my father,
The worm, my mother and sister?
15. Ah! Where then would be my hope?
Who ever would see my wish?
16. To the bars of the grave they descend,
Together go down to the dust.

390. Job even goes so far as to express the wish that resurrection were conceivable and possible.

xiv. 13. Oh that thou wouldst hide me in Sheol,
. Wouldst conceal me, till thine anger were past,
Wouldst set me a time and remember me!

---

[1] Prov. xii. 31.   [2] Job viii. 8; xv. 18.

absent from the Septuagint translation; nor do Jewish commentators adduce this passage in support of the doctrine.[1] In view of Job's desire throughout the book to see God and enjoy restitution and vindication, before his death—a desire gratified (xlii. 5) in accordance with the prophecy of the three friends, at the close of their three first speeches—we can only suggest the following as somewhat conveying the author's idea:

> I know that my avenger liveth,
> And an heir shall stand my grave;[2]
> And after he hath *relaxed* this encircling net,
> Then still in my flesh shall I see God.

The guesses of the versions, and the difficulties that attend the reasonable interpertation, not to say translation, of this passage, sufficiently attest the presence of some corruption; and justify the suggestion that *sherah* should be read for *'ori*, especially as some *verb* is imperatively required in this clause; similarly in verse 29 we should probably read *shannetha* for *'avenoth*.

393. WHAT BECAME OF THE SOUL?—If then the Israelites were not assured of a belief in Immortality, what views did they hold as to the action of death upon man? At the creation of man, we read,[3] "And Yahveh God formed man of dust from the earth, and blew into his nostrils the breath of life." Death should be the converse of this, and so we find in the Sequel to the Book of Job, which contains the Elihu discourses.

---

[1] Pearson "On the Creed," p. 664.
[2] xviii. 20; xx. 21; Psa. xlviii. 14. [3] Gen. ii. 7.

> xxxiv. 11. If He turn His attention to man,
> And gather to Himself his spirit and *breath*;
> All flesh would die together,
> And man would *return* to *dust*.

Apparently this also is opposed to the idea of immortality, God withdraws the animating principle, and man ceases to be. More fully and clearly is this expressed in the Psalms, where the reference to the Genesis narrative is more pronounced:

> civ. 29. Thou hidest thy face, they are troubled;
> Thou gatherest their breath, they expire,
> And return to their dust.
> 30. Thou sendest forth thy breath, they are *created*:
> So thou renewest the face of the earth.

This passage appears to savour of a traduciary theory, the animating principle, withdrawn from one generation is transferred to the next. The earth is renewed, and not suffered to be depopulated. The individual is mortal, the race alone immortal. It is thus we must understand the answer which the Preacher gives to the question previously propounded by himself.

> Ecc. iii. 21. Who knoweth the breath of the sons of men
> that mounteth upwards,
> And the breath of the beasts, that descendeth
> downwards to the earth?
> xii. 7. The dust returneth to the earth, as it was,
> And the breath returneth to God who gave it.

We need not dwell on the passage Proverbs xii. 28:

> In the course of righteousness is life,
> And its way is a path *not unto death*,

which it has been attempted to render "a path unto *no death*" = immortality. As the supposed support in the Phœnician inscription on the sarcophagus of

Aschmanuzar[1] is withdrawn by the reading of the most competent critics, "an orphan the son of a *widow*." Besides we should expect *lo-maveth* not *al-maveth*, in accordance with usual Hebrew idiom. The LXX. antithetic parallel, "and the way of sinners leads unto death," probably represents the original.

394. IMMORTALITY OF FAME AND NAME.—Before we proceed to record the late expressions of this doctrine, and the vague popular belief that seems to have existed long before it was admitted by authority, we will consider the restricted view of immortality, as enjoyed by man, through never-dying fame and endless posterity. In the Book of Wisdom, we read :

> viii. 13. By Wisdom, shall I have immortality,
> And leave an eternal memory to my descendants.

When we further read, "Righteousness is immortal" (i. 15), "Virginity is immortal" (iv. 1), we cannot but feel that the phrase "hopeful of immortality" (iii. 4), beautifully suggestive as it is, was intended to convey no more than the idea, that the memory of the deeds of the righteous shall never perish, and that they are supported in afflictions and persecutions by this confidence in the immortality of their fame.[2] On the other hand, the wicked are said to die without hope (iii. 11, 18), *i.e.*, of this immortality; for as the wicked perish without attaining wisdom[3] they are deprived of this hope of eternal fame.[4] Very strongly is this reiterated as a refrain in Psalm xlix. 13, 21 :

---

[1] C. I. P., iii. line 3. [2] *Cf.* Isa. xxiii. 16; Psa. xlv. 18.
[3] Job iv. 21 ; xxxvi. 12. [4] Job xxiv. 20 ; Prov. x. 7.

> A man lacking wisdom, though in honoured position,
> Must be likened to the beasts that perish;

There is no further remembrance of such after death. The cynical author of Ecclesiastes goes further indeed, asserting (ii. 16) that "there is no remembrance of the wise more than of the fool for ever."

395. Beside personal immortality through fame, there was an indirect immortality, by means of posterity, or, as the Hebrew would express it, the immortality of name. The Israelites, like the Chinese, were very anxious to have posterity, especially sons, that the family name might not become extinct. It was for this purpose that the rights of inheritance and entail were observed so strictly. A man could not dispose of his property, as it belonged to his son; if, through stress of poverty, it was compulsorily lost by distraint for debt, theoretically it must return to him at the year of release,[1] or at the latest at the year of jubilee.[2] It was, too, to ensure posterity, that concubinage was permitted. Saul makes David swear[3] not to cut off his seed after him, nor destroy his name from his father's house. Absalom reared up a pillar in his lifetime for a monument, "for he said I have no son to keep my name in remembrance."[4] It has been pointed out that half the bitterness of death felt by Hezeqiah was due to the fact that at that time he had no son, Manasseh being born three years subsequently. God also vouchsafes to employ this phraseology, and promises that his people shall be a name to him for ever.[5] The son of Sirach expresses this idea plainly: "A father died, and is as though he had not died, for he left his likeness behind

---

[1] Deut. xv.   [2] Lev. xxv.   [3] 1 Sam. xxiv. 22.
[4] 2 Sam. xviii. 18.   [5] Jer. xiii. 11; Zeph. iii. 20.

him" (xxx. 4); while Wisdom states a father's extreme love for his son to have been one of the incentives to idolatry: "For a father smitten with inconsolable grief for his son, suddenly snatched from him by death, made an image of him, and honoured as God the man then dead." (xiv. 15.)

396. All this is strong evidence, that the Hebrew idea was the immortality of the race, not of the individual. A man without family, or who had lost his family by catastrophe, is viewed as chastened by God, if he is a righteous man, or as accursed of God, if he is a worldly liver. It was on this account that whole families are represented as perishing for one man's sin; as in the insurrection of Qorah, Dathan, and Ahiram, and the affair of Achan; for wicked doers shall be extirpated.[1] In Psalm xli. 5, we find as a strong form of curse, "When shall he die, and his name perish?"[2]

397. LATER DEVELOPMENT OF THE IDEA OF IMMORTALITY.—During the Exile, and later, we for the first time find definite statements regarding the future existence; and even these are employed either allegorically or in the highest flights of rhetoric:

> Isa. xiv. 9. Sheol, from beneath, is stirred for thee, to meet thy coming;
> It hath aroused for thee, the Shades, all the chiefs of earth;
> It hath caused all the kings of nations to stand by their thrones.
> 10. They will all of them answer and say unto thee
> Yea, thou too hast been weakened as we, and made like unto us.

---

[1] Psa. xxxvii. 28; Job. xviii. 17; Prov. ii. 22.
[2] Cf. Jer. ii. 19.

Isa. xiv. 11. Thy pride, the clang of the cymbals, hath
been brought down to Sheol,
Worms are spread for thy bed, and worms
form thy coverlet.

So also Ezeqiel xxxii. 21 : " The gallant heroes shall speak to him from the midst of Sheol." We involuntarily feel that we are in a new atmosphere. This is not Hebrew but foreign thought.

398. M. Halevy[1] gives an Assyrian legend about the mountain of the universe, where reigns the god Nergal, with his wife Allat, sister of Astarte, and where the dead warriors are the object of the pious and devoted attention of the wives and relations. He applies this to the mount of congregation in the recesses of the north[2] which is indeed attractive, as the mount is mentioned in connection with an assembly of dead warriors. But what appears inimical to this application is the fact, that the Babylonian monarch *aspires* to sit in the recesses of the north; this is denied him, and he is *thrust down* to *Sheol*, where he meets the departed heroes. The Hebrew prophet either misunderstood the Assyrian legend, or had some other legend at his disposal; Sheol and this mountain are with him two different places. The rare Rabbinical legend that there was in Zion a cleft rock, the foot of which was the entrance to Sheol, is discussed by Derenbourg and Halevy, and is supposed by them to throw light on this passage in Isaiah, and on the difficulty in Ps. xlviii. 3, " Beautiful of elevation, the joy of the whole earth, mount Zion, the recesses of the north, the city of the great king." (Cheyne.) Is not this, however, a pathos? Does

---

[1] "Comptes Rendus Académie des Inscriptions," 1880.
[2] Isa. xiv 13.

an allusion to the site of Sheol accord suitably with the praise of the magnificent Holy City? Both the Prophet and the Psalmist require rather an Oriental Olympus, the seat of the gods, than a place of assembly for the shades of heroes in Sheol.

399. There are, moreover, some passages which employ death and resurrection allegorically of the past and future, religious and political, of the children of Israel. Hosea vi. 2 is frequently taken in this sense, and would be the most interesting, being the most ancient, but we have seen above that death and resurrection are not referred to here. There can, however, be no doubt about Isaiah xxvi. 19:

> Thy dead men shall live, my corpses shall arise,
> Awake and sing, inhabitants of the grave!

and the vision of dry bones in Ezeqiel (xxxvii.), where the house of Israel in captivity is viewed as dead, and the nation, bereft of its former glory, is compared to an army of skeletons; but as God would not forsake his people, and had promised their restoration, the beautiful parable is completed by the rehabilitation of the bones and the revival of the corpses, the return from exile being described as a resurrection.

400. Though such is undeniably the primary meaning and object of these two passages, it is hardly conceivable that these two great prophets would have employed such imagery without some inner consciousness, however faint and undefined, of a hope of immortality, if not of resurrection, for the servants of God, if not for the whole human race. These passages doubtless, and the conception that inspired them, paved the way for subsequent trains of thought, which finally culminated, though fully two centuries later, in the first clear utterance concerning resurrection and immortality: "And many that sleep in the dust of the earth shall awake, some to everlasting life, and some to shame and everlasting abhorrence."[1]

401. POPULAR BELIEFS AS TO A FUTURE STATE.—But because of the silence of the prophets and philosophers on the subject of immortality, we are not justified in assuming that the doctrine was unknown amongst the current popular beliefs even at an early period. The nations around entertained this belief in various forms; the Egyptians, the Assyrians, and, as has been more recently maintained, the Phœnicians also. The Israelites, who were ever ready to welcome new forms of worship and prone to fall easy victims to the seductive rites of strange gods, would hardly remain proof against the fascination of the doctrine of a future life, rendered doubly attractive by the attendant superstition of having recourse to the dead, to obtain information about the unknown issue of events in this life. That necromancy is prohibited[2] is evidence of its existence at least as late as the days of Jeremiah. King Saul had put to death several who practised this art; and the episode of his interview with Samuel, raised by the incantations of the witch of Endor, shows distinctly the popular idea of the continued existence of the departed, and of their power to resume their former appearance and costume.[3] Isaiah (viii. 19) refers to this as a well-known practice: "When they say to you, 'Seek

[1] Dan. xii. 2, 3; *cf.* 2 Macc. vii. 9. [2] Lev. xx. 27.
[3] 1 Sam. xxviii. 14.

ventriloquists and wizards that chatter and groan, should not a people seek to *its gods*, viz., *the dead*, on behalf of the living?' Then put them to the test. To the Law and the Testimony seek; if they do not speak in accordance with the message there, it is because there is no dawn of revelation for them." The dead are called gods in several passages; the witch of Endor cries, "I see gods ascending out of the earth"; also what are called "sacrifices to the *dead*," in Psalm cvi. 28, are spoken of as "sacrifices to *gods*" in Numbers xxv. 2, and in Deuteronomy xxxii. 17 as "sacrifices to *devils*."

402. Further, the narratives of the restoration by Elijah and Elisha of children manifestly dead,[1] evince a clear belief that the personality does not perish at death, but is mysteriously somewhere else, whence it can return by divine power to re-inhabit its former tabernacle. We have another instance of miraculous recovery of the dead in the case of the man cast into the sepulchre of Elisha, who as soon as he came in contact with the bones of the saint, returned to life.[2] Much more remarkable in this connection is the translation of Enoch and Elijah; the race who believed that these two saints were bodily taken up into heaven must have had some notion of a future life. Dorner regards the translation of Enoch as not only typical of resurrection and immortality, but as indicative of the manner in which mankind would have been removed from this earth to a higher sphere of existence, if sin had not subverted the original plan. These legends attest the popular imaginations upon this interesting subject.

[1] 1 Kings xvii. 22; 2 Kings v. 35.   [2] 2 Kings xiii. 21.

405. We have then, on the one hand, distinct traces of the presence of the belief in immortality amongst the people from early times, and yet, on the other, no allusion to it, much less statement of it, made by the Hebrew prophets and poets before the time of the Exile. An interesting discussion on this anomaly arose between MM. Halevy and Derenbourg. The position of the former is : " Granted the great affinity between Hebrew and Assyrio-Babylonian legends, there is no reason for making an exception of belief in immortality of the soul, as this belief existed among the Assyrians long prior to the formation of Syro-Phœnician nations. Pentateuch and Prophets seek to repress and destroy the worship of the dead, which they rank with idolatry, hence this cultus must be deeply imbedded in the hearts of the people. And we know that the Prophets are often opposed to national belief." To this Derenbourg replies : " Popular thought is *not* Jewish thought. If Israel has a genius of its own, it is that of the prophets and poets who created its literature. Inasmuch as the people preferred idolatry to monotheism, they are in no way distinguished from Assyrians, Amorites, and Phœnicians." He perhaps mentally included that the popular ideas about immortality differed nothing from those of the heathen nations surrounding Palestine. We have no hesitation in accepting the conclusion of Halevy in preference to that of Derenbourg. Adopting a parallel line of argument to the latter, we might deny that the popular creed in the reign of Edward VI. was Catholic, because the Court and some prominent bishops were Protestant, and because Protestantism subsequently prevailed. It is necessary then that some attempt should be made to explain how it comes to pass that the doctrine of Immortality, triumphant in the New Testament, and known to have been held about two centuries before the birth of Christ, should have been suppressed by Moses and the Prophets.

406. Ewald observes:[1] "Yahvism is a religion of life, the Egyptian religion, a religion of death. The Egyptian nation like all others, when grown effeminate and luxurious, busied itself more with the unseen future than with present action. Is it not then conceivable that Moses, knowing the ill-effect in Egypt produced on the ignorant by an undue regard to the future existence, was apprehensive of a similar result among the people he was leading forth, who were already too prone to idolatrous worship, and whose courage and persistence might have been unnerved and relaxed in the long struggle before them if their gaze had been diverted from the earthly Canaan, not yet acquired, and they had indulged in dreams of bliss in a future unseen world, which in their then state of mind they would have debased and materialised? Can this be viewed as an entirely gratuitous assumption, when we remember the notoriety of Baal-Pe'or for a heinous crime, which in Numbers (xxv. 2) is described as simply worshipping *gods*, presumably Moabitish, but in Psalm cvi. 28[2] is denounced as "eating the sacrifices of the *dead*"? The heathen paid divine rites to the dead, should we then be wrong in concluding that to avoid the temptation to so awful an iniquity, the doctrine of Immortality was not promulgated?

407. We turn in vain to Rabbinical commentators for light on the Old Testament standpoint with regard

---

[1] Hist. ii. 134.   [2] *Cf.* Rev. ii. 14.

to this doctrine. It is true that Maimonides[1] makes the unsupported statement that "the resurrection of the dead is a fundamental article of our teacher Moses— on whom be peace!—but it happens to the righteous alone." Bishop Pearson, however, justly remarks:[2] "The Jews insist upon such weak inferences out of the Law, as to show that the resurrection was not clearly delivered by Moses. As because in the formation of man, Moses wrote *wayyiitser* with *two* yods and in the formation of beasts with but *one*, *wayyitser*, therefore the beasts are made but *once*, but man *twice*, once in his generation, and again in his resurrection. So from Ex. xv. 1, it is not said Moses *sang*, but he *shall* sing, viz., after the resurrection, in the life to come. Derenbourg asserts that the " Rabbinical idea of immortality was derived from Plato through Alexandria." This surely requires some qualification, for the ideas of a future life reserved to the righteous of Israel, of annihilation of the wicked, or of their purgation in Gehenna, are all of them, with many others, interconflicting, manifestly derived by expansion from well-known passages of Scripture.

408. To a child, or young man, the prospect of death is intended by nature to be distasteful. Love of life is implanted by God as the mainspring to quicken life and vigour. In youth the main religious sentiment should be to seek the divine blessing on the opening life, and so to live as to expect some measure of success as a token of divine approval. With advance of years, with experience of disappointment and defeat, baffled in conflict with insoluble moral problems, the soul of the mature man hears a voice within him

---

[1] Weber, p. 372.   [2] "On the Creed," p. 660.

proclaim: "This is not your rest"; and he finds support and comfort in the doctrine of immortality.

409. The youth of mankind too, as the apostle would say, required to be fed with milk, and not with meat. In accordance with the principle of evolution which God has been pleased to authorise or direct in connection with the development of religious as of other conceptions, we observe that the doctrine of immortality was not formulated till after the loss of the incentive to virtue and morality, afforded by the promises of earthly prosperity, intimately connected with and attendant upon the observance of social and religious laws. It was in the maturer age of the Israelite people, when they lay crushed under the disappointment of hopes cherished for centuries, that the new moral motive became necessary. May it not be said, that it was as fitting that the doctrine of immortality should first have dispelled the gloom and cheered the hearts of the returning exiles from Babylon, as that the Messiah should come just before the final dispersion of the Hebrew race?

INDEX

The Numbers refer to the Paragraphs only.

AARON, 207
Abel, 61
Abiathar, 145, 247
Abraham, 184-185
Abram, 182-183, 340
Accada in, 304, 324
Adam, 58
Akzib, 244
Altars, 142
Amram, 33
Amraphel, 71
Anaq, 253, 256, 272, 276
Anath, 255
Ancestral Worship, 138, 326, 369
Apocrypha, 308
Ark, 136, 223-224
Asherah, 139, 196
Axioms, 269

BAAL, 156, 266
Babel, 68
Bamboo Annals, 313
Bathshua, 230
Bede, 37
Beer-Lachai-roi, 80
Beer-Sheba, 79
Benjamin, 252, 257, 276
Benoni, 256, 276
Bethel, 82, 340
Bilhan, 198, 251
Bohan, 198

CAIN, 61
Caleb, 180, 216, 236-237
Call of Abram, 174, 305
Canaan, 65, 257
Canon, 308
Carmel, 202, 231, 276
Cherubim, 136
Cheyne, 171, 245, 255, 325, 399
Chinese references, 23, 117, 137, 297-328, 368, 369, 395
Chronology, 102-105, 277-279
Circumcision, 122-127, 339
Creation, 2, 165, 324

—D, 67, 81, 251
Damascus, 189 *n*, 340
Dan, 258-261
Daniel, 242, 347, 400
Deborah, 137
Decalogue, 119, 160
Definitions, 270
Derenbourg, 398, 404-405, 407
Deussen, 171
Deuteronomist, 116
Divination, 323
Driver, 40, 112, 116, 123, 230, 243
Duke of Argyll, 39

EDOM, 194
Ehud, 257
—el, 94, 191

Elohist, 116
Ephraim, 244
Ephratah, 236 (3); 244
Equinox, 131, 326
Esau, 193
Eseq, 79, 193, 253
Eshbal, 253
Eve, 61
Evil, 167-168, 171, 327
Ewald, 35, 40, 63-64, 66, 70, 73, 77, 130-131, 135, 183, 185, 188-189, 199-200, 228, 245, 247, 262, 285, 288, 336, 340, 360, 406
Exodus, 178, 248, 280, 330, 357, 270

FALL OF MAN, 2, 167-171, 327
Filial piety, 325, 369
Firstborn, 132, 284 (4)
Flood, 2, 172-173, 303
Fustel de Coulanges, 295

Gabelentz, 305
Gad, 263
Genealogies, 63, 70, 85-101, 108-113, 219, 325, 330
Gershom, 217
Gibeah, 33, 73
Gideon, 139
Gilead, 81
Gilgal, 125
God, 152-164, 320-321, 324
Grove, 139

HAGAR, 185
Halevy, 388, 398, 405
Ham, 65
Hamerton, P. W., 25
Hammurabi, 71, 277, 353
Hebron, 210, 213, 216, 222
Herder, 289
Hezron, 202-253
High Priest, 144-147

Higher Criticism, 14-15, 18, 21, 29-30, 343, 347-350
Hills, 141
Hinton, Dr. James, 169
Hippopotamus, 165
Historico-Geographical, 92, 198, 202-203
Historiographers, 314
History Composition, 37, 42, 46, 50, 69, 82-83, 89, 96, 114-115-116, 120, 133-134, 155, 158, 161, 165-166, 176, 223, 256, 311-318, 332, 340, 342, 344, 359
Holy Place, 137-143
Horace, 196, 300
Hyksos, 189, 203, 273, 275, 279

IMMORTALITY, 149, 322, Appendix
Innocence, 60
Inspiration, 149-151, 310, 318, 341, 364, 366
Isaac, 189
Iscah, 188
Ishmael, 191
Israel, 196, 276, 283-284
Issachar, 265
Ithamar, 145, 207

JACOB, 90, 195
Jair, 249, 285
Japhet, 66
Jasher, 166, 196 (3*b*)
Jehovah-Nissi, 248
Jephunneh, 238
Jesse, 219
Jezebel, 266
Job, 383, 388
Jochebed, 33
Joseph, 90, 176, 242-251, 282-283
Judah, 227-241, 244, 283, 293, 249, 295-296

Keil, 101, 106, 123, 127, 173, 188, 193, 202, 238, 259, 326, 334
Kuenen, 32, 89, 102–103, 159, 170, 178, 180, 199, 206, 210, 226, 230, 234, 268, 278, 281, 290, 330, 336, 338, 348, 350, 356

LECHI, 80 (4)
Levi, 204–206, 210, 214–215, 220,
Lewan, 205
Libnah, 217
Life, 169
Lost Tradition, 90, 126, 212, 234, 244, 271, 274, 285–286
Lot, 71–72
Lot's wife, 72

MAACHAH, 250
Mahaneh, Dan, 261
Manasseh, 248
Manasseh, Samaritan, 205
Manoah, 261
Martial, 184, 193
Matri, 108
Matztzeboth, 138
Melchizedeq, 156, 358
Mephibosheth, 156
Metre, 319
Miracles, 360
Miriam, 216, 218
Mitchell, 169
Moabite Stone, 159, 264
Moral Corruption, 151
Moreh, 78, 137
Moriah, 74
Moses, 33, 177, 219
Mosites, 219
Mountain of the north, 324, 398

—N, 93
Nachshon, 236 (4–5)
Naphthali, 262

Newman, Cardinal, 7
Nimrod, 67
Noah, 64
No'am, 64

Oehler, 11
Offering of Isaac, 33, 74, 228, 364
Og, 287
Osarsiph, 242
Ovid, 19, 66, 184

PARALLELISM, 319
Parody, 43
Passover, 128, 133, 326, 331, **339**
Pearson, 392, 407
Penuel, 83
Perizzites, 232
Phinehaz, 102, 145, 207
Postulates, 268
Priestly code, 116, 172
Propagation, rate of, 106–107
Prophecy, 543, 316, 328, 361–363
Puns, 45

—Q, 189, 253
Qenites, 210–211, 215, 240
Qenizzites, 274. See Caleb
Qish, 219
Qohath, 216, 246
Qorach, 221–222
Quousque tandem, 364–366

RACE NAMES, 191, 232
Rachab, 202
Rebecca, 190
Rechoboth, 79, 200–201, 190
Reductio ad absurdum, 47
Renan, 61, 65, 158, 184, 189, 191, 246, 285, 291, 336
Renouf, 25, 28
Rephaim, 254, 404
Reuben, 197–202, 294

Reuchlin, 11, 366
Revelation, 36, 52, 148, 162, 164-165, 169, 173-174, 310, 341, 364
Rubel, 197, 199
Ruchubi, 200

SABBATH, 117-121, 324, 339
Sacred fire, 135
Sacred trees, 137
Sacrifice, 134-135
Samuel, 208, 240
Sarah, 187
Satan, 171
Saturn, 153
Sayce, 71, 117, 120, 156-157, 161, 174, 176, 178-179, 182, 191, 201, 205, 213, 228, 242, 272, 275-280, 304, 345-355
Schrader, 67-68, 71, 80, 117, 120, 153, 158-159, 200, 230
Seir, 192, 254
Semele, 191
Serpent, 170
Shaddai, 158
Shammah, 80 (5)
Shechem, 276, 340, 284, 296
Shelah, 241, 244
Shiloh, 207, 245-246
Shobal, 253
Shuach, 236 (4), 260
Shuthelach, 241, 253
Sihon, 287, 356
Simeon, 203
Sodom and Gomorrha, 33, 73

Sothic Cycle, 278
Sselophehad, 251
Stone knives, 122, 126
Stopford Brooke, 2
Sun, 154, 166

TABERNACLE, 225, 256
Tamar, 230
Ten Plagues, 178, 289
Terioth, 222
Threshing-floor, 76
Tradition, 31-34, 67
Truth, 16-17
Tyre, 187, 355

VERDICT OF THE MONUMENTS, 264, 277-278-279, 284, 351-359

WANDERINGS, 179, 281
Weber, 132, 407
Wellhausen, 128, 132, 146, 157, 206, 226, 280, 289, 331, 336, 348, 350
Woman, 59

YAHVEH, 153, 159-164, 377
Yahvist, 58, 116, 230
Yechudh, 157, 228-229, 257

ZEBULUN, 266
Zerach, 218, 231
Zilpah, 251
Zoar, 73
Zur, 157

PASSAGES OF SCRIPTURE SPECIALLY REFERRED TO

GENESIS—	PAR.
ii. 23	59
iii. 15	170
iv. 26	62
x. 30	189 n
xv. 13	104
xvi. 13	80 (1)
xvii. 5	185
xxv. 25	193
xxvii. 11	195
xxix. 1	195
xxx. 8	262
xxxviii. 5	244
xlvi. 27	106
xlviii. 22	235
xlix. 4	200
xlix. 9, 22	235
10	245, 246
13	266
21	262

EXODUS—	
xiii. 12	132
xxii. 29	132

LEVITICUS—	
xxiii. 34–39	133

NUMBERS—	
x. 35, 36	154
xxi. 17, 18	52

JOSHUA—	PAR.
vi. 25	202
x. 13	166
xv. 6	198
xxiv. 31	122

JUDGES—	
xii. 4	248
xvii. 17	80 n

2 SAMUEL—	
vi. 3	223
vi. 13	136
xix. 44 (43)	243
xxiii. 24	156

1 KINGS—	
v. 11 (iv. 31)	101

1 CHRONICLES—	
ii. 50	236 (3)
ii. 55	211
iv. 19	256 (5)
vi. 10 (v. 36)	110
vii. 12	259
ix.	111
xv. 15	224
xxiv. 21	219
xxvi. 31	209

Passages of Scripture specially referred to

	PAR.
2 CHRONICLES—	
iii. 1	75
NEHEMIAH—	
11.	111
ESTHER—	
ix. 19	232
JOB—	
xix. 25, 26	392
xxxiv. 26	404
PSALMS—	
xxxvii. 37	196
xlviii. 15 (14)	379
lxxxviii. 6 (5)	378
13 (12)	376
cvi. 28	401–406
cxxxix. 8	379
PROVERBS—	
xii. 28	393

	PAR.
ISAIAH—	
vi. 13	138
viii. 19	401
EZEKIEL—	
xx. 18	132
HOSEA—	
vi. 2	385
AMOS—	
v. 25, 26	153
MICAH—	
i. 10	45
WISDOM—	
iii. 4	394
ix. 15	403
xiv. 15	395
SIRACH—	
xxx. 4	395

Printed by BALLANTYNE, HANSON & CO.
London and Edinburgh.

www.ingramcontent.com/pod-product-compliance
Lightning Source LLC
Chambersburg PA
CBHW041437300426
44114CB00025B/2906